# Lyndon Baines Johnson
## 1908–1973

# Lyndon Baines Johnson
# 1908–1973

## Reflections in History: A Personal Collection

By Dwayne A. Bridges

# Lyndon Baines Johnson 1908–1973

Reflections in History: A Personal Collection

Manufactured in Singapore.

For information, please contact:
Brown Books Publishing Group
16200 North Dallas Parkway, Suite 170
Dallas, Texas 75248
www.brownbooks.com
972-381-0009
A New Era in Publishing™

Paperbound Edition ISBN: 1-933285-24-9
Hardbound Edition with DVD ISBN: 1-933285-25-7
LCCN 2005906886
1 2 3 4 5 6 7 8 9 10

First Edition
The special hardbound edition with DVD insert is limited to one thousand copies.

www.reflectionsinhistory.com

*To all White House photographers*
*past, present, and future*

# Table of Contents

Introduction.................................................................................VIII

Acknowledgements............................................................................IX

The Johnson Family..........................................................................1
    a) Lyndon Baines Johnson............................................................2
    b) Lady Bird Johnson................................................................4
    c) Lynda Bird Johnson...............................................................6
    d) Luci Baines Johnson.............................................................7

The Photographers...........................................................................9
    a) Abbie Rowe......................................................................10
    b) Frank Muto......................................................................11
    c) Arnold Newman...................................................................12
    d) Robert Knudsen..................................................................13
    e) Cecil Stoughton.................................................................14
    f) Yoichi Okamoto..................................................................15
    g) Frank Wolfe.....................................................................16
    h) Kevin Smith.....................................................................17
    i) Michael Geissinger..............................................................19

The Collection..............................................................................21
    a) The Frank Muto Collection.......................................................22
    b) The Robert Knudsen Collection...................................................22
    c) The Congressman George Mahon Collection.........................................22
    d) The Sanford Fox Collection......................................................22
    e) Biography of Sanford Fox.........................................................23
    f) Biography of Congressman George Mahon............................................24

The Art and History of Photography..........................................................27
    a) Black and White Photography.....................................................28
    b) Color Photography...............................................................28
    c) Official White House Photographs................................................29
    d) White House Photography Today...................................................29

The Congress and Senate Years...............................................................31
    a) The 1946 Congressional Campaign.................................................33
    b) The 1948 Senate Campaign........................................................38
    c) The 1960 Presidential Candidate.................................................42
    d) The 1960 Democratic National Convention.........................................45
    e) The 1960 Presidential Campaign..................................................45
    f) Religion as an Issue in the 1960 Campaign.......................................45
    g) The Campaign Agenda.............................................................64
    h) The 1960 Televised Debates......................................................73
    i) The 1960 Whistle-Stop Tour......................................................82
    j) The 1960 Election Results.......................................................90

The Vice Presidency 1961–1963...............................................................93
    a) The German Chancellor...........................................................95
    b) The Chinese Premier.............................................................100
    c) Neiman Marcus...................................................................102
    d) The Space Program...............................................................108
    e) First American Manned Orbital Flight............................................111
    f) Final Visit to NASA.............................................................121

The Trip to Texas—November 1963.............................................................123
    a) Chronology......................................................................124
    b) The Motorcade...................................................................125
    c) A New President.................................................................127
    d) Recollections of Congressman George Mahon.......................................128
    e) Helen Mahon Remembers That Day..................................................130
    f) Memorial Address................................................................131
    g) Citizens Respond................................................................132
    h) Christmas 1963..................................................................133
    i) Pageant of the Peace............................................................134

The Presidency 1963–1969....................................................................137
    a) The 1964 Presidential Campaign..................................................138
    b) The Lady Bird Special...........................................................140
    c) The President's Inaugural Address: January 20, 1965.............................145
    d) Presidential Pets...............................................................147
    e) Luci's Wedding Day—August 6, 1966...............................................151
    f) Charles S. Robb.................................................................154
    g) Lynda's Wedding Day—December 9, 1967............................................157

Closing Days of the Presidency..............................................................159

Christmas Greetings.........................................................................167

Back at the Ranch—The Retirement Years (1969–1973)..........................................177
    a) The Presidential Memoirs........................................................180
    b) Memorial Tributes..............................................................182

Signature Study.............................................................................187
    a) LBJ Signature Study Analysis....................................................188
    b) The M-60 Autopen Machine........................................................196
    c) Lyndon B. Johnson Signatures....................................................205
    d) Lady Bird Johnson Signatures....................................................213
    e) Lynda Bird Johnson Signatures...................................................220
    f) Luci Baines Johnson Signatures..................................................222

White House Photographer Identification Stamps..............................................225

Notes and Sources...........................................................................229

Bibliography................................................................................243
    a) Books...........................................................................244
    b) Magazines, Newspapers and Periodicals...........................................246
    c) Interviews and Correspondence...................................................247
    d) Public Transcripts..............................................................247
    e) Internet Sources................................................................248

# Introduction

This book is the product of many years of collecting photographs and other material relating to the history of Lyndon B. Johnson. The history of LBJ has been widely written and discussed by many well-known authors. However, it is my intention to present the story of Lyndon Baines Johnson from a different perspective, a history that can be followed through the photography and gifts sent by the first family to friends and constituents. These photographs and handwritten mementos offer a unique insight into an era and a man who was literally thrown into the presidential arena under extraordinary circumstances. Many of these insights are told through the photographers themselves who were there to capture the moment.

The collection of material displayed throughout this text is my own and was obtained from several prominent sources. The first source came from a very good friend, Ernie Trujillo. The purchase was a large family album containing political photographs and memorabilia spanning the years from Dwight D. Eisenhower to Gerald Ford. This expansive album of material became the cornerstone of the collection. The contents of the album were from the estate of the late Texas district judge, Duncan Holt, who had married Daphne Mahon, the daughter of the late Congressman George Mahon of Lubbock, Texas. The collection would indicate that Daphne Mahon inherited the album from her parents. As will be shown, Congressman Mahon and his wife were very good friends and close political associates with the Johnson family.

A second and equally important source of material came from a purchase at an antiquarian bookstore. The purchase was a three-ring binder containing twenty-five original black and white photos and proof sheets of then-Senator Lyndon B. Johnson. The photographer who had taken these photographs was the late Senate Democratic photographer, Frank Muto. A large portion of these photographs was taken during the 1960 campaign when LBJ was seeking the Democratic nomination for president. Some were taken later when he became John F. Kennedy's vice presidential running mate. The majority of these photographs have never been published.

Other important and significant material came from the estate of Robert L. Knudsen, a White House photographer, and from the estate of Sanford Fox, the White House social director, whose estates were sold at public auction through Guernsey's auction house in New York City in November 2002.

All remaining material came from various public and private sales. I have made every attempt to catalog and substantiate original provenance for all the pieces. If the original provenance could not be determined, I have simply noted the pieces as being from my personal collection.

# Acknowledgements

As with any large endeavor, there are many people to thank. The first and most important recognition must go to my wife Renee. This book would not have been possible if it were not for her support.

A big round of thanks must be extended to the library staff at the Lyndon B. Johnson Library and Museum. Special thanks are extended to Phillip Scott and Kyla Wilson in the audiovisual archives department, for they were largely responsible in assisting me with the photographic research. The LBJ Library and Museum houses the Frank Muto collection of photographs, which was an invaluable asset to this study. I think it quite appropriate to thank the Frank Muto family for donating such a wonderful collection to the museum; it is truly an important part of American photographic history. Thanks are also extended to Bob Tissing, Claudia Anderson, Char Derricks, and Michael MacDonald, who assisted me with much of the literary research and Lindsay De Shazo, of Automated Signature Technology, who restored the M-60 Autopen machine.

Thanks are also extended to Alan Goodrich and James Hill with the audiovisual archives department at the John F. Kennedy Library and Museum. Their assistance with the Cecil Stoughton and Robert Knudsen collection was very much appreciated.

I would like to thank Andy Reisberg at Photographic Archives in Dallas, Texas, who assisted in the authentication, restoration, and cleaning of several of the Frank Muto photographs. His experience with historical photographic techniques was extremely valuable. Andy was one of the early staff photographers working with the company hired by the LBJ Library and Museum during the Frank Muto photo acquisition in the 1980s. He and other photographers in the early 1980s assisted in cataloging and printing the collection from the original negatives. This early "hands-on" experience makes Andy uniquely qualified in authenticating these particular photographs.

A very special thanks goes to Cecil Stoughton for the rare and special opportunity to hear firsthand his recollections of history, especially those events of November 22, 1963. Thanks are extended to Michael Geissinger, whom I had the pleasure to meet, and to Frank Wolf and Kevin Smith, who took time to speak with me as well. To all of these men who chose photography as their profession, we owe a great deal of gratitude for their service and documentation of history.

To George Meyer and his wife Barbara, a world of gratitude is extended for their wonderful friendship and generosity.

Thanks are also extended to NW Communications of Austin, Inc. on behalf of its television station KTBC for a portion of the material represented within this book. A special thanks is offered to 12Forward, Inc. who assisted with the final production of the Yoichi Okamoto DVD presentation.

To all those who I have met and worked with over the years, to those with whom I have engaged at libraries and other institutions, to the many friends and family who took the time to listen, and to those who have inspired me along the way, please accept my sincere gratitude.

# The Johnson Family

# Lyndon Baines Johnson (1908–1973)

Much has been written about the life and character of Lyndon Baines Johnson. There is no middle ground when attempting to characterize Lyndon B. Johnson. Throughout his political career, he had more than his share of opposition. That's just something that comes with the territory of politics. But Lyndon Johnson was truly a unique and controversial person living during an exceptional and tumultuous period of American history.

"Johnson was much loved and greatly hated—not just liked and disliked but adored by some and despised by others. Some remember him as kind, generous, compassionate, considerate, and a decent man devoted to advancing the well-being of the least advantaged among us. Others describe him as cruel, dictatorial, grandiose, and even vicious."[1]

"Bryce Harlo, a House and Senate staffer, and later a White House counsel under Eisenhower, remembers LBJ as having a unique character: 'Wherever he'd sit down there was a cloud of dust. Something was happening all the time, even if he were seated . . . He was talking to the guys next to him . . . He was getting up; he was sitting down . . . His alarm clock watch, which he loved to harass people with . . . It was a stunt . . . he always set it off at some propitious time to attract attention to himself. He couldn't stand being the cynosure of all eyes. He had to be at the head of the table . . . And people had to do what he thought they should do. And ordinarily he made them do it. You never know anybody like that, because they don't make them like that. But once in a millennium, they do. That's Lyndon.'"[2]

"A Great Society for the American people and their fellow men was the vision of Lyndon B. Johnson. In his first years of office he obtained passage of one of the most extensive legislative programs in the nation's history. Maintaining collective security, he carried on the rapidly growing struggle to restrain the Communist encroachment in Vietnam.

"Lyndon Johnson was born on August 27, 1908, in central Texas, not far from Johnson City, which his family had helped settle. He felt the pinch of rural poverty as he grew up, working his way through school at the Southwest Texas State Teachers College. There he learned compassion for the poverty of others and taught students of Mexican descent.

"In 1931, Lyndon got his first taste of politics when he became the secretary to Congressman Richard Kleberg. He was so successful, he was voted Speaker of the Little Congress, which consisted of all the congressional secretaries in Congress. The catalyst that kicked his political career into high gear was when President Roosevelt appointed him as the Texas director of the National Youth Administration. This was the experience and spotlight he needed. Then in 1937, he successfully campaigned for the House of Representatives on President Roosevelt's New Deal platform, effectively aided by his wife, Claudia "Lady Bird" Taylor, whom he had married in 1934.

"During World War II, he served briefly in the navy as a lieutenant commander, winning a Silver Star in the South Pacific. After six terms in the House, Johnson was elected to the Senate in 1948. In 1953, he became the youngest minority leader in Senate history, and the following year, when the Democrats won control, he became the majority leader. With very rare skill, he obtained passage of a number of key Eisenhower measures.

"In the 1960 campaign, Johnson was selected as John F. Kennedy's running mate. When Kennedy was assassinated on November 22, 1963, Lyndon B. Johnson became our thirty–sixth president. First he obtained enactment of the measures President Kennedy had been urging at the time of his death—a new civil rights bill and a tax cut. Next he urged the nation "to build a great society, a place where the meaning of man's life matches the marvels of man's labor." In 1964, Johnson won the presidency with 61 percent of the vote, which was the widest popular vote margin in American history—more than 15 million votes."

Lyndon Baines Johnson ★ USIA Photograph #64-2529, 1964 - Photograph by Cecil Stoughton

"The Great Society program became Johnson's agenda for Congress in January 1965. The program encompassed aid to education, attack on disease, Medicare, urban renewal, beautification, conservation, development of depressed regions, a wide-scale fight against poverty, control and prevention of crime and delinquency, and removal of obstacles to the right to vote. Congress, at times augmenting or amending, rapidly enacted Johnson's recommendations. Millions of elderly people found relief through the 1965 Medicare amendment to the Social Security Act. Under Johnson, the country made spectacular explorations of space in a program he had championed since its start. When three astronauts successfully orbited the moon in December 1968, Johnson congratulated them: "You've taken . . . all of us, all over the world, into a new era . . ." Nevertheless, two overriding crises had been gaining momentum since 1965. Despite the beginning of new antipoverty and antidiscrimination programs, unrest and rioting in black ghettos troubled the nation. President Johnson steadily exerted his influence against segregation on behalf of law and order, but there was no early solution. The other crisis arose in Vietnam. Despite Johnson's efforts to end Communist aggression and achieve a settlement, fighting continued. Controversy over the war had become acute by the end of March 1968, when he limited the bombing of North Vietnam in order to initiate negotiations. At the same time, he startled the world by withdrawing as a candidate for reelection so that he might devote his full efforts, unimpeded by politics, to the quest for peace. When he left office, peace talks were underway, but he did not live to see them successful. Lyndon Johnson died of a heart attack at his Texas ranch on January 22, 1973."[3]

(This historical profile was quoted from the White House Web site)

http://www.whitehouse.gov/history/presidents/lj36.html

# Lady Bird Johnson
## (Claudia Alta Taylor)

"Mrs. Lyndon Baines Johnson was born Claudia Alta Taylor in Karnack, Texas, on December 22, 1912. Mrs. Johnson's father was Thomas Jefferson Taylor, owner of a general store, who declared himself "dealer in everything." Her mother, Minnie Pattillo Taylor, had died when Lady Bird was only five years old. She had two older brothers, Tommy and Tony. After her mother's death, Mrs. Johnson's aunt Effie Pattillo moved to Karnack to look after her. At an early age, a nursemaid said she was "as purty as a lady bird"—and thereafter she became known to her family and friends as "Lady Bird." Mrs. Johnson grew up in a modest home and attended a small rural elementary school in Harrison County, Texas. She graduated from Marshall High School in 1928, and attended Saint Mary's Episcopal School for Girls in Dallas from 1928 to 1930.

"Mrs. Johnson entered the University of Texas in 1930 and received a Bachelor of Arts degree in 1933, with a major in history. She then earned a journalism degree in 1934. Many colleges and universities have since awarded Mrs. Johnson honorary degrees.

"After a whirlwind courtship, Claudia Alta Taylor and Lyndon Baines Johnson married on November 17, 1934, at Saint Mark's Episcopal Church in San Antonio, Texas. Two daughters were born to the Johnsons: Lynda Bird Johnson in 1944, (now Mrs. Charles S. Robb), who resides in Virginia; and in 1947, Luci Baines Johnson (now married to Ian Turpin), who lives in Austin, Texas. Mrs. Johnson has seven grandchildren—one boy and six girls—and five great-grandchildren.

"Mrs. Johnson is the author of *A White House Diary*, a record of her activities, which she kept during the years when her husband served as the thirty–sixth president of the United States. About writing *A White House Diary*, Mrs. Johnson has said, "I was keenly aware that I had a unique opportunity, a front row seat, on an unfolding story, and nobody else was going to see it from quite the vantage point that I saw it." She also coauthored *Wildflowers Across America* with Carlton Lees.

"During her White House years, Mrs. Johnson served as honorary chairman of the National Head Start Program, a program for underprivileged preschool children that prepares them to take their place in the classroom on a par with their peers. In 1977, President Gerald Ford presented Mrs. Johnson with this country's highest civilian award: the Medal of Freedom. Mrs. Johnson also received the Congressional Gold Medal from President Ronald Reagan in 1988. In January 1971, Mrs. Johnson was appointed to a six-year term as a member of the University of Texas System Board of Regents. She is a life member of the University of Texas Ex-student Association, and has been a member of the International Conference Steering Committee (1981–82) and the University of Texas Centennial Commission. For many years, Mrs. Johnson was a trustee of the National Geographic Society, and continues as a trustee emeritus. She also served as a member of the National Committee for the Bicentennial Era and as cochairman of the Advisory Council of the American Freedom Train Foundation. President Ford had appointed Mrs. Johnson to the Advisory Council to the American Revolution Bicentennial Administration, and in 1977, President Jimmy Carter appointed Mrs. Johnson to the President's Commission on White House Fellowships.

"In 1966, Mrs. Johnson was presented the George Foster Peabody Award for the television program, "A Visit to Washington with Mrs. Lyndon B. Johnson on Behalf of a More Beautiful America." She received the Eleanor Roosevelt Golden Candlestick Award from the Women's National Press Club in 1968.

"First and foremost, Mrs. Johnson is an environmentalist, and has been an active worker on innumerable projects. In Washington, she enlisted the aid of friends to plant thousands of tulips and daffodils, which still delight visitors to our nation's capital. The Highway Beautification Act of 1965 was the result of Mrs. Johnson's national campaign for beautification.

"Mrs. Johnson was honorary chairman of the LBJ Memorial Grove on the Potomac in Washington, D. C., and also chaired the Town Lake Beautification Project, a community effort to create a hike-and-bike trail along the Colorado River in Austin, Texas. She became a member of the National Park Service's Advisory Board on National Parks, Historic Sites, Buildings, and Monuments in 1969 and served on the council for many years."

Lady Bird Johnson ★ Photograph by Robert L. Knudsen - LBJ Library Photo #C9172-13

"In 1969, Mrs. Johnson founded the Texas Highway Beautification Awards, and for the next twenty years, she hosted the annual awards ceremonies and presented her personal checks to the winners. She is also a trustee of the American Conservation Association.

"On her seventieth birthday in 1982, Mrs. Johnson founded the National Wildflower Research Center, a nonprofit environmental organization dedicated to the preservation and reestablishment of native plants in natural and planned landscapes. She donated sixty acres of land and a sum of money to establish the Center, which serves as a clearinghouse of information for people all over the country. She realized her long-held dream in 1995 when the Center moved into its larger facility where she is the chairman of the Wildflower Center's board of directors.

"In honor of her eightieth birthday and the many contributions to the betterment of our environment, the LBJ Foundation Board of Directors established the Lady Bird Johnson Conservation Award in 1992.

"In December 1972, President and Mrs. Johnson gave the LBJ Ranch house and surrounding property to the people of the United States as a national historic site, retaining a life estate in the Ranch. Mrs. Johnson also maintains a house in Austin. Today, Mrs. Johnson supports and continues to be very interested in the activities of the Lyndon B. Johnson Library and Museum, and in the Lyndon B. Johnson School of Public Affairs, both located on the University of Texas campus in Austin."[4]

(This biography was quoted from the Lyndon Baines Johnson Library and Museum Web site)

http://www.lbjlib.utexas.edu/johnson/archives.hom/biographys.hom/ladybird_bio.asp

Lynda Bird Johnson
White House Staff Photo ★ From Photo C-6787-0
September 30, 1967

## Lynda Bird Johnson

Lynda Bird Johnson was born March 19, 1944 in Washington, D.C., when her father was a congressman. She was only nineteen when her father became president and she had been attending the University of Texas at Austin when John F. Kennedy was assassinated. She had been engaged to a young naval officer named Bernie Rosenbach, but broke that engagement off in early April 1964. Lynda then dated actor George Hamilton, which the press had a field day with. That romance also came to an end when she fell in love with Captain Charles (Chuck) Robb, who was a member of the Marine Corps Honor Guard stationed at the White House. Lynda and Chuck Robb eventually married in a military ceremony at the White House on December 9, 1967. Their wedding was of special note, as there had not been a wedding at the White House in fifty-three years. Shortly after the wedding, Captain Robb left for Vietnam, where he served with distinction. Upon returning home from the war, and with his own interest in politics, he became lieutenant governor and then later governor of the State of Virginia. He also served as a U.S. senator from 1989–2001.[5]

"Lynda Johnson had first attended George Washington University and then graduated from the University of Texas in 1966. She has been awarded an honorary Doctor of Humane Letters from Washington and Lee University and an honorary Doctorate of Public Service from Norwich University in Vermont. As a young lady, she worked as a writer for *McCall's Magazine* from 1966 to 1968, and then as a contributing editor for *Ladies Home Journal* from 1969 through 1981. In 1979, President Jimmy Carter appointed Lynda as the chair of the President's Advisory Committee for Women. She served in that appointment until 1981. She left *Ladies Home Journal* in 1981 to campaign with her husband when he became the governor of Virginia. From 1982 to 1985, she was the chair of the Virginia Women's Cultural History Project where she chaired the Virginia Task Force on Infant Mortality. From 1989 to 1996, she served as the commissioner on the National Commission to Prevent Infant Mortality.

Mrs. Robb is fond of listing her profession as "professional volunteer," and she has indeed, served many organizations over the years, always focusing on the condition of children and women, including Reading Is Fundamental, the nation's largest children's literacy organization. She served as chairman of the board of directors from 1996 until her term ended in 2001. She is a past member of the board of Ford's Theatre, the past co-vice chairman of America's Promise, and a current member of the board of the Lady Bird Johnson Wildflower Research Center. In addition to her continued work as a member of the board on behalf of RIF, Mrs. Robb is president of the National Home Library Foundation."[6]

Lynda and Chuck Robb have three daughters: Lucinda Desha Robb, Catherine Lewis Robb, and Jennifer Wickliffe Robb.[7]

Luci Baines Johnson

White House Staff Photo ★ From Photo C-6787-0
September 30, 1967

## Luci Baines Johnson

Luci Baines Johnson, originally spelled "Lucy," was born in Washington, D.C., on July 2, 1947. She changed the spelling of her first name when she was a teenager. Although her parents were non-denominational while in office, the family's religious background was Episcopalian and Disciples of Christ. Luci, however, took an interest in the Catholic Church. She received Catholic rights of baptism on her eighteenth birthday at Saint Mathews Church in Washington, D.C. Luci was only sixteen when President John F. Kennedy was killed and her father took office. At the time of the tragedy, she was attending the National Cathedral School in Washington. Since her father had been in office all of her life, she was already accustomed to politics. Luci was interviewed by *LIFE* magazine in early 1964 and commented, "I know I'm different from the rest of the family. My interests are not the same and my physical appearance is not the same. I am a blue-eyed child in a brown-eyed family. Sometimes I think I scare them. Lynda is interested in her schoolwork and she is a good student. I am not. I am extremely impulsive and Lynda isn't. I am a high-strung person who likes to be happy. I don't try to hide my emotions. My worst point is that I am headstrong. I don't listen enough. I love to talk and I talk too much. I don't take advice very well either. I have to learn things the hard way."[8]

These comments characterized Luci Baines Johnson very well. She dated a number of young men during her White House years, but it was during a party arranged by some friends that she met Patrick Nugent. Patrick and Luci would be married on August 6, 1966. The first Johnson grandchild was born a year later on June 21, 1967, and was named Patrick Lyndon Nugent,—"Little Lyn," as he was called by his grandfather. Luci and Pat moved to Austin, Texas, where they made their home, but by mid-1968, when Patrick went to Vietnam, Luci and Little Lyn moved back to the White House.

Luci and Pat Nugent would have three more children: Nicole, Rebekah, and Claudia. In 1979, Luci and Patrick Nugent had their Catholic marriage annulled. Luci would later marry Ian Turpin, a Canadian financier.[9] Today, Luci Johnson Turpin, who simply goes by Luci Johnson, is the chairman of the board of the LBJ Holding Company, is the vice president of The Business Suites, and is a member of the board of directors of LBJ Broadcasting. She currently serves the public and the local Austin community in a number of capacities. She is a member of the board of directors of the National Wildlife Research Center and is on the board of visitors for the Georgetown University School of Nursing. She is also a trustee of Boston University, an advisory chairman for the Endowment Fund for KLUR-TV in Austin, a member of the advisory board for the Center for Battered Women and Believe in Me, and is a life trustee of the Seton Fund.[10]

# The Photographers

(Abbie Rowe Biography Compiled from the Truman Presidential Museum and Library) **Abbie Rowe Collection**

# Abbie Rowe (1905-1967)

"Abbie Rowe was born in Strasburg, Virginia, on August 23, 1905. He spent most of his career in government service and was first hired in 1930 by the Bureau of Public Roads. Although partly crippled by polio, he went on to become a noted photographer. When he happened to photograph First Lady Eleanor Roosevelt riding on horseback along the Mount Vernon Highway in March 1938, she wrote of the incident in her newspaper column "My Day." Subsequently, Rowe appealed directly to her for a change of job status because of his difficulty performing heavy manual labor. He was eventually reassigned as a photographer for the National Capital Parks of the National Park Service. Many of his photographs documented public buildings and roads in and around the nation's capital. In December 1941, as America entered World War II, Abbie Rowe received a challenging new assignment. At the request of President Roosevelt, the National Park Service assigned Rowe to provide photographic coverage of the president's activities, particularly those that occurred away from the White House. Gradually, his duties were expanded to include the documentation of events that took place within the White House. By the Truman years, he was called upon to document the president at many official ceremonies, both in and away from the White House. His work continued through the Eisenhower, Kennedy, and into the Johnson administrations prior to his death in April 1967.

"From 1941 through 1967, Abbie Rowe photographed hundreds of events, including official ceremonies, the visits of foreign dignitaries, the enactment of important legislation, and many other state functions both large and small. He covered history-making events like the funerals of Franklin Roosevelt and John Kennedy, Harry Truman's announcement of the surrender of Japan that ended World War II, and presidential inaugurations. But he also covered smaller ceremonies as well—Presidents pardoning Thanksgiving turkeys, welcoming groups of Girl Scouts, accepting small gifts from admirers, and performing the countless little ceremonial functions that are part of the pomp and symbolism of the presidency."

The above biography is quoted from

http://www.trumanlibrary.org/abierowe/abierowe.htm

Frank P. Muto

This photograph of Frank Muto was taken when he was a major in the U.S. Army. ★ National Archives & Records Administration, Photograph #111-P-10579

## Frank Patrick Muto (1909-1980)

"Frank Patrick Muto was the senate Democratic photographer for eighteen years before his retirement in 1975. Mr. Muto had covered World War II as a news photographer and later directed the still pictures branch at the old War Department.

"Mr. Muto was born in Princeton, New Jersey, in 1909. His first job was working as an office boy for the *New York Daily News* at the age of fifteen. He later worked as a photographer and photo editor. In the 1930s, he worked as a picture editor for several screen magazines on the West Coast and as the director of tourist photography for the Italian government before joining the International News Service as a war correspondent. He covered the Polish and Norwegian campaigns as well as the Finn-Russian war. He was later captured and held as a POW before returning to the United States. As a former army major, Mr. Muto served as a public relations and still-photograph officer, beginning the still-picture public relations section for the old War Department, later known as the Army Pictorial Service. While serving at the Army Pictorial Service during World War II, he attained the rank of captain. During that time, and until the end of World War II, he went on special assignments to all theaters of operations, including the official surrender of Japan. After the war, Mr. Muto worked as a freelance photographer before becoming the senate Democratic photographer in 1957.

"A former resident of Falls Church, Virginia, he and his wife Anne T. Muto moved to Las Vegas in 1979. Frank Muto received medals from Poland and Finland for his humanitarian service to their countries during World War II and was a member of the White House News Photographers Association. A year later after moving to Las Vegas, Frank Muto died of congestive heart failure on Wednesday October 8, 1980, at Sunrise Hospital in Las Vegas, Nevada. Mr. Muto's photographic collection of some 5000 photographs resides at the Lyndon B. Johnson Library and Museum in Austin, Texas."[1]

Arnold Newman

Self-portrait of photographer Arnold Newman, taken in New York City, 1987. ★ Copyright Arnold Newman, Getty Images.

## Arnold Newman

Arnold Newman was born March 3, 1918, in New York City, New York. Although Mr. Newman was never a White House photographer, his photography is one of the most widely collected and exhibited photographic works of art today, and he has photographed many presidents over the years. Considered to be one of the most influential photographers of the twentieth century, his formal education and study began at the University of Miami in Coral Gables, Florida, in 1936. He began his professional career shortly after school while working in portrait studios around West Palm Beach and in studios around Philadelphia and Baltimore. It was during these early years that Mr. Newman began forming his own particular form of "environmental portraiture." In 1941, he got his first break when Beaumont Newhall from the Museum of Modern Art, along with another famous photographer, Alfred Stieglitz, recognized his extraordinary talent for portraiture. With their assistance, Arnold Newman was given his first photography exhibit at the A.D. Gallery in New York. It was at this gallery that he began to refine his own style of photography.

"Mr. Newman has owned and operated his own gallery out of New York City since 1945. His work has been featured in nearly every major publication around the world. Publications such as *LIFE*, *Look*, *Fortune*, *The New Yorker*, *Esquire*, and *Vanity Fair* have all printed his work over the years."[2] Exhibits of his work have traveled around the world several times. Arnold Newman has said, "We don't take photographs with our cameras, we take them with our hearts and our minds. They are a reflection of ourselves, what we are, and what we think. A preoccupation with abstraction, combined with an interest in the documentation of people in their natural surroundings, was the basis upon which I built my approach to portraiture. The portrait of a personality must be as complete as we can make it. The physical image of the subject and the personality traits that image reflects are the most important aspects, but alone they are not enough. We must also show the subject's relationship to his world either by fact or by graphic symbolism. The photographer's visual approach must weld these ideas into an organic whole, and the photographic image produced must create an atmosphere which reflects our impressions of the whole."[3] Arnold Newman's photographic style is reflected exceptionally well in the photograph he took of Senator Lyndon Johnson in 1953 **(see page 40)**. Mr. Newman captured Senator Johnson within his environment. The photograph conveys with great symbolism the man who was considered the master of the Senate. In one single moment and in one single frame of photographic history, Arnold Newman captured a great American statesman in a way that portrays his subject as if he were a fixture of the environment. The same way a nature photographer captures his subject in the wild, a portrait that expresses in our mind's eye, that which we call American politics.

Robert L. Knudsen

From Photo Courtesy of John Fitzgerald Kennedy Library ★
Taken September 22, 1962

# Robert L. Knudsen
# (1921–1989)

Robert LeRoy Knudsen worked as a White House photographer from 1946 to 1974, the longest tenure of any White House photographer in American history. Mr. Knudsen served as part of the White House photography staff under five presidents, beginning with President Truman, and then he retired during the Nixon administration. Mr. Knudsen graduated from Omaha North High School in 1945 and then joined the navy. He became a navy photographer and graduated first in his class at the Naval Photographic School in Pensacola, Florida.[4] He served in Guam and in the Philippines before being reassigned to Washington, D.C. While working in Washington, the navy required him from time to time to take photographs at the White House. It was during these assignments that President Truman noticed his outstanding work and formally requested his service on a regular and more continuous basis. Thus, Robert Knudsen became the very first "official" White House photographer.[5]

Robert Knudsen probably photographed more important political and White House events than any single photographer to date. When asked during a telephone interview how many photographs he took during his tenure, he said, "I couldn't venture to guess. Some days it was probably four hundred pictures a day, depending on the occasion. But I would say it might average about one hundred pictures a day.[6] "Chief Knudsen, as some called him, held the rank of chief petty officer until he retired from the navy in 1965, but continued to work at the White House under the Civil Service. Robert Knudsen photographed many historical moments. He was there to take the first White House photos of John Kennedy Jr. taking his first

steps, he was there when Harry Truman and Dwight D. Eisenhower were sworn into office, and he was there to photograph three White House weddings of presidential daughters Lynda and Luci Johnson and Tricia Nixon. He was also there to photograph the bad times.[7] He photographed the firing of Douglas McArthur by President Truman, he photographed the events surrounding the early Cold War era under Eisenhower, and he was there during the troubling times of Vietnam under the Johnson administration. He was also there for the most difficult assignment of his career—photographing the autopsy of President John F. Kennedy.[8] During one particular interview, Robert Knudsen spoke of the presidents he served. With Truman he said, "With him, you always knew where you stood. If he didn't like what you were doing, he told you." With Eisenhower, "He was a typical military general in the White House. But when he was at the farm at Gettysburg, Ike just wanted to be one of the guys." With Kennedy, "He loved sailing. He was happiest when he was out there sailing, and he loved to take pictures that weren't necessarily official." With Johnson, "He was stubborn, hard-nosed and ornery on the outside, but inside he was just a pussycat. He fired me four different times. I remember what the Vietnam War did to Johnson. It was killing the man." With Nixon, "The thing I remember most is the inaccessibility to Nixon. With the other four presidents, I could just wander into the Oval Office most of the time. With Nixon, if I really wanted something, I usually had to ask his daughter Julie."[9] Robert Knudsen said he was amazed by the diversity of the men he had served. There was really nothing to compare them by, because they had so little common ground other than the office they held.[10] Robert L. Knudsen died of a heart attack at age sixty-one on January 27, 1989.

Cecil W. Stoughton

From Photo Courtesy of John Fitzgerald Kennedy Library ★ Taken September 22, 1962

# Cecil W. Stoughton

Cecil W. Stoughton was born January 18, 1920, in Oskaloosa, Iowa, a small town just south of Des Moines. Mr. Stoughton's interest in photography began as a teenager in the mid-1930s when he was the high school photographer. Mr. Stoughton says, "For those times, that was small potatoes compared to what they are now. We used an old folding camera which had only one exposure, one f-stop, and only one shutter speed."[11] "Cecil Stoughton's professional career began in 1940 when he enlisted in the U.S. Army Air Corps and was assigned as a combat photographer. For training, the army sent him to a LIFE magazine training session after which he was sent to the South Pacific to cover the war effort. He decided to make the military a career and was stationed in Hawaii until 1951. Later in 1951, he was assigned to the joint chief of staff as a motion picture photographer, which was supervised by the public relations branch of the office of the secretary of defense."[12]

In 1957, Cecil Stoughton accepted a commission in the army signal corps and became a first lieutenant. From 1957 to 1961, he reported to the deputy chief of information for the army, General Chester (Ted) V. Clifton. During this time, General Clifton had Lieutenant Stoughton work at Cape Canaveral, Florida, photographing much of the growing space initiative. In 1961, when John F. Kennedy became president of the United States, General Clifton was appointed President Kennedy's military aide. General Clifton recommended Cecil Stoughton to the president and was quickly assigned to the White

House as a personal photographer. The work of White House photographer was shared between himself and Robert Knudsen. Cecil Stoughton says, "Bob and I were buddies from way back. We knew each other well before the White House. In the public relations branch of the secretary of defense they would hold a school for photographers and bring guys in from all around the world in order to give them a chance to be exposed to the brass and hierarchy. It was at one of these classes back in the 1950s when Bob and I first met. During the White House years, we would share the load. Bob covered much of the social side, dinner arrangements, and such. Much of the time we were both together, even on trips. We both wore civilian clothes and everyone knew us, so we never had to compete with anyone."[13] Cecil Stoughton worked as a White House photographer through the Kennedy years and was in the press car behind the president's limousine that fatal day in Dallas. Robert Knudsen was not on the trip because he was recovering from an eye injury. Cecil was the photographer who took the famous photograph seen around the world of Vice President Johnson being sworn into office on Air Force One, with Lady Bird Johnson standing on one side and the shocked and grieving First Lady Jacqueline Kennedy standing on the other.

After the assassination of President Kennedy, Cecil Stoughton stayed on as a White House photographer under President Johnson until 1965. By 1967, Cecil had retired from the Army and went to work for the National Park Service as their chief photographer. Cecil Stoughton retired altogether from civil service in 1973.

Yoichi Okamoto

Photographer Yoichi Okamoto taken November 22, 1965 at the LBJ Ranch in Stonewall, Texas. ★ Lyndon Baines Johnson Library, Photo # A1604-35a.

# Yoichi Okamoto
# (1915–1985)

Yoichi Okamoto was born July 5, 1915, in Yonkers, New York, and was a graduate of Colgate University. Mr. Okamoto first served in the army during World War II as a still and motion picture photographer, and he headed the army signal corps's photo office in occupied Austria. He then worked for a brief time as a photographer for the local newspaper in Syracuse, New York. After that, he went on to work for the United States Information Agency (USIA), where he served as a photographer stationed in several locations throughout Germany and Austria. He later became the Chief of the Visual Materials Branch of the USIA in Washington, D.C., where he and Lyndon Johnson became acquainted. It was in 1961 when he accompanied Vice President Lyndon Johnson on an official visit to West Berlin. Vice President Johnson was so impressed with Mr. Okamoto's work that he requested him on other official trips. When Lyndon Johnson became president, he appointed Mr. Okamoto, "Oke" as he was called, as his official White House photographer. In 1969, when President Johnson retired from office, Mr. Okamoto, along with two other men, started Image Labs in Washington, D.C., where he did freelance work for magazines and corporations.[14]

"Yoichi Okamoto's photography reveals a gift for capturing his subject's personality. This is especially true of his work as chief White House photographer, where he gained unprecedented access to Lyndon Johnson. Mr. Okamoto was able to anticipate the president's changeable moods, and his candid images tell us much about LBJ's personal and political style. His goal, he told President Johnson, was not just to take portraits, but also "to hang around and try to document history in the making." "Yoichi Okamoto's photography is well represented in the holdings of the National Archives. In addition to his White House photographs that are preserved at the Lyndon Baines Johnson Library in Austin, Texas, his work as a USIA staff member, as well as some of his later freelance photographs, are among USIA photographic files at the National Archives at College Park. In 1973, Mr. Okamoto completed several assignments for the Environmental Protection Agency's DOCUMERICA project. These photographs and some of his letters can also be found in the National Archives."[15]

*Please see the DVD presentation by Yoichi Okamoto at the back of the hardbound book. The DVD is available only with the special limited edition hardback series of this book.*

# Francis (Frank) L. Wolfe

Francis L. Wolfe

Portrait Taken by Peg Tharp April 29, 2003

Francis (Frank) L. Wolfe was born September 30, 1940, in York, Pennsylvania. It was Yoichi Okamoto who tagged him with the name of Frank during his White House years.[16] Shortly after graduating high school, Frank went to work in a local manufacturing plant. He soon realized that this was not what he wanted to do the rest of his life, and like many young men, he joined the army. It was during his time in the army that Frank was introduced to photography. While in basic training, a request came down for a volunteer to be stationed in Washington, D.C. Frank happened to be the first to raise his hand and was assigned to the White House on November 10, 1959, under the Eisenhower administration. His job was a military courier, a "military postman," as Frank puts it. He served in that capacity until the Kennedy administration. When Cecil Stoughton was appointed as a photographer, Cecil needed assistance in the photo lab, so the army sent Frank to photo lab school to help support the lab operations. It was while working in the White House photo lab that Frank took a serious interest in photography.

The White House photo lab at this time was located in a part of the city called Foggy Bottom, "In an old firehouse across from a wax museum. It was a unique part of town, located right along the river."[17] "Today, the Foggy Bottom Historic District is roughly bounded by 25th St., NW, on the east; New Hampshire Ave. and H St., NW, on the south; 26th St. on the west; and K St. on the north. In the late 1800s, the area originally housed workers from nearby industries like the Godey's Lime Kilns, the Washington Gas and Light Company, the Glass Works, the Abner/Drury and Christian Heurich breweries, and Cranford's Paving Company. Foggy Bottom was described in the early days as being low and swampy with fogs settling in over the river banks that mixed with smog from the gas works."[18] The White House photo lab was located in Foggy Bottom until the Johnson years, when it moved to Georgetown. During the Kennedy administration, Frank worked in the photo lab, supporting Cecil Stoughton's work, but he eventually started taking photographs on his own. The lab technicians would take their own photographs and would hold competitions between themselves. Cecil would judge and critique their work. When Frank started entering photography contests sponsored by the *Washington Post* and he won several of the contests, Cecil took notice and began to give Frank assignments at the White House. Eventually, Frank became a full-time White House photographer, and he resigned from the photo lab completely. Frank worked as a White House photographer through the Johnson administration. When President Johnson retired in 1968, Frank got word that a photographer was needed at the LBJ Library and Museum in Austin, Texas. Frank took the position and worked at the LBJ Library, taking photos for the president and for the library. He not only took photos for the president and the library during this tenure, but he also assisted in the archiving of the library's large photographic collection. Frank Wolfe retired from the LBJ Library and Museum in 1994.

Kevin S. Smith

Self Portrait Taken in 2003

## Kevin S. Smith

Kevin S. Smith was born June 3, 1942, in Berkley, California, and acquired an interest in photography at an early age. His father had practiced photography all his life and when Kevin was a child, his father gave him a Kodak Pony camera. Kevin's first photograph was that of a dead house sparrow, which he carefully positioned as naturally as possible for the snapshot. When Kevin was in his junior year of high school, his grandfather sent him his first professional camera. It was this gift that sparked a serious interest in photography. Kevin's second interest was in nature and the environment. After high school, much to the consternation of his high school music teacher who was grooming him for the opera, he was far more interested in nature than singing, and he enrolled in the wildlife management curriculum at Michigan State University. Two years later, he transferred to the University of Montana where he received his Bachelor of Science degree. In 1963, during his senior year of college, the draft board called upon him. But since he was a full-time student, he did not have to serve. When Kevin did graduate, he knew the draft board might come looking for him again. Since there were no jobs being offered in wildlife management, he took interest in the military just to see what they had to offer. This was a very difficult period of time, especially since the Vietnam War was at its peak and Kevin knew that if he had to join the military, he wanted to do it on his own terms. The army was offering occupational guarantees for those that would enlist, so Kevin joined the army and signed up to be a photo lab technician.

The army sent him to Leonardwood, Missouri, for basic training. His fate as a professional photographer was sealed while in basic training. One morning as the recruits were filing into ranks, the company commander informed Kevin that he was to stay back at the barracks, and at one o'clock report to this military Quonset hut. Well, Kevin showed up at one o'clock, along with about twenty-five other recruits, all of them sitting there looking at each other wondering what was about to happen. Shortly after, this civilian walked through the door and stepped up to the podium. The gentleman's first words were, "If there are any of you here today not interested in working at the White House in Washington, D.C., you can get up right now and leave with no questions asked." Almost immediately, thirteen recruits got up and left the room. Kevin thought to himself, "How dumb can you get? We are in the middle of a war and these thirteen guys get up and leave!" None of them were really sure why the recruits left, but Kevin and the remaining recruits spent the afternoon in interviews, and at the end of the day, there were only four of them. The next day they were subjected to polygraph tests, and at the end of those tests, there were only three of them. They don't know what happened to the fourth guy. Nonetheless, the three of them went on to finish basic training, with two of them being assigned to cryptology training, while Kevin was sent to photo lab school in New Jersey. As luck or fate would have it, the two other recruits ended up working as cryptologists at the White House, directly across the hall from the photographer's office.

Kevin reported to the White House photo lab in January of 1965. He wasn't in the photo lab more than six weeks when Cecil Stoughton retired from the White House. This created a need for another photographer. The photo lab decided to hold a

To Kevin
Who makes them like I like them.    *[signature: Lyndon Johnson]*

Photograph of President Lyndon B. Johnson handing out a photo of his grandson to the press corps. November 30, 1967 - LBJ Library Photo #C7663-11 ★ Photograph by Kevin Smith

Kevin returned from the trip, Oke noticed that the only photo he had taken was that of the grandchild, and Oke was fuming mad about it. Oke said, "What in the hell were you doing down there for an entire week? You didn't take any photos of the president. All you return with is just a few snapshots of the kid!" About ten minutes later, the phone rings with orders to report immediately to the Oval Office. Kevin and Oke grab their cameras and run up to the president's office. They get to the office to find the entire press corps there. President Johnson had copies of one of Kevin's photographs of Little Lyn sitting in the rocking chair and was handing them out to the press corps. The president, in his southern drawl, said, "By God, if you boys could take pictures like this I wouldn't have any trouble with you!" Kevin looked over at Oke who was just looking up at the ceiling in disbelief. Kevin then took a photo of the president handing out his photographs. Later that week the president kindly sent Kevin a signed print that reads, "To Kevin, who takes them like I like them," signed Lyndon B. Johnson.

Kevin retired from photography after leaving the White House in 1969 and decided to give his college education in wildlife management a try. He became a National Park ranger and worked at the Mount Ranier National Park in Washington State. He soon decided that being a park ranger was not his cup of tea and he moved to Portland, Oregon, where he returned to college and received a degree in mechanical engineering. With his new degree, he worked for twenty-three years as a commercial building inspector for the City of Beaverton, Oregon. In 1990, Kevin was diagnosed with cancer, but with early detection, a good doctor, and a healthy outlook toward life, he remains cancer free. Kevin took early retirement and has returned to what he loves best,— he now specializes in nature photography.[19]

photography contest for the open position, and Kevin won. So it was, Kevin became part of the White House photography team, which consisted of Yoichi Okamoto, Bob Knudsen, Frank Wolfe, and a part-time navy movie photographer named Don Stoderl. Michael Geissinger would not get assigned to the White House photography staff until 1966.

One of Kevin's favorite pictures was a photograph he took of President Johnson handing out a photo of Little Lyn, the president's grandson. Kevin had been sent to the LBJ Ranch with the president and his family for a short visit. While at the ranch, the only photos Kevin took was that of Little Lyn sitting in a rocking chair at the ranch house. When

Michael A. Geissinger

Photograph by Dwayne Bridges, taken at the LBJ Library and Museum on July 31, 2003.

## Michael A. Geissinger

Michael Geissinger was born September 11, 1942, in Huntington, Pennsylvania. Michael got started in photography during his junior year of high school. Reminiscing, he said, "I remember starting out with a Polaroid camera, which I had asked my parents for. I am not sure why, probably because of the instant gratification. Now we are back with that same instant gratification with digital cameras. I started out with that Polaroid camera and then got serious with it in my senior year. I also started looking around for a college to attend. My options were either history or education, but that did not interest me as much as photography."[20] After high school, Michael attended Rochester Institute of Technology (RIT) and majored in photography. He graduated from RIT in 1964 and then entered the air force. He joined the air force by choice, not by draft. His aspiration was to become a pilot. Unfortunately, becoming a pilot did not work out and instead he chose to take the specialist's test for photography. Michael easily passed the test and was sent to Roswell, New Mexico, for his first duty assignment.

By mid-1966, a temporary duty assignment came down from headquarters requesting a photographer in Washington, D.C. The assignment was not specific and none of the staff at Roswell thought it had anything to do with the White House. There were only three photographers at Roswell qualified for the position, and Michael only had a few months remaining with his enlistment. He was really looking forward to getting out in September, but the timeframe for the assignment was from June to December. Michael said he would accept the assignment if it didn't require him to extend his enlistment for an entire year. The air force agreed and extended his enlistment only to January of 1967, just enough time to cover the assignment. Michael also knew that he had a better chance of finding a job in Washington than in New Mexico, once he fulfilled his enlistment. The assignment only stated that he was to report to an address on "M" Street in Georgetown, which just happened to be where the White House photo lab and the White House communication agency were located. Of course, Michael didn't know that at the time. Once he arrived and started working, he quickly realized the unique opportunity. When January 1967 came and the assignment was technically finished, Michael went to Bill Maravek who was the White House chief for the photo lab, and requested to stay on. He told Mr. Maravek that he had a degree in photography from RIT and would like a chance to take pictures at the White House. Bill discussed the idea with Yoichi Okamoto and they both agreed to keep Michael on. They started him out with weekly rotations to the White House with an army sergeant who had just came in to assist with the photography. Fortunately for Michael, "This sergeant didn't know whether to take pictures or salute. So, he lasted about a couple of weeks and he was gone. Michael kept rotating to the White House to take pictures and kind of just rolled into the mix of things." [21]

The White House photographer staff at this time consisted of Yoichi Okamoto (Oke)—who was the chief White House photographer,—Frank Wolfe, Kevin Smith, Bob Knudsen, and Michael. Oke covered the president and the more important events while Bob primarily covered events with Mrs. Johnson and her two daughters. The other staff photographers, Frank, Kevin, and Michael, would rotate on events and on presidential trips with Oke. Frank Wolf and Kevin Smith were both military, while Bob Knudsen was classified as civil service. Oke and Michael were civilian appointees.

When January 20, 1969, arrived, and President Johnson retired from office, Richard Nixon replaced most of the photography staff with his own appointments.

After the White House, Michael took a position as the head of the public relations photo operations at Virginia Tech. He did this for a few years and then went back to his alma mater, Rochester Institute of Technology, where he taught for fifteen years. In 1985, he participated in a faculty exchange program between RIT and Shanghai University of Technology and spent several months teaching and traveling in China. While in China, he took more than three-hundred rolls of film and once again realized his love for photography. When he returned from China in 1986, he moved to Washington, D.C. and began his own freelance photography business. While still freelancing today for publications like the *Financial Times* of London, *Newsday*, and the *New York Times*, he owns and publishes the *Alexandria Guide*, a regional publication that focuses on tourism for the Alexandria, Virginia, area.

# The Collection

The collection of material provided within this text includes original photographs, letters, and other political memorabilia obtained primarily from four distinct and significant sources: 1) The Sanford L. Fox collection, 2) The Robert L. Knudsen collection, 3) The Congressman George Mahon collection, and 4) the Frank P. Muto collection. Another smaller collection worthy of note came from the estate of a lady who had worked for Neiman Marcus in Dallas, Texas. Neiman Marcus assisted with much of the wardrobe worn by Mrs. Johnson and her two daughters.

---

## The Frank Muto Collection

The Frank Muto collection consists of all original black and white photographs (and contact sheets) taken of Lyndon Johnson during his 1960 Democratic campaign for president.

These photographs cover a very short period of time beginning in November 1959 with only a handful covering the timeframe when LBJ was a Democratic candidate for president. Three contact sheets in the collection cover the first few months, when Lyndon Johnson was vice president.

## The Robert Knudsen Collection

The Robert L. Knudsen collection of original and vintage photographic prints were obtained from the estate of Robert Knudsen, which was sold at public auction by Guernsey's auction house in New York on November 16–17, 2002.

## The Congressman George Mahon Collection

The Congressman George Mahon collection of signed photographs, letters, and other material spans the political era from President Dwight D. Eisenhower to President Gerald Ford. The collection consists of fifteen formally signed and unsigned White House photographs, many of which depict the congressman and his wife with President and Mrs. Johnson at various functions. Other photographs are more personal, such as the Johnson family photos that were sent to George and Helen Mahon during special occasions.

Also included in the collection are a full series of official White House Christmas cards that were sent to Congressman Mahon and his wife over the years from the president and first lady.

## The Sanford L. Fox Collection

The Sanford Fox collection of signed photographs, letters, notes, and other political autographs were all obtained from the estate of Sanford Fox that was sold at public auction by Guernsey's auction house in New York on November 16–17, 2002.

Sanford L. Fox

Chief of the Social Entertainment Office ★ White House
Staff Photograph, John Fitzgerald Kennedy Library and Museum,
Boston, MA

# Sanford L. Fox
# (1919–1996)

Sanford L. Fox (Sandy, as he was called) was the chief of the social entertainment office, the director of protocol, and the coordinator of graphics for the White House from 1960 until his retirement in December 1974. "Mr. Fox was the fourth person to occupy the position since it was created in 1881 as support to the social secretary and to the first family. Prior to heading the office, Mr. Fox was 'on loan' from the State Department, the navy, and the CIA throughout most of the 1940s and 1950s. From his office in the northeast corner of the east wing of the executive mansion, Mr. Fox contributed to and participated in historic events for seven administrations—those of Presidents Franklin D. Roosevelt, Harry S. Truman, Dwight D. Eisenhower, John F. Kennedy, Lyndon B. Johnson, Richard M. Nixon, and Gerald Ford."[1]

"His office produced by hand and by letterpress all the exquisite invitations, menus, place cards, escort cards, and programs that helped make a White House social or state occasion a memorable event. The talents of Sanford Fox were brought to the attention of the White House in 1942 when he was an Army Corps lieutenant en route to the World War II Teheran Conference as a member of Franklin D. Roosevelt's flight crew. Part of his assignment was to teach the president how to don a life jacket in the event that the plane went down. Mr. Roosevelt, on learning of Mr. Fox's calligraphy skills, engaged him to pen the place cards for a stopover dinner in Cairo. Here Franklin Roosevelt met Churchill before going on to the Teheran Conference. Following the war, Sanford Fox was detailed to the White House and was later "borrowed" by the White House from time to time to assist in the calligraphy for special occasions."[2]

"Sanford Fox, a resident of Alexandria, Virginia, was renowned for his calligraphy and artistic abilities. His duties over the years in the White House included the design and calligraphy used for the proclamation of U.S. citizenship awarded to Winston Churchill as well as the design for the prayer card issued for President Kennedy's funeral. He also coordinated the weddings for the daughters of both President Johnson and President Nixon. Aside from his artistic duties, during Christmas at the White House he would play Santa Claus for the visiting underprivileged children. Mr. Fox, who suffered from Alzheimer's disease, died at the age of seventy seven on December 29, 1996."[3]

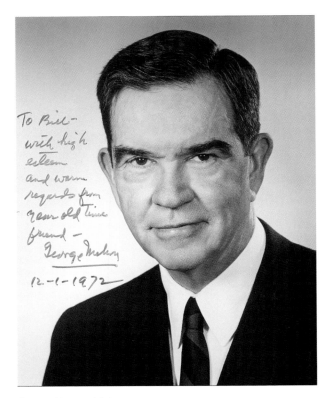

George Herman Mahon

Congressional Photograph by Anton Studio 1966 ★ Library of
Congress Number LC-USZ62-107883)

# George Herman Mahon
# (1900–1985)

"Congressman George Mahon was born September 22, 1900, in a small town named after his ancestors: Mahon, Louisiana, which is near Haynesville, Louisiana. He and his family moved to Loraine, Texas, when he was eight years old and he attended public school. Congressman Mahon graduated college from Hardin Simmons University in Abilene, Texas, and went on to study law at both the University of Texas and at the University of Minnesota. Upon his return to Texas from Minnesota, he set up his first law practice in Colorado City, Texas. He successfully campaigned and served as the county attorney and later served as the district attorney. His campaign for Congress began in 1934, which he successfully won and was sworn into office on January 3, 1935, representing the nineteenth district of Texas. Congressman Mahon would serve forty-four consecutive years in congress, under eight presidents, until his retirement in 1979. He became a leading member of the House Appropriations Committee in 1939 and later served as the chairman of that committee from 1963–1978. During his tenure as congressman, he was considered one of the four or five most powerful men in national government."[4] Congressman Mahon also served on what was called the "Committee of Eight." This committee was a small select group of men chosen by President Truman and "entrusted with providing the funds for, and keeping secret the atomic bomb project—known as The Manhattan Project."[5] Congressman George Mahon was also in the Dallas motorcade that fateful day when President John F. Kennedy was shot and killed. Congressman Mahon recalls that he was riding about four or five cars behind the president.[6] Helen Mahon recounts that her husband was also present on Air Force One after Lyndon Johnson was sworn into office. "He flew from Dallas to San Antonio on the plane with President Johnson. He then flew in the vice president's plane from San Antonio to Houston. When they left Houston that night, he flew back to Fort Worth on the president's plane, where he and the president talked most of the way."[7] George Mahon married Helen Stevenson of Loraine, Texas, in 1923. Her father was a former county judge.[8] Their only child, Daphne, who was born in 1927, later moved to Dallas and married Judge Duncan Holt. Congressman Mahon died November 19, 1985, and is buried in Loraine, Texas. His portrait hangs in the Appropriations Committee Chamber on Capitol Hill in recognition for his many years of public service. Although George Mahon served in congress for more than forty years, the availability of political material for the congressman is quite scarce. Since the time I acquired the Mahon family photo album, I have continued to search for material by the late congressman. I have determined that congressional material for George Mahon is extremely rare and quite difficult to find. The reason for this scarcity is unknown and rather unusual, given the many years he served as congressman.

The portrait shown above is an 8x10 black-and-white photograph obtained from the estate of a Dallas attorney and longtime friend. This photograph was personally signed and dated by Congressman George Mahon. The inscription reads, "To Bill, with high esteem and warm regards from your old time friend, George Mahon, 12-1-1972."

# The Art and History
# of Photography

There are several key characteristics to look for when authenticating original photography versus contemporary or later prints. The first requirement is to have a good understanding of the processing techniques used during a particular period in time. I will not go into all of the various processing techniques used throughout history, because there are a multitude of books available that address that topic. I will elaborate on what to look for in photographic prints common to the 1960s. The photograph itself will usually have indications of the processing technique used, and thus its approximate age.

Once these older photographic techniques are understood, one will gain a much greater appreciation for the art and technique of earlier photography.

## Black and White Photography

The most common black and white photographic paper used during the 1960s was a silver bromide, fiber-based, graded paper. All of the Frank Muto prints in this collection were processed using a single weight, grade 2 fiber-based paper. The glossy surface found on these photographs was created through an old technique called glazing or ferrotyping. To create a glossy surface, the photographer would squeegee the photograph face down on a metal sheet called a ferrotype plate. Once done, the photographer could then choose to either soak the print in a glazing solution or place the print onto a heated glazing machine that baked a glossy surface to the print. By the early 1970s when variable contrast and resin-coated papers came onto the market, the need for this tedious glazing process was eliminated.[1]

Contemporary black and white photographs can be differentiated from older or pre 1970s photography through inspecting the paper and the surface textures that were created through these specific processing techniques.

## Color Photography

During the 1960s, mass production of color photography was just coming of age. The color processing techniques at this time still required more work than black and white photography. For the less experienced photographer, it could take as much as an hour to process and print just one unfamiliar color negative.[2]

Color photography and the modern processing techniques we know today originated from the research and development at Kodak and Agfa during the 1940s. By the 1950s Kodak and Agfa had developed specific proprietary techniques for their color photography. These developments gave the professional photographer the capability to process color prints more independently. But, it was not until the 1970s when color processing techniques and equipment costs were reduced enough for widespread use.[3]

The most common processing technique used during the 1960s was the chromogenic technique. For this process, the color film and paper consisted of three silver halide emulsion layers, each layer being sensitive to blue, green, or red light. The natural spectrum of light would affect each of these emulsion layers to form specific color images. In the beginning, the three-layer technique required the creation of three separate negatives. Each negative would be used independently to create different colors for a final transfer to paper. By the 1950s, Kodak and Agfa developed their own chemicals called couplers that combined all three emulsion layers into a single form, called a tri-pack.[4]

There were two types of paper available for color printing—positive and reversal paper. Positive paper was used for printing from color negatives while reversal paper was used to create color prints from transparencies. Positive papers were the most common and easiest to use. In general, the color papers had fewer surface textures compared to black and white papers. Most of these papers would yield a matte finish because creating a glossy finish through the "glazing" method had the potential to destroy a color print. Although glossy color prints were made, they took a much longer time to process.[5]

## Official White House Photographs

When looking at official White House photographs, the name of the photographer and, in almost every case, the date and photo number will be stamped on the back. This was a standard practice for the White House photo lab and is a quick means by which to determine an official photograph. Photographs intended for mass public distribution by the White House would usually have only the date and photo number stamped on the back. (**See the section, starting on page 225, for some examples of the photographer's stamps that can be found on the reverse side of official White House photographs.**)

During the Lyndon B. Johnson administration, most official White House photographs were printed at 11"x14". Yoichi Okamoto mentions this point in his 1970 slideshow presentation, and Michael Geissinger and Kevin Smith have mentioned this during interviews. Although 8"x10" and 5"x7" photos were printed and can be considered "official," these sizes were usually printed in larger quantities and were intended for public distribution. Contact and proof sheets were generated specifically for the lab or for the staff photographers themselves and were seldom, if ever, distributed or offered to the general public.

The ability to determine a contemporary photographic print from an original takes a keen eye and a reasonable understanding of both the history and the photographic techniques used during a particular period in time. If one decides to undertake the venture of collecting original photography, approach it no differently than collecting any other work of art. Do your homework first. With today's sophisticated use of technology, the layman and professional alike can sometimes be fooled.

## White House Photography Today

Susan Kismaric, who is the curator of photography at the Museum of Modern Art in New York, said it best in her book *American Politicians—Photographs from 1843 to 1995*, when she said: "…photographers will continue, in the near future anyway, to make meaningful and important photographs of politicians. It is their job as journalists and artists to report and comment on what interests the public and that which consumes images. And as a public, our desire for photographs of our leaders has not abated. The people we select to represent us symbolize that which we hope for. As a group, photographers remain profoundly important in telling us how successful we are in our choices. They will make photographs that describe campaigns, influence elections, document terms of office, and portray the man or woman behind the image. They will make photographs that will help create and then confirm our image of ourselves through our politicians, the photographs that will exist in our museums and in newspapers and magazine archives as history."[6]

# The Congress
# and Senate Years

Lyndon B. Johnson got his first job in Washington, D.C., in 1931, when Congressman Richard Kleberg hired the young Lyndon as his congressional secretary. By 1934, at the age of twenty-six, Lyndon Johnson was elected as the speaker of the Little Congress. The Little Congress was the association composed of secretaries to the congressmen.[1] In that same year, Lyndon Johnson married Claudia Taylor, better known as Lady Bird. By 1935, Lyndon Johnson became the director of the National Youth Administration (NYA) through the appointment of President Franklin Roosevelt. Lyndon worked as the director of the NYA for two years until the 10th Congressional District of Texas was suddenly left vacant by the death of Congressman James Buchanan. Lyndon resigned as the director of the NYA to campaign for the congressional seat, which he successfully won. In 1941, when Texas Senator Morris Sheppard passed away, Lyndon campaigned for that seat, but lost the Senate race to the former Texas governor, W. Lee O'Daniel. While in Congress, Lyndon and Lady Bird Johnson gave birth to two girls—Lynda Bird Johnson, born on March 19, 1944, and Lucy Baines Johnson, who was born three years later on July 2, 1947. In 1948, Lyndon Johnson decided to try his hand again at winning a seat in the Senate. This time he would win, but with much controversy. He beat the very popular former Texas Governor Coke Stevenson by only eighty-seven votes.

Regardless of this narrow victory, Lyndon Johnson's tenure in the Senate is considered legendary. In 1951, he was elected the majority whip, and then in 1953, he was elected as the minority leader. By 1955, he was elected the Senate majority leader, which made him the youngest senator to ever have been elected to that position. In 1960, Lyndon Johnson campaigned as a Democratic candidate for president, but lost the party vote to John F. Kennedy. John F. Kennedy in turn asked Lyndon Johnson to be his running mate for vice president. LBJ accepted the offer and when John Kennedy won the presidential election, Lyndon Johnson ended his long and successful career in the Senate and became the vice president of the United States."[2]

# The 1946 Congressional Campaign

The 1946 campaign for Congress occurred during a time when the country was reorganizing after the war. Many of the men were returning home, looking for jobs and a means to build a family. Many feared that the sudden decline in military production would cause massive unemployment and return the country back to the depression days.

At this time, Lyndon Johnson had just lost his father figure, President Franklin D. Roosevelt, on April 12, 1945. Congressman Johnson had served under no other President. He and President Roosevelt were close, and the president had taken the young Lyndon under his wing as if he were a son. For the first time, Lyndon Johnson was on his own with no political muscle at the top, with the exception of Sam Rayburn who resided in the House of Representatives.

The 1946 Johnson campaign was up against a man named Hardy Hollers. Mr. Hollers was the son of a 'circuit-riding preacher' who had assisted in the prosecution of German war criminals after the war.[3] Hardy Hollers himself was a well-known attorney and a recently discharged army colonel. He campaigned against Lyndon Johnson on two issues. One, that he was a veteran, and two, that Lyndon Johnson was a crook.[4]

Willard Deason, an attorney and old college friend of Lyndon is said, "The 1946 campaign was very bitter, not on Mr. Johnson's part, but on the part of his opponent. Hollers accused Lyndon of everything under the sun, including his war record. He said he had been in the army for four years, and that Lyndon had been in the navy for just a few months. And that while he hadn't been making any money, Lyndon had been getting rich, and he accused Lyndon of being close to Roosevelt and then close to Truman, and so on."[5]

Jake Pickle, a personal friend to the Johnson family and later a congressman said, "All kinds of rumors were floating around town, that Lyndon owned *this* building and owned *that* apartment house; and that he was the front man for several big investors; and that he was just growing rich in office. That was the theme used more than any other during the campaign. No actual charges were ever made against Lyndon, just implied statements that he had feathered his nest and was getting rich. Lyndon felt that it was a campaign by some of the major oil companies that didn't like some of his votes, and he in turn attacked the oil companies and campaigned against them far more than he campaigned against Colonel Hollers."[6]

Lyndon Johnson focused on the rural districts and on behalf of the farmer. He spoke of "farm-to-market roads, low interest farm loans, crop insurance, and school lunches for farm children."[7]

To spice up the campaign trail, Gene Autry, the cowboy musician and actor appeared with Congressman Johnson during twelve of his campaign rallies.

The following exhibits are unpublished photographs of one of the campaign rallies held in Texas in July of 1946. These photographs came from a personal photo album of a local Texas resident who had attended the rallies.

These photographs provide an unprecedented view and unique perspective of Lyndon Johnson during his early years. These early "hometown" photos represent what Lyndon B. Johnson was all about. Yoichi Okamoto pointed this perspective out in his 1970 slideshow presentation, referring to a photograph he had taken in Fredericksburg, Texas. Okamoto said, "This is Johnson country, this is Johnson people. You have to understand this when you think of Johnson. These are the people he was born and brought up with."[8]

This first exhibit is an original 5"x7" black-and-white photograph of Congressman Lyndon B. Johnson, taken in July of 1946 during a campaign stop in Texas. The photograph shows Lyndon Johnson on stage with a microphone hanging around his neck, addressing a crowd of supporters. The photograph was signed by Lyndon Johnson at the lower right portion and says, ". . . from his friend—Lyndon B. Johnson."

**Exhibit #1** ★ an original 5"x7" black and white photograph of Congressman Lyndon B. Johnson, taken in July of 1946 during a campaign stop in Texas.

**Exhibit #2** ★ Gene Autry (1907–1998) This is an original 3"x5" black-and-white photograph of Texas cowboy actor and musician Gene Autry.

Exhibit #2 is an original 3"x5" black-and-white photograph of Texas cowboy actor and musician Gene Autry. The photograph shows Gene Autry on stage in Texas where he performed during a 1946 campaign rally for Lyndon Johnson. Gene Autry was a well-recognized Texas celebrity. He was born and raised in Tioga, Texas, just north of Dallas. Lyndon Johnson had helped Gene Autry during the war by getting him assigned to the air transport command and then later assisting him in speeding up his discharge at the end of the war so he could get back to singing and acting. When Gene Autry asked Lyndon if he could help with his 1946 campaign, he gladly accepted.[9] Lyndon Johnson's organizers would send out postcards inviting people to hear his speech. Advertisements would appear in the local newspapers, handbills would be distributed, and telephone calls would be made on the day of the event to remind voters to come. A few hours before the event, the four-man band called "Johnson's Hill Billy Boys" would ride around town playing music to let everyone know that the rally was about to begin. During the rally, Gene Autry would sing old time favorites like "I'm Back in the Saddle Again," and say to the crowd, "Let's put my friend Lyndon back in the saddle again, because that's where he belongs."[10]

Other well-known songs such as "Sioux City Sue" and "Home on the Range" were played, as well as other favorites. When all was said and done, "You couldn't tell a rally from a roundup." Lorraine Barnes, a feature reporter for the *Austin American* newspaper, reported in an article after the rally, on Saturday July 27, 1946, "Lyndon Johnson, that old vote-wrangler from Johnson City, paced a fast election-eve campaign Friday through seven central Texas towns to the lyrical refrain: 'I'm back in the saddle again, Out where a friend is a friend . . .' That voice was the clear tenor of another Texan of some renown—Gene Autry, top movie cowhand, who played through seven successive mob scenes at the hands of central Texas youngsters 'Just a ridin', rockin', and a ropin', 'Autry sang. 'Poundin' leather all day long . . .'"[11]

The third exhibit is an original 3"x5" black-and-white photograph showing Lyndon Johnson sitting in the backseat of his car, reaching out to shake the hand of a young supporter.

Lyndon Johnson had a very warm spot in his heart for young folks. Having been a teacher and the director of the National Youth Administration before becoming a congressman, he recognized the importance of those who would someday be the next generation of voters.

**Exhibit #3** ★  Photograph of Congressman Lyndon B. Johnson, taken July 1946. Lyndon Johnson sitting in the backseat of his car, reaching out to shake the hand of a young supporter.

The fourth and final photograph in this series is an original 3"x5" black-and-white photograph that shows a 1946 election return board that was erected outside a Texas county courthouse. Two men can be seen reviewing the latest results.

Lyndon B. Johnson won his congressional seat for the 10th District in 1946 with 65 percent of the vote.[12]

**Exhibit #4** ★ Photograph of a 1946 Election-Return Board that was set up outside a Texas county courthouse

## The 1948 Senate Campaign

The 1948 Texas Senate campaign "was one of the toughest, most dramatic, most complicated, and most disputed elections in Texas history."[13] At first, Lyndon Johnson did not want to run for Senate. To do so, he would be required to give up his current seat in Congress. If he lost the Senate election, he would lose everything. On May 11, 1948, John Connally and several other Texas Senate campaign supporters met to discuss whether Lyndon Johnson should be the candidate. When the group told Lyndon they thought a younger man such as John Connally should be the candidate, the very next day, on May 12, 1948, Lyndon Johnson announced his candidacy for U.S. Senate.[14] The 1948 Texas Senate campaign stage was set, with Lyndon Johnson running against a very popular former Texas governor, Coke Stevenson. Johnson exploited his campaign agenda with two issues against Coke Stevenson—the labor union and the issue of communism in government.[15] The campaign reached its summit in August 1948 with LBJ campaigning by helicopter and visiting as many as ten to twenty towns a day. The runoff election was held on Saturday, August 29, 1948. The voting was very close. On the evening of the election, Stevenson led by 8000 votes. The next day, Stevenson's lead fell to only eight votes. At that point, a critical set of votes from Duvall County put Johnson in the lead again. After the vote count continued back and forth for nearly a week, the state Democratic Executive Committee, on September 14, 1948, certified the final votes with Lyndon Johnson winning the election by just eighty-seven votes.[16] Stevenson contested the election and took the challenge all the way to the Supreme Court. Johnson's lawyer, Abe Fortas, convinced the court that it had no jurisdiction to review the ballots and on November 3, 1948, Lyndon Johnson was proclaimed the winner. This set of circumstances earned him the nickname of "Landslide Lyndon."[17] LBJ's primary staff at this time consisted of Mary Rather as his personal secretary, Leslie Carpenter as publicity manager, his brother Sam Houston Johnson as an "all-around troubleshooter," John Connally as his administrative assistant, Horace Busby as his speech writer, and Walter Jenkins and Warren Woodward as his seconds-in-command.[18]

**State Headquarters**

# LYNDON B. JOHNSON

## FOR

## UNITED STATES SENATE

301 WEST EIGHTH ST.          TELEPHONE 5333

AUSTIN, TEXAS

July 26, 1948

Vice-President and
Managing Director
Baker Hotel
Mineral Wells, Texas

My dear Friend:

Thanks so much for your letter
of the 23rd. Wish I had time to
take that rest, but I am leaving
for Washington today. I appreciate
your good wishes and hope to see
you soon.

Sincerely,

Lyndon B. Johnson

*"It's Time For a Man with a Platform"*

**Exhibit #5** ★ Letter sent by Congressman Lyndon Johnson on his Senate Campaign letterhead, dated July 26, 1948.

Exhibit five is an original letter written to a supporter from Lyndon Johnson on his Senate campaign letterhead, dated July 26, 1948. These original letters are extremely rare since the campaign headquarters were in operation for only a few short months.

**Exhibit #6** ★ Photograph is copyright Arnold Newman, Getty Images. Senate Minority Leader Lyndon B. Johnson, taken July 12, 1953, in the President's Room

Exhibit six is an original vintage 10.5"x13.5" color photograph of Senate Minority Leader Lyndon B. Johnson, taken July 12, 1953, in the President's Room located in the Senate office building, Washington, D.C. The photograph was taken by the famed portrait photographer Arnold Newman in 1953 and was published in the February 10, 1954, issue of *Holiday Magazine*. This original Arnold Newman photograph was mounted in the mid-1950s to a photo matboard and was signed at the bottom by Senator Lyndon Johnson to a friend. This particular photograph is quite scarce. Only a handful of these "original" vintage prints are known to exist. It is now thought that many of these prints came from *Holiday Magazine*. *Holiday Magazine* had the original Arnold Newman negative for a period of time as they prepared the February 1954 issue. How many of these large color prints were made for LBJ is unknown, but certainly very few. Placing a favorite photograph on a mat and then autographing the photograph was a common gift the Johnsons would use throughout their political career. This particular inscription reads, "To Charles . . ., from his friend, Lyndon B. Johnson." In 1953, Lyndon Johnson was elected minority leader of the Senate. By 1954, when this photograph was published, he had been elected to the Senate for a second term. By the next year, in 1955, Lyndon Johnson was elected the Senate majority leader and became the youngest man to have been elected majority leader in U.S. Senate history. This particular photograph is listed in the LBJ Library and Museum as photograph #54-2-2 and is copyright Arnold Newman, Getty Images.

**Exhibit #7** ★ Photographer's proof sheet of four large-format 120mm photographic negatives taken November 1, 1959, during the Texas Jaycee Citizenship Seminar held in Austin, Texas. ★ Photographs by Frank Muto

Exhibit seven is an 8"x10" proof sheet of four large-format 120mm photographic negatives taken November 1, 1959, during the Texas Jaycee Citizenship Seminar held in Austin, Texas. On the reverse of the contact sheet is the photographer's handwritten catalog number, FM-537. The top left photograph shows the entertainer Arthur Godfrey receiving an award from Jack Miller, the Jaycee president. The top right photograph shows from left to right, Jack Miller, Jaycee President; Tom Miller, the Austin mayor; Arthur Godfrey; and Senator Lyndon Johnson. The lower left photograph shows Senator Thomas Dodd from Connecticut speaking with Arthur Godfrey. The lower right photograph again shows Arthur Godfrey receiving an award from the Jaycees.

Just fourteen days earlier on, October 17, 1959, the Speaker of the House of Representatives, Sam Rayburn, announced the formation of the "Johnson-for-President Committee" at a press conference in Dallas, Texas.

The Lyndon B. Johnson campaign for the 1960 Democratic presidential election had just begun.

These photographs can be referenced in the Lyndon Johnson Library and Museum, audiovisual archives, reference numbers 59-11-2FM, 59-11-7FM, 59-11-6FM, and 59-11-14FM.

**Exhibit #8** ★ Photograph Taken November 4, 1959, during LBJ's Democratic Presidential Campaign through Texas ★ Photograph by Frank Muto

## The 1960 Presidential Candidate

Exhibit eight is an 8"x10" photograph taken November 4, 1959, during LBJ's campaign swing through Texas as a Democratic presidential candidate. This photograph shows Senator Lyndon Johnson shaking hands with an unidentified supporter in Corpus Christi, Texas. On the reverse of the photograph is the photographer's catalog number, FM-601. The LBJ Library photograph reference number is 59-11-95FM.

Exhibit nine is an 8"x10" photograph taken November 5, 1959, probably in Sinton, Texas. The Lyndon B. Johnson Library and Museum does not indicate a specific location for this photograph. The photograph shows

**Exhibit #9** ★ Photograph Taken November 5, 1959, during LBJ's Democratic Presidential Campaign through Texas ★ Photograph by Frank Muto

Lyndon and Lady Bird Johnson speaking before a small group of students during his campaign as a Democratic presidential candidate.

Lyndon Johnson always had an interest in the welfare and education of American youth. Lyndon's own experience as a teacher in Cotulla, Texas, in his early years of college left a lifelong impression that molded a great respect for the teaching profession and an appreciation for the student/teacher relationship. Many years later, Lyndon Johnson would say, "I still see the faces of the children who sat in my class . . . I still see their excited eyes speaking friendship."[19]

The LBJ Library and Museum reference and catalog number for this photo is 59-11-125FM.

**Exhibit #10** ★ Presidential Candidate Lyndon Johnson Speaking to Reporters on May 6-7, 1960 ★ Photograph by Frank Muto

Exhibit ten is an 8"x10" photograph taken May 6–7, 1960, en route to Pennsylvania and West Virginia on board a Convair aircraft during LBJ's campaign as a Democratic candidate for president. The Democratic Convention was only two months away and would be held in Los Angeles, California. In this photograph, Senator Lyndon Johnson is seen speaking to a group of reporters. From left to right are Bill Secrest, Bob Vermillion, Bob Baskin, LBJ, John Mathis, and Mary M. Wiley. Mary Margaret Wiley would later become Mrs. Jack Valenti. Mary Wiley was Senator Johnson's secretary for many years. She and Jack Valenti would later marry in Houston, Texas, on June 1, 1962, when LBJ was vice president. Mary asked the vice president to give her away.[20] It was at this time that Marie Fehmer took over as LBJ's executive secretary. Eventually Jack Valenti would be appointed as LBJ's personal assistant during his administration. Mary and Jack were very close friends to the Johnsons. They had a daughter named Courtenay who was very close to the president. The White House staff had standing orders to notify him when Mary and Jack brought Courtenay to the White House. He was known to get angry if he discovered she had been there and he had not been informed.

On the reverse of this photo is written FM-CS-255-6. The LBJ Library and Museum reference and catalog number is 60-5-5 FM, 1960 Campaign Strip #10.

## The 1960 Democratic National Convention

The Democratic National Convention was held on July 11, 1960, in Los Angeles, California. On the second day of the convention, Sam Rayburn formally placed Lyndon Johnson on the Democratic ballot as a presidential candidate. As history indicates, John F. Kennedy would win the nomination on the first ballot, with 806 votes to Lyndon Johnson's 409 votes.

Senator Johnson had stiff competition in 1960. Other notable men on the Democratic presidential ballot included Stuart Symington, Adlai Stevenson, and Hubert Humphrey. Although there was much speculation and hype surrounding the 1960 Democratic Convention, the two front-runners were clearly John Kennedy and Lyndon Johnson.

Much has been written about the events leading up to John Kennedy's asking Lyndon Johnson to be his running mate. Debate still exists on exactly how Lyndon Johnson came to accept the offer. Nevertheless, here was Lyndon Johnson, the most powerful and experienced majority leader of the Senate, being offered the least politically influential position in the executive branch, the vice presidency. Why did Lyndon Johnson accept John Kennedy's offer to be his running mate? Sam Rayburn and others told him not to accept it. Kennedy caught hell from his inner circle including his brother Bobby for even considering LBJ.

I believe Theodore Sorenson summed up Kennedy's position best: "The selection of the vice president is not the clean slate that one thinks it is. After a while, you get down to the choice of who is going to hurt you the least. So the list narrows down rather quickly. In 1960, it was particularly important that the vice presidential candidate be a protestant and not be from the Northeast. Johnson was the logical person to ask. He was the runner-up at the convention. He was the leader of the party where Kennedy had little strength—the South, and to some extent the West. He was the majority leader of the Senate. He was a man with whom Kennedy had worked in the Senate. They were compatible, and Kennedy admired and respected Johnson. He had the greatness and the stature. So, for all these reasons, it was logical to go first to Lyndon Johnson and ask him if he would be vice president."[21]

Why did LBJ accept Kennedy's offer? LBJ would be giving up his very powerful position of Senate majority leader. "Why was it accepted? The answer to this question goes beyond JFK's reasons for making the offer. Lyndon Johnson agreed with the argument that he would strengthen the Democratic ticket, but his reasons were far reaching. He knew that by 1968, he would be sixty years old and if he wanted to be the president of the United States, he needed to position himself for it. The office of the vice president, if used correctly, could aid in that goal. He knew and understood the depth of the liberal Democrats who were opposed to him. He believed that he could use the eight years as vice president to demonstrate to these groups that he was not the enemy. As a Senator from Texas, even being the Senate majority leader, he could not be too far ahead of his Texas constituents. He knew and understood the first two rules of politics: (1) represent your constituency, and (2) do not break until you are strong enough at home to withstand the challenge. Having won the 1948 election by only eighty–seven questionable votes, LBJ was in no position to challenge the conservative Texas electorate. His three-to-one victory in 1954 had made it possible to start moving away from the conservative voting patterns and toward the center of the national Democratic Party. As vice president, he would no longer be tied to a purely Texas voting base."[22]

## The 1960 Presidential Campaign

These next series of photographs (exhibits 11–18) were all taken during the month of September 1960. The campaign was at its height of activity with the November primary just around the corner. As can be seen in these photographs, large crowds of supporters came out to greet the popular candidate.

## Religion As an Issue in the 1960 Campaign

The 1960 presidential campaign was surrounded with controversy over John F. Kennedy's being Catholic. Lyndon Johnson, on the other hand, was a member of the Disciples of Christ from his hometown of Johnson City. LBJ was raised in a small town where half the residents were Baptist and the other half were Methodist or Disciples of Christ.[23] Religion played an important role in American politics during the 1960 campaign. Many voters turned out to vote their religion rather than their politics. A stark example to the deep emotions surrounding this topic was noticed in a campaign sign held by an elderly lady in Sutton, West Virginia, that read: "We've never had a Catholic president and I hope we never do. Our people built this country. If they had wanted a Catholic to be president, they would have said so in the Constitution."[24]

On September 12, 1960, the day before JFK arrived in Austin, Texas *(see Exhibit #11)*, John F. Kennedy agreed to meet with the Ministerial Association of Houston, Texas, to offer his views on the issues of religion as it related to politics. In his speech, "He clearly favored the separation of church and state, opposed federal aid to parochial schools, opposed sending an ambassador to the Vatican, and put his oath to the Constitution over the dictates of the church in the realm of politics."[25]

# ADDRESS OF SENATOR JOHN F. KENNEDY TO THE GREATER HOUSTON MINISTERIAL ASSOCIATION
## Rice Hotel, Houston, Texas ★ September 12, 1960

*Reverend Meza, Reverend Reck, I'm grateful for your generous invitation to speak my views.*

*While the so-called religious issue is necessarily and properly the chief topic here tonight, I want to emphasize from the outset that we have far more critical issues to face in the 1960 election; the spread of Communist influence, until it now festers 90 miles off the coast of Florida—the humiliating treatment of our President and Vice President by those who no longer respect our power—the hungry children I saw in West Virginia, the old people who cannot pay their doctor bills, the families forced to give up their farms—an America with too many slums, with too few schools, and too late to the moon and outer space.*

*These are the real issues which should decide this campaign. And they are not religious issues—for war and hunger and ignorance and despair know no religious barriers.*

*But because I am a Catholic, and no Catholic has ever been elected President, the real issues in this campaign have been obscured—perhaps deliberately, in some quarters less responsible than this. So it is apparently necessary for me to state once again—not what kind of church I believe in, for that should be important only to me—but what kind of America I believe in.*

*I believe in an America where the separation of church and state is absolute—where no Catholic prelate would tell the President (should he be Catholic) how to act, and no Protestant minister would tell his parishioners for whom to vote—where no church or church school is granted any public funds or political preference— and where no man is denied public office merely because his religion differs from the President who might appoint him or the people who might elect him.*

*I believe in an America that is officially neither Catholic, Protestant nor Jewish—where no public official either requests or accepts instructions on public policy from the Pope, the National Council of Churches or any other ecclesiastical source—where no religious body seeks to impose its will directly or indirectly upon the general populace or the public acts of its officials—and where religious liberty is so indivisible that an act against one church is treated as an act against all.*

*For while this year it may be a Catholic against whom the finger of suspicion is pointed, in other years it has been, and may someday be again, a Jew—or a Quaker—or a Unitarian—or a Baptist. It was Virginia's harassment of Baptist preachers, for example, that helped lead to Jefferson's statute of religious freedom. Today I may be the victim—but tomorrow it may be you—until the whole fabric of our harmonious society is ripped at a time of great national peril.*

*Finally, I believe in an America where religious intolerance will someday end—where all men and all churches are treated as equal—where every man has the same right to attend or not attend the church of his choice—where there is no Catholic vote, no anti-Catholic vote, no bloc voting of any kind—and where Catholics, Protestants and Jews, at both the lay and pastoral level, will refrain from those attitudes of disdain and division which have so often marred their works in the past, and promote instead the American ideal of brotherhood.*

*That is the kind of America in which I believe. And it represents the kind of Presidency in which I believe—a great office that must neither be humbled by making it the instrument of any one religious group nor tarnished by arbitrarily withholding its occupancy from the members of any one religious group. I believe in a President whose religious views are his own private affair, neither imposed by him upon the nation or imposed by the nation upon him as a condition to holding that office.*

*I would not look with favor upon a President working to subvert the first amendment's guarantees of religious liberty. Nor would our system of checks and balances permit him to do so—and neither do I look with favor upon those who would work to subvert Article VI of the Constitution by requiring a religious test— even by indirection—for it. If they disagree with that safeguard they should be out openly working to repeal it.*

*I want a Chief Executive whose public acts are responsible to all groups and obligated to none—who can attend any ceremony, service or dinner his office may appropriately require of him—and whose fulfillment of his Presidential oath is not limited or conditioned by any religious oath, ritual or obligation.*

*This is the kind of America I believe in—and this is the kind I fought for in the South Pacific, and the kind my brother died for in Europe. No one suggested then that we may have a "divided loyalty," that we did "not believe in liberty," or that we belonged to a disloyal group that threatened the "freedoms for which our forefathers died."*

*And in fact this is the kind of America for which our forefathers died—when they fled here to escape religious test oaths that denied office to members of less favored churches—when they fought for the Constitution, the Bill of Rights, and the Virginia Statute of Religious Freedom—and when they fought at the shrine I visited today, the Alamo. For side by side with Bowie and Crockett died McCafferty and Bailey and Carey—but no one knows whether they were Catholic or not. For there was no religious test at the Alamo.*

*I ask you tonight to follow in that tradition—to judge me on the basis of my record of 14 years in Congress—on my declared stands against an Ambassador to the Vatican, against unconstitutional aid to parochial schools, and against any boycott of the public schools (which I have attended myself)—instead of judging me on the basis of these pamphlets and publications we all have seen that carefully select quotations out of context from the statements of Catholic church leaders, usually in other countries, frequently in other centuries, and always omitting, of course, the statement of the American Bishops in 1948 which strongly endorsed church-state separation, and which more nearly reflects the views of almost every American Catholic. I do not consider these other quotations binding upon my public acts—why should you? But let me say, with respect to other countries, that I am wholly opposed to the state being used by any religious group, Catholic or Protestant, to compel, prohibit, or persecute the free exercise of any other religion. And I hope that you and I condemn with equal fervor those nations which deny their Presidency to Protestants and those which deny it to Catholics. And rather than cite the misdeeds of those who differ, I would cite the record of the Catholic Church in such nations as Ireland and France—and the independence of such statesmen as Adenauer and De Gaulle. But let me stress again that these are my views—for contrary to common newspaper usage, I am not the Catholic candidate for President. I am the Democratic Party's candidate for President who happens also to be a Catholic. I do not speak for my church on public matters—and the church does not speak for me.*

*Whatever issue may come before me as President—on birth control, divorce, censorship, gambling or any other subject—I will make my decision in accordance with these views, in accordance with what my conscience tells me to be the national interest, and without regard to outside religious pressures or dictates. And no power or threat of punishment could cause me to decide otherwise.*

*But if the time should ever come—and I do not concede any conflict to be even remotely possible—when my office would require me to either violate my conscience or violate the national interest, then I would resign the office; and I hope any conscientious public servant would do the same.*

*But I do not intend to apologize for these views to my critics of either Catholic or Protestant faith—nor do I intend to disavow either my views or my church in order to win this election.*

*If I should lose on the real issues, I shall return to my seat in the Senate, satisfied that I had tried my best and was fairly judged. But if this election is decided on the basis that 40 million Americans lost their chance of being President on the day they were baptized, then it is the whole nation that will be the loser, in the eyes of Catholics and non-Catholics around the world, in the eyes of history, and in the eyes of our own people.*

*But if, on the other hand, I should win the election, then I shall devote every effort of mind and spirit to fulfilling the oath of the Presidency—practically identical, I might add, to the oath I have taken for 14 years in the Congress. For without reservation, I can "solemnly swear that I will faithfully execute the office of President of the United States, and will to the best of my ability preserve, protect, and defend the Constitution . . . so help me God.*[26]

**Exhibit #11**  ★  John F. Kennedy and Lyndon B. Johnson at the Austin Municipal Airport, September 13, 1960.  ★  Photograph by Frank Muto

Exhibit eleven is an 8"x10" photograph taken September 13, 1960. This photograph shows Democratic presidential candidate John F. Kennedy and vice presidential candidate Lyndon B. Johnson addressing a crowd of supporters at the Austin municipal city airport during their campaign swing through Texas the day after Kennedy made his historic speech before the Greater Houston Ministerial Association.

This photograph can be found in the Lyndon B. Johnson Library and Museum in a series of photos with reference numbers 60-9-160 through 60-9-184. On the reverse of this original photo is the photographer's handwritten number FM-CS-243-5.

# SENATOR JOHN F. KENNEDY

## Speech Given to the Public on the Steps of the Texas State Capitol on September 13, 1960

*"Governor Daniel, Senator Johnson, Congressman Thornberry, Lieutenant Governor, General Wilson, distinguished guests, ladies and gentlemen I want to express my warm appreciation to your distinguished governor for his generous welcome this morning. The U.S. Senate is filled with Governors that wanted to get to the Senate. He is the only one I know in the Senate who wanted to come back here and be Governor of a great State. I can understand why. We have been traveling since the night before last, when we came into the Pass of the North, from El Paso down through San Antonio, Houston, and today in Austin. One of the things that has impressed me most about Texas, which I regard as a forward looking and progressive State has been the care and attention which the people of Texas have given to the past. Yesterday we visited the Alamo. Coming into the city of Austin last night, the Governor pointed with pride to a building which has been developed under his administration, which will house the Archives of Texas, which will house, as said, the letter which Travis wrote from the Alamo, which will house the documents which Houston wrote, which will house the documents which have helped build the State of Texas. Why would a State like Texas, which lives on a frontier, which has had a record of progress, look to the past? The reason is simple. We look to the past so we will know where we are going in the future. We look to the past because it tells us what we have been able to do. We look to the past because it gives us confidence that this country has been built by men of courage, men of character, men who are willing to risk all to develop the State of Texas and the United States. We look today to the past, both as Democrats and as Americans, because it is the past that tells us most about what the future can be. I look to the past of the Democratic Party as the standard bearer of that party. I look to the record of Lyndon Johnson as the Vice Presidential candidate of this party because I think that record has been a good one for Texas and the United States. The resources of this district were developed in part by the initiative of Lyndon Johnson, followed by a distinguished Congressman, Homer Thornberry. The resources of this State were developed in part under the leadership of Sam Rayburn. The Democratic Party and history, the Democratic Party and Texas, have been jointed intimately together. Therefore, I consider it a source of strength to the party nationally as well as in the State of Texas, as well as in the State of Massachusetts, as well as in the State of Florida, as well as in the State of Washington, that the Democratic Party on this occasion presents a united national front to the country. We are able to serve the people because the people belong to the Democratic Party. We include Yankees from the North and Texans from the South. We include farmers from Lubbock, we include rangers from California. We include citrus growers from Oregon. We include all of the people. And because we include every interest and every group we speak for the people, in the Congress and in the executive branch. Texas has sent 21 Democratic Congressmen to the Congress, and 1 Republican, a fair proportion, a good average. You have elected two Democratic Senators, Senator Johnson and Senator Ralph Yarborough, with whom I serve on the Committee on Labor and Public Welfare. You have elected a man who is the Speaker of the House. You have elected a Senator who leads the Democratic Party, both unanimously, both chosen by Democrats in all parts of the United States to lead them in the House and Senate and speak for them. Now, if the Democratic Party and Texas have been so intimately joined, it seems to me that you can place your confidence in the Democratic Party in the future. We seek to lead not merely one section of the United States or one interest. We see, Senator Johnson and I seek to lead the United States in a difficult and dangerous time. We do not do so saying that if we are elected the problems of Texas will be over, the problems of the United States will be solved, because they will not be solved in our generation or our time. But we do promise that if we are elected that this country will be strong, and this country will present an image to the world of vitality and energy, that we will represent to the world not only our own interests, but also extend a hand to all those who wish to associate with us, in the great fight for freedom and independence. The Democratic Presidents in this century have been successful here in the United States: Wilson, Roosevelt, and Truman. They have been successful around the world because they were successful here, because they moved this country ahead, because they demonstrated that here in this country we were still revolutionaries, that we still believed in the doctrines which are far more progressive and vigorous than the doctrines of the Communists. Mr. Khrushchev came to the Senate Foreign Relations Committee and he predicted that our children would be Communists. He went to China after a visit to the United States and said that the capitalistic system is a sick and dying and faltering horse that is about to collapse to the ground. I do not agree with him. I think our brightest days are ahead. I think it is incumbent upon us to demonstrate that this system of ours can work, that it can work in a period of danger, that it can work at a time when it is being challenged all over the globe, that we can hold out a hand of friendship to those to the south of us, to those in Africa, those in Asia, that we represent the way to the future, and that the Communist system is as old as Egypt. I ask your support in this election not merely for the State of Texas, but also for the United States; not merely for the United States, but for all those who desire to join us in a great effort to maintain their freedom. The hard, tough question for the next decade, for this or any other group of Americans, is whether a free society can maintain itself, whether we can demonstrate to a watching world as we sit on a most conspicuous stage, that the future and the United States are one.*

*I ask your help in this campaign. I ask you to join us in turning this State and this country back on the road of progress. Thank you."*[27]

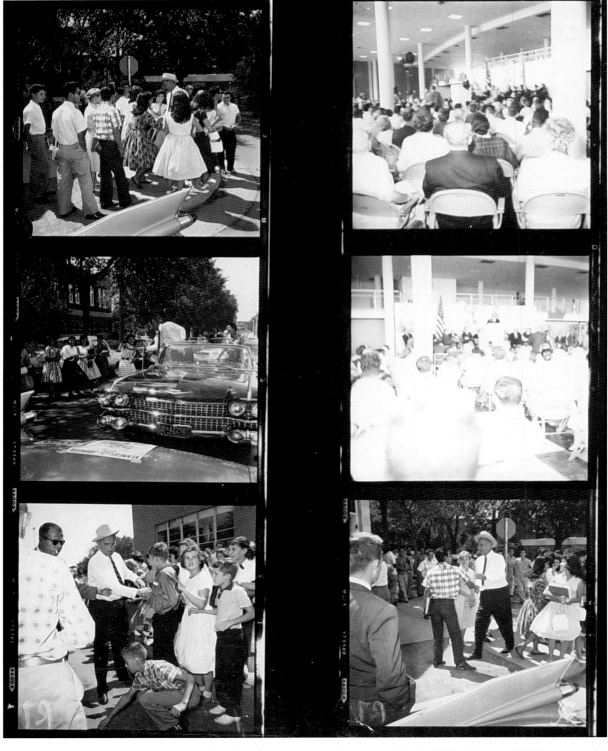

**Exhibit #12** ★ Negatives that were taken with a large-format camera on September 13–14, 1960, during the JFK/LBJ presidential campaign. ★ Photographs by Frank Muto

Exhibit twelve is an 8"x10" proof sheet of six 120mm negatives that were taken with a large-format camera on September 13–14, 1960, during the JFK/LBJ presidential campaign. In these photographs, LBJ is shown campaigning in Albuquerque and Artesia, New Mexico. Frank Muto again has captured that energy and excitement that seemed to radiate from LBJ, especially when he was among a crowd of supporters. He particularly enjoyed speaking to young people.

This series of photographs can be found in the Lyndon B. Johnson Library and Museum, reference numbers 60-9-259 through 60-9-264.

# SENATOR LYNDON B. JOHNSON

### Speech Given at the Democratic Rally in Albuquerque, New Mexico, on September 14, 1960

*Your state of New Mexico occupies a unique role in our national life. More than any other of the fifty states, New Mexico is the link between our nation and the Latin world with the Western Hemisphere. Today I believe we need to talk frankly to Americans about our relations with our oldest friends—the lands of the South.*

*The oldest, proudest and most important foreign policy of our land—for nearly 160 years—has been our pledge to maintain the integrity of the independence of our Latin neighbors. Except for the Monroe Doctrine, except for the peace and order which it has assured in our community of nations, the United States would never have been able to fulfill the role of world leadership for the cause of freedom in this 20th Century. The United States could never have undertaken the war to make the world safe for Democracy 40 years ago. The United States could never have answered the challenge of the Axis powers 20 years ago and won the liberation of Western Europe. The United States could never have risen to meet the cold war challenge of international communism in Greece and Turkey, in Italy or Berlin, in France or Iran. The United States would never have attained its position of leadership among the members of the United Nations. The United States could never have done any of these things except for the fact that—through the Monroe Doctrine–we have maintained in our own neighborhood of nations a bond of mutual trust, mutual respect and mutual cooperation such as no other great power in history had ever had from its neighbors.*

*Some may have forgotten this—or overlooked it—through the years, but the enemies of the United States have never underestimated this source of American strength. Every totalitarian of this century has recognized the surest road to the isolation–and ultimately the subjugation—of the United States is the road to the heart of Latin America. There may be explanations for the diplomatic defeats in other areas. The United States may survive losses of position in other sections of the world, but the United States cannot forgive—the American people cannot forgive–the loss of this nation's position in its own hemisphere. The American people cannot forgive such a loss because the American system—and the entire American position in the world—ould fall over such a loss. Today the American people are faced with the inescapable reality that the administration now in power in Washington has permitted—and must accept the responsibility for—the most critical setback ever administered by the United States leadership in this hemisphere.*

*Today Communism has a foothold only 90 miles from the shores of the United States. The bearded dictator under the umbrella of Communism thumbed his nose at our country. In one fell swoop—without firing a shot—Khrushchev has moved across continents and oceans to stand nearly as close to the mainland of the United States as Hitler ever got to the mainland of England. Cuba may be small. The use of Cuba as a military operating base for Communism may be implausible, but these are the facts which we in the United States must face squarely.*

*For the first time, every home, every church, every school in the continental United States is potentially within the range of operational weapons of destruction. For the first time, the military security of the United States is compromised from within the neighborhood of the American Republics. Most important of all, is our position of leadership among our own neighbors which today is compromised as it has never been compromised in all our history.*

*Where there has never been doubt before, today there is doubt about the extent of the inter-American support of the position of the United States on questions affecting the direction of this hemisphere. Because of that doubt, no informed person in any branch of your national government will feel certain that Cuba is the last as well as the first American state to turn its face toward Moscow. Other nations stand on the brink and we know it. By every reasonable standard, we may well be facing the beginning of the most difficult, trying and demanding period known by free men in the Western hemisphere.*

*This is realism and only realism. The question this places before the American people in this election year is a question of the greatest gravity. Is there to be—or not to be—a reckoning by the American electorate with those who have permitted this compromising of the American position in this hemisphere. This leadership is not the national leadership America needs to day.*

*Our United States is a land of two cultures—not one. One hundred years before the Anglo-American heritage found its roots at Plymouth Rock, Spanish explorers were founding the Latin American culture on the borders of our own United States—here in New Mexico and in Texas and in Arizona and in all the regions bordering the Gulf. The ties of history which bind us to the Latin world in friendship and mutual respect are as great as those that tie us to the cultures in Western Europe.*

*If the United States is to maintain a position in this hemisphere which has been traditionally ours, we shall do so by the quality of leadership we display—not by the quantity of wealth, population, and productivity which has always been our advantage in the past. We can no longer say that the first requisite of American leadership is the ability to stand face to face and debate with the Soviet Premier. A greater challenge and more pressing challenge is fighting American leadership which can sit down together—face to face with our own American neighbors and restore the spirit of trust and cooperation essential to living together as good neighbors.*

*Seven years and seven months ago, when the present administration came to power, America stood at the very pinnacle of trust and friendship with the lands to the South. The responsibility for the deterioration of the United States position in these lands falls squarely upon the administration now in Washington.*

*Because of this, I say certain things are essential—*

1) *By their votes next November, the American voter must speak to the people of the Americas—and speak to Khrushchev in Moscow—by refusing to ratify again the leadership responsible for this deterioration of the United States position at home.*

2) *The United States must not delude itself in believing that the friendship of the Latin nations can be bought with any massive spending program alone.*

3) *It must be the purpose of the government of the United States to set about in the Western Hemisphere to build an American community with their universal basic standards of health, standards of opportunity for all the children of the Americas, whether their family name derives from Spanish or English.*

4) *Most important of all, we must recognize that the true answer to the serious threat cannot be resolved solely between Washington and Havana or Washington and the other capitals of Latin America. This threat is a by-product of the cold war and a great part of the answer lies between Washington and Moscow.*

*Khrushchev has dared to move within 90 miles of our shores because he has seen our government in Washington cut into the vitals of our military strength, impounding funds voted by the Democratic Congress to provide a stronger military force. Khrushchev has been encouraged to think that the Americas may someday be his because he had heard our leadership in Washington saying for seven years and seven months that the American economic system may not have the capacity to meet the security needs of this nation.*

*If we want to keep Communism out of the Western Hemisphere, we must make our will felt at the capital of Communism—not among the capitals of our best and closest friends. The day and hour has come when the Americas must have leadership which will carry the people forward to the brighter new day which that first light of the Atomic Age promised to these Mexico skies fifteen years ago. Sixty years ago a young man from a wealthy family in the east charged up San Juan Hill in Cuba and helped to set the people of that nation free. At the age of 43, that young man became President of the United States. Under his leadership this nation moved forward in new directions across new frontiers and toward a position of integrity and respect in the world.*

*America needs again the leadership of vigor—of purpose and vitality and decisiveness.*

*And that is the leadership offered by the man who represents the integrity, the self-confidence, the courage and the boldness of imagination of the American people today—the next President of the United States—John F. Kennedy.*[28]

**Exhibit #13** ★ Lyndon B. Johnson Campaigning in Tucson, Arizona, on September 15, 1960 ★ Photograph by Frank Muto

Exhibit thirteen is an 8"x10" photograph taken September 15, 1960, when vice presidential hopeful Lyndon

Johnson was campaigning in Tucson, Arizona.

This photograph can be found in the Lyndon B. Johnson Library and Museum, reference number 60-9-283FM.

# SENATOR LYNDON B. JOHNSON

## Draft of Speech Written for Public Address in Tucson, Arizona, on September 15, 1960

*The issues that we will decide in this coming election reach into the household of every American. When I say "every American" I mean to exclude none, from the descendants of the First American who watched Columbus land, to the last immigrant to our side of the ocean or border.*

*Far too often, in distinguishing the shares of our national abundance, the first have been made last and the last have been forgotten. The American Indian has been shoved from the table and the late settler has found no room. The view has too often prevailed that separation is a complete answer to the problems of minorities—that injustice and suffering are tolerable if they are only moved out of sight. So the reservation and "foreign" quarter have been left to care for their own.*

*This may satisfy a republican conscience, but the Democratic Party has a broader range of vision. As the Party of all the people, our eye must find the sparrow as well as the hawk. We cannot be content as long as any group—no matter how small in numbers or power—is left out of America's future.*

*In talking about the problems and needs of the Indian people, I do not propose to linger over old grievances and ancient wrongs that were done in the haste to build a new nation. They have burned deeply into the heart of America and are known to every schoolboy.*

*But few Americans know much about the barriers that face the Indian family today in securing suitable employment, decent housing and medical care, education for its children and opportunity for its youth. So I want to talk about their modern grievances and modern needs, and what John Kennedy and I propose to do about them come next January.*

*The Indian people know that for seven and a half years there has been no room for them at the Republican table, which is reserved for the spokesmen of financial power and privilege. They have a right to know what they can expect of a Democratic administration. As one who has proved his friendship where it counts most, in the halls of Congress, I say that they can look forward to an era of unparalleled progress.*

*The concern of the Democratic Party for the Indian welfare is not an empty campaign gesture, to be abandoned the day after the election, but a matter of long record.*

*When Franklin D. Roosevelt entered the White House in 1933, the condition of the Indian people was desperate. Abject poverty, disease and illiteracy were their common lot, and whole tribes were threatened with extinction.*

*With the leadership of Harold Ickes as Secretary of the Interior and John Collier as Commissioner of Indian Affairs, a great revival began. For the first time, the Indian affairs of the Federal government were in the hand of the genuine friends of the Indian, and administered by men who understood and valued his culture and traditions. With the support of Democratic Congresses, new programs of tribal rehabilitation, medical services, sanitation, education and other forms of aid were inaugurated, and a system of effective self-government developed. The Federal government and Indian institutions worked together to raise the status of the India people to a level of social, economic and political parity with the rest of American society.*

*Here in Arizona, where more Indians reside than in any other state, Democratic policies and Democratic programs brought new hope and new opportunities in place of generations of neglect. In 1948, a landmark decision by Judge Udall, the father of your great Congressman Stewart Udall, gave the reservation Indians of Arizona the right to vote and the means to influence their own destinies as full and equal citizens.*

*In 1950, a Democratic administration and a Democratic Congress enacted a long-range rehabilitation program for the benefit of the Navajo and Hopi Indians of Arizona, which has helped to meet the urgent needs of these neglected people and the restore them to a position of dignity and self respect.*

*But in 1952, there came the big change, and the heart went out of the administration for Indian Affairs in Washington. Under the Republican Party and Republican appointees, programs created by Democrats for the benefit for the Indian people, became centers for the operations of their enemies. Each nickel earmarked for Indian welfare rather than the banker's profit has been subjected to the begrudging will of a Budget Bureau controlled by men who meet Indians only at cigar stores and believe they are all made of wood.*

*The Republican concept of the perfect solution for all Indian problems is to repeal the Indian. This is what they mean by "termination" and "setting the Indian free." To "set the Indian free," of course, means to free him of his lands, mineral rights, schools, legal clams, and system of self-government—in short, to strip him bare.*

*When tribal leaders have asked Republican officials for Federal help in the development of their reservation so as to create opportunities for their members, they have been told not to try to develop jobs for their people at home, but to ship them to Chicago, or Detroit or some other industrial city to look for work.*

*During the past seven and a half years, one thing and one thing alone has stood in the way of Republican efforts to wash out all Federal services and programs for the benefit of the Indian population—a Democratic majority in the Congress. If Democrats in Congress—and most particularly your own fine Representative, Stewart Udall—had not been alert and active in the defense of Indian rights, all progress made during the previous twenty years would have gone right down the drain.*

*Just by way of example, in 1956 when the Congress was considering legislation to extend the life of the Indian Claims Commission, Republican administration spokesmen did their level best to have the rues of the game changed so as to foreclose and prohibit certain types of Indian claims against the government. Congressional Democrats resisted this attempt to undermine the legal rights of Indian citizens, and enacted the legislation in a form, which assured that every Indian tribe could continue to present its grievances for a full and fair determination.*

*While standing firm against administration attacks upon Indian rights, Democrats in Congress have been able to make some legislative advances in this field. In the 86th Congress, again due in large part to the energetic support of Stewart Udall—we enacted legislation to permit the long-term leasing of Navajo lands, so as to promote the construction of new Indian homes and to make it possible for industry to be brought to the reservation. The result, we hope and believe, will be the creation of more jobs and better living conditions, and a real boost to the whole economy of that part of your state.*

*As a direct result of Congressional pressure and action, behind Democratic leadership, an expanded program of medical services for all Indians has been undertaken. We have increased appropriations for hospitals and general health facilities so as to serve more effectively the serious health needs of all Indian tribes. Already, this program has substantially lowered the incidence of tuberculosis and aided in the prevention of other diseases which have plagued our Indian population.*

*What we have been able to do with a Democratic Congress in the face of a hostile, nothing-doing administration—is just a sample of what we can and will do after the coming Democratic victory at the polls. With a united government, joining White House leadership and Congressional support in the pursuit of a common purpose, there will be a new birth of progress for the American Indian as well as his immigrant brothers, both early and late.*

*Our aim in this regard is clear. As our platform states, we recognize the unique legal and moral responsibility of the Federal government for Indians in restitution for past injustices as well as the reality of present needs. We pledge the prompt adoption of a program to assist Indian tribes in the full development of their human and natural resources, and advance their health, education and economic welfare while preserving the priceless quality of their cultural heritage. Our treaties and contractual relationships will be held inviolate, save with the free consent of the tribes concerned.*

*This new Democratic administration will bring competent, sympathetic and dedicated leadership to the administration of Indian affairs—a leadership that will not tolerate practices that have, under Republican domination, eroded Indian rights and resources, reduced their land holdings, and repudiated federal obligations. Indian claims against the United States can and will be settled fairly and promptly, whether by negotiation or other means, in the best interests of both.*

*That platform is our personal pledge. Neither John Kennedy nor myself will rest until we translate it into history.*[29]

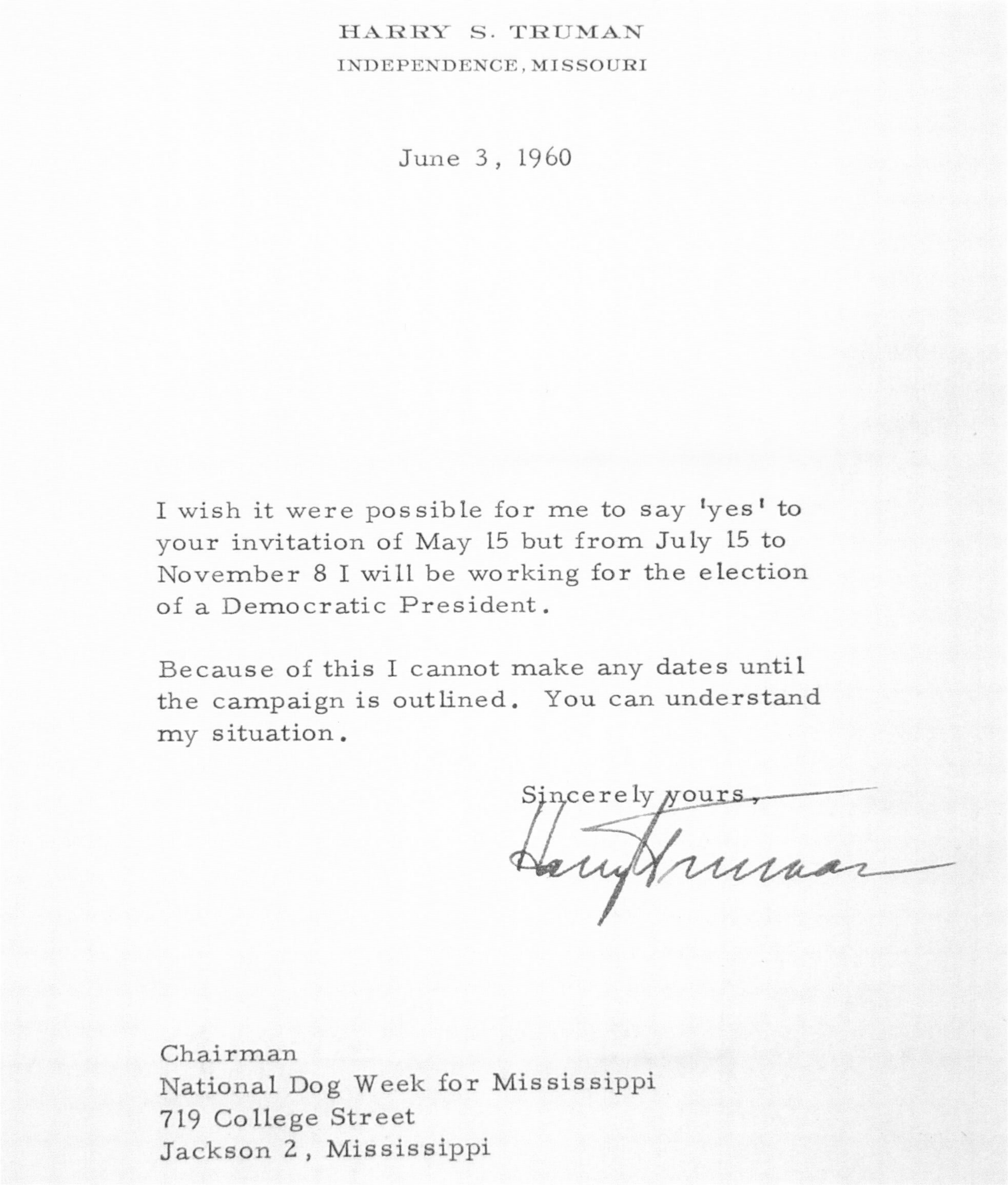

HARRY S. TRUMAN
INDEPENDENCE, MISSOURI


June 3, 1960


I wish it were possible for me to say 'yes' to
your invitation of May 15 but from July 15 to
November 8 I will be working for the election
of a Democratic President.

Because of this I cannot make any dates until
the campaign is outlined. You can understand
my situation.

Sincerely yours,

Harry Truman


Chairman
National Dog Week for Mississippi
719 College Street
Jackson 2, Mississippi

**Exhibit #14**

Exhibit fourteen is a letter dated June 3, 1960, from former President Harry Truman. The importance of this letter is in its content. The former president mentions he cannot attend an invitation due to his involvement in the 1960 campaign. He states, "I wish it were possible for me to say yes to your invitation of May 15 but from July 15 to November 8, I will be working for the election of a Democratic President."

The date of July 15 is significant because the Democratic Convention was held the week of July 11 to July 15. Harry Truman had already decided not to attend the convention because he thought the convention was rigged for Kennedy. President Truman also had met with Lyndon Johnson back in the late fall of 1959 at the LBJ Ranch. [30] Most assuredly, one topic of discussion was the election year. President Truman offered his time and experience to Lyndon by appearing at several rallies during the 1960 campaign.

# Senator Lyndon B. Johnson and former President Harry Truman

## Transcript of Recorded Remarks Made at a Press Conference in Kansas City, Missouri, on July 29, 1960

### Senator Johnson:

*I want to thank you for your courtesy and your indulgence and your understanding of me. I have had a delightful visit with one of my old and most beloved friends, one of the greatest living Americans. I feel like I have learned a great deal from you during the time you were in Washington. And he calmed me about as much as any father I ever had in the last thirty minutes on what to do and what not to do in this campaign. He demonstrated that he knew how to run everything from precinct to President—those great qualities that have been the bulwark of the Democratic government. He had the courage to stand up to the dictators of the world and every decision he made was a big one and it was a good one. And I came here to ask him first what he thought the Congress ought to do when we get back in session; how he campaigned for Vice President; how he thought we could return the government to the dynamic leadership of the Democratic Party. He gave me good advice and sound advice and I invited him to come to Texas to visit with me and with his much beloved Speaker Sam Rayburn. We hope that circumstances will permit the acceptance of that invitation because we always enjoy his visits . . .*

*Now we discussed the platform and I'll go into it in a little more detail with you as we get on the plane.*

*I'm ready to answer any questions may want to ask after the President makes his statement if he cares to. I want to thank him again on his hospitality and for the counsel that he has given me through the years, and particularly my Party that he has served from Precinct to President.*

### Harry Truman:

*Thank you very much Lyndon. I am very happy to be with you today. Senator Johnson and I have been friends for a long time and I was most happy to receive him . . .*

### Press Questions:

**Question:** *Mr. President, you yourself have been in office. What is your general opinion of the Kennedy-Johnson Ticket?*

**Truman:** *Well it's going to win! What other opinion could I have!*

**Question:** *Carl Friend from the* Fort Worth Press. *You are quoted as making certain comments about the Democratic Convention, do you have any views about the Republican Convention?*

**Truman:** *The Republican Convention is one of the worst that's ever been and they have elected the worst ticket this country has ever been offered. Does that answer your question?*

**Question:** WFAA Dallas. *Do you feel that Khrushchev and foreign issues is the mainstay of this campaign?*

**Truman:** *No, I do not. Domestic issues are the main things in this campaign. Foreign policy is something that the President of the United States must decide on. And when we get a new President maybe we will have a foreign policy. Does that answer your question?*

**Question:** *Mr. President, Jess Baker, has anything happened since the convention to change your opinion?*

**Truman:** *No. Period!*[31]

Exhibit fifteen is an original 8"x10" proof sheet of six 120mm negatives that were taken September 22, 1960, of Lyndon Johnson, Lady Bird Johnson, and former President Harry Truman, in the midst of a crowd at a campaign rally in Kansas City, Missouri. The Glennon high school band can be seen in the background with some of the students holding banners that say "Glennon Students Greet Johnson."

These negatives and set of photographs can be found in the Lyndon B. Johnson Library and Museum, reference numbers 60-9-372 to 60-9-377.

**Exhibit #15** ★ September 22, 1960, of Lyndon Johnson, Lady Bird Johnson, and former President Harry Truman, in the midst of a crowd at a campaign rally in Kansas City, Missouri. ★ Photograph by Frank Muto

**Exhibit #16** ★ Lyndon B. Johnson and Harry Truman at a Campaign Rally in Quincy, Illinois, September 27, 1960 ★ Photograph by Frank Muto

Exhibit sixteen is an 8"x10" photograph taken September 27, 1960, of Lyndon Johnson at a campaign rally at Washington Park in Quincy, Illinois. In the foreground is former President Harry Truman.

This photograph can be found in the Lyndon B. Johnson Library and Museum, reference number 60-9-436FM.

At the time this photograph was taken, John F. Kennedy was preparing for his second televised debate with Richard Nixon. The Kennedy/Nixon debates were the first televised presidential debates in this country. The first debate was held the day before in Chicago, on September 26, 1960.

# SENATOR LYNDON B. JOHNSON
### Transcript of Speech Delivered at Washington Park, Quincy, Illinois, on September 27, 1960

*Down in my hill country of Texas, that I left about daylight this morning, we had one of our young fellows that was out riding the range bring in his pony and then took the afternoon off. Now when he got back the boss man said, "Tommy, where have you been all afternoon?" He said, "I've been over to the old settlers' reunion." "Well, what have you been doing at the old settlers reunion?" Tommy said, " I was listening to United States Senator Joseph Weldon Bailey make a mighty powerful speech." The boss said, "Senator Bailey didn't speak all afternoon did he?" "Almost!" The boss said, "If that's true, what did Senator Bailey talk about all afternoon?" Tommy scratched his head, started thinking about it and couldn't remember exactly what the Senator had said. Tommy said, "Boss I can't quote verbatim what the Senator spoke about, but the general impression I got was that he recommended himself most highly." Now, I have not come here today to recommend myself most highly, but I have come here today to make some recommendations to you. First, this is the week and this is the place where the 1960 Democratic campaign goes into high gear and I want you to know it. This is a great district where Abraham Lincoln and Douglas had one of their historic debates and this is the district that I remember in my time that produced the great Speaker of the House, that wonderful gray haired leader known as Henry Rainey. Mr. Rainey's successor in the House of Representatives, went on to be the Majority Leader of the United States Senate and I am proud to honor and salute the man you have made Majority Leader of all the Senators—Scott Lucas of Illinois. Now, the next job you have to do and the first one on the agenda is to take this affable, this able, this man of the people, Montgomery Carrott and send him to Washington in January as a Democrat from his Congressional District. The other day when I opened this campaign I went from Austin, Texas on to Boston—one end of the nation to the other, across the country from the South to the North, from Texas to Massachusetts, and more than a hundred thousand people came out and gave me their hand and their welcome. You don't know how proud it made me feel this day when we are being divided and when the Russians are challenging us and when the Communists are within ninety miles of our shore line to know that the Protestant grandson of a Confederate soldier could be welcome with open arms in the cradle of liberty, Boston, Massachusetts. I am here today as I told Bern Sandford, for two reasons: First, I was invited and Second, I wanted to come. I wanted to come because in this final decision you have a real responsibility to your community. I hope Jack Kennedy, the next President of the United States, comes out here to see you. When this Irish Catholic grandson of a poor Irish immigrant came to Texas, a hundred and seventy-five thousand Texans tipped their Stetsons to him and the women yelled. It is not important where the Kennedy's live or where they worship their God. But what is significant, and what I want you young people to remember about this speech is that this is important and it is an indication that we have gotten away from the prejudices of a hundred years ago, the prejudices of 1860 with the War between the Sates. What is equally important is that we have gotten away from the prejudices of 1928 and Al Smith, and I think that we are going to bury that issue with this election and you young people are going to help us do it. Today there is a meeting in the United Nations that may involve and may well determine whether we live in war or peace, or whether we live at all. Premier Khrushchev has proven beyond any doubt that this spokesman of the Soviet Union, this spokesman of the atheistic Communists, came to New York for the sole purpose of destroying the United Nations. He has made a brazen move to take over the United States lock stock and barrel, and I say as a good American, and I ask you to join me as good Americans, regardless of party, that we say to Mr. Khrushchev, "You had better stop, look, and listen." Mr. Khrushchev will not succeed—there is no doubt about that—but the thing that we in America should be concerned about is the fact that Premier Khrushchev was allowed to get into a position where he would even dare make this proposal. For many years the Communists have been probing for soft spots in the Free World. Over the years some of their efforts have been successful, some have been unsuccessful, but in recent years the Communists have become bolder and bolder. Our own President was forced to cancel a trip to Japan and had to turn around in the Philippines because of the riots in Tokyo. Our own Vice President was run out of South America and the Marines had to protect him and his wife. The Communists have reached half way around the world and today they have set up operation just ninety miles from our shores. Mr. Khrushchev did not make any snap decisions. He did not wake up one morning and decide to push America around. Communists have been planning and they have been scheming for many years to push and shove and drive at every opportunity, as part of their master plan of what Mr. Khrushchev says is to bury America. They will keep doing it as long as they can get by with it. They do not care who shakes the finger at them in the kitchen. They do not care whom they insult. The Communists understand and respect strength and respect it in capital letters. They understand and respect the rocket and the missile system that will match and overpower their own and we've got to have one. They understand and respect education and schools, and they respect those who stay ahead of them in this field and we've got to stay ahead of them. They respect and understand industries that are running at full capacity, and we have got to put our unemployed back to work and raise the income of our farmer. In seven years and seven months under Ezra Taft Benson and Mr. Nixon's advice, farm incomes have gone down thirty-three and a third percent. Farm mortgages have gone up fifty percent, and the farmer cannot live long in that kind of economy. The Democrats are going to put a stop to it.*

*We are concerned over the strength of our economy, our schools, and our farm income. Concerned over our future growth as much as we are concerned over our military strength. Our total strength as a nation and as a leader of the world will be the deciding factor in the struggle with Communism. The best way to take the initiative from Mr. Khrushchev is to get busy and develop America—go forward instead of standing on high center, and I think you are ready to go with it, aren't you? Well, I'll tell you this—this kind of language the Communists understand, and the Democratic Party intends to speak to them in no uncertain terms through positive and constructive action to build a stronger America, and in the words of a great American and I hope you listen and remember, "It is time for America to move—to move forward—to move ahead–but to move now." And the American who said that is the next President, your friend, Jack Kennedy. There are two basic differences between the Democratic Party and the Republican Party. One is the Republican Party is satisfied to stay where you are. A fellow in Oklahoma told me the other day, "The Republicans are going to get some of these folks around here over fifty—they are looking toward retirement—but those under fifty want to move ahead, grow stronger, do better, have a greater America, preserve democracy—and Jack Kennedy is going to get their votes. The Democratic Party is the party that cares about educating the young. So I say to you boys and girls, give us your help, give us your voice, go out there and talk to your uncles, your cousins and your aunts, and your mothers and your fathers and your grandpas and your grandmas and get them to vote for Congressman Carrott, for Jack Kennedy and the greatest Democratic victory this nation has ever heard. Goodbye and God bless you.*[32]

# SENATOR LYNDON B. JOHNSON

**Presentation of Award to Senator Lyndon B. Johnson from the Young Democratic Club of Adams County, Quincy, Illinois, on September 27, 1960**

*I want to thank all of you very much. Lady Bird and I are going to come back after we are Vice President and in the meantime, tonight, before I go to bed I am going to talk to friends of yours, particularly you young folks that are not willing to let the Communists move in close to us, and you folks that want to move forward. I am going to tell Jack Kennedy tonight when I talk to him that I asked you if he could count on you, and I want to hear your answer. Can he? You are going to roll up the biggest majority of the Democratic Party beginning on November 8 that this town has ever given any ticket since 1845. Now, there are two points that I want to make with you. We have twenty-one Democratic Congressmen and they all have different viewpoints, they represent different sections, have different interests, and are led by the greatest living Democrat, Sam Rayburn. Whether they are conservative or liberal, every single one of the twenty-one Democrats in Congress, without exception, are for Jack Kennedy for President. Now, we have some problems in Texas and our state officials don't always agree. I can remember when some of them supported the great crusade and some of them voted Republican in 1952. I want you to remember this, the men that you have selected to speak for you, from the Governor to the lowest office on the state ticket, have endorsed Jack Kennedy. The third point, and I don't know how many of you out there are familiar with the political activities or political races, but we had a fine clean fight in Los Angeles. We gave them all we had. I never made a speech that I didn't say Jack Kennedy is the nominee and that I would support enthusiastically. Well, he was the nominee by a vote two to one and after I was defeated and I was stretched out on the floor, and it was all over, this fellow from Massachusetts, the cradle of liberty, picked up the telephone and said he wanted to come to my room. I don't know how many men in political life have gone to the man that fought him, to the man that opposed him, to the man that stayed in there and pitched until even the Canal Zone voted, but Jack Kennedy came down and said, "Our Country is in trouble. I need all the help I can get. I want to be President of all the people. I don't want to be a sectionalist. I don't want regional government. I want to look after all Americans. You got 400 votes and I got 800 votes, and that made up most of the votes that were cast at the Convention. Why don't we join together—unite America—unify the Democratic Party, both of us sit on the jury and do what's best for our country. I ask you to come and be my running mate." Now I thought that was a pretty big thing for a pretty big man to do. If you don't think it is, you just look around and see how many men elected to public office and their first official act is to get the man that tried to defeat him. Lift him up and say, I want a partnership with you. I want to say today, if you think our country is in trouble—and I do—if you think we've got problems with Khrushchev and I do, if you think we have a series of crises and I do, then it's important that we close ranks and unite to preserve the freedoms of the republic that we love. And that's why I am here. I would be less frank if I didn't say to you that in my political experience I have never liked to wind up second, but I wouldn't be honest with you if I didn't tell you this. With the problems that are ahead of us, it's going to take all the leadership that we've got in the Democratic Party...[33]*

**Exhibit #17** ★ Lyndon B. Johnson in downtown Columbus, Ohio, taken September 29, 1960 ★ Photograph by Frank Muto

## The Campaign Agenda

By September 1960, the campaign agenda was clear. Kennedy and Johnson had a lengthy domestic agenda—higher teacher salaries, more aid to public schools, reduced federal aid to parochial schools, renewal of urban areas, a stronger civil rights bill, a consumer protection council, health insurance for senior citizens leveraged through Social Security, more jobs, and a national Peace Corps. Kennedy and Johnson favored limits on campaign contributions, more protection for the environment and natural resources, and wanted to accelerate the U.S. space program. They wanted to reduce the "missile gap" that was forming between the United States and the Soviet Union. And finally, they wanted to provide aid to underdeveloped countries and avidly supported the anti-Castro movement.[34]

Exhibit seventeen is an 8"x10" photograph taken September 29, 1960 in downtown Columbus, Ohio. Lyndon Johnson is seen leaving the podium where he had just addressed a large crowd of supporters. This photograph can be found in the Lyndon B. Johnson Library and Museum, reference number FM-CS-44–6.

# SENATOR LYNDON B. JOHNSON

## Transcript of Speech Delivered at City Hall in Downtown Columbus, Ohio, on September 29, 1960

*Governor LaSalle, my old and trusted friend of many years. The Democratic Congressman that belongs to the people, Dick Lyon, and my fellow Americans. In case a few Republicans are present I want to include them too. This is a great event in my life. I went to the town that my grandfather founded more than a hundred years ago and we had a centennial the other day. The population hasn't gone up, and it hasn't gone down much either. It's about 671. So, when I see all these folks out here surrounding me, it just makes me think that we are getting ready to cut the "old red rooster". You are the folks that own this town. You are the people that produced the sons that won the war. You are the people that are going to be called upon in November to make a fateful decision. A decision that may well determine whether we serve freedom or whether Communism continues to expand. I want to tell you two or three stories, and I will try to be rather brief because you have a good heart and you have touched me deeply by coming here, to manifest your interest in your country and in your flag and in your government under which you live. President Truman will soon be 78 years old. I went out to the farm where he was born and raised, and where he plowed the soil where a modern supermarket now stands. I asked him for some advice. He told me that he thought that Jack Kennedy and I ought to carry our story to the people because the press, according to their own press, the editors and publishers of magazines, said that four out of five newspapers in this country were Republican. So it is pretty hard to get the true story to the people. He suggested that I go from the southland to the northland and as far as I could go, and meet the people there. So he said that he had been all over this country and there are about the same kind of folks wherever you go—99 percent of them are good people who want to do what is right. So I went from Austin, Texas to Boston and from Boston to Austin. I was surprised and delighted and thrilled that the Protestant grandson of a Confederate soldier could be received with bands playing, with girls singing, and with people welcoming him with open arms. So Lady Bird asked Jack Kennedy's sister and Bobby Kennedy's wife to come to Texas and meet our ladies. Every place they went from Houston to Dallas, from El Paso to Wichita Falls, all across that big state of the union, south to the North Pole, the headlines said, "We like the Kennedy Gals". By that time we thought it was safe for Jack to come in. I remember that we had some warming up exercises and some preliminaries before Los Angeles. So Jack came in and I never was so proud of my state in all its entire history to observe that 175,000 Texans, according to the Dallas "Republican" Morning News, came out to welcome enthusiastically, this Roman Catholic grandson of a poor Irish immigrant. So in Boston it made me think perhaps we had developed and improved and marched along and enlightened ourselves and gotten away from the prejudices of the 1860's. Maybe in Austin we had gotten away from the prejudices of Al Smith in 1928. And I pray to God that we have. I will tell you a little story because it is not important what church you worship in. What is important is that you believe in God and that you worship him. The fight in this world today is not between those who believe in God, whether they are Baptists or Methodists or Catholics or members of the First Christian Church as I am. The fight in this world today is not between those who believe in God, but between those who know no God, the Atheistic Communists, and those who worship God in any way. At the beginning of this campaign I made one point clear. It was, during all my travels from north to south and from east to west, I was not going to speak as a southerner to a southerner, as a white to a white or as a Protestant to a Protestant. My sole objective was, and now is, to always proudly speak as an American to Americans. Anything else by a man who is seeking the support of his fellow countrymen in times like these, could be disastrous to his country and destructive to the flag. We are living in times that truly can be called an age of national peril. A very cold and a very determined dictator is stepping up his moves to destroy freedom in the world. He is walking down the path which has been trod by all the dictators in history. He is in the United Nations today trying to blow it up. He is there with his friend, Mr. Castro, who holds a beachhead ninety miles off our own shore. Someone asked Mr. Truman, I am told the other day, what he thought should be done with Castro. He said, "Well, the first thing I would do is shave him. The next thing I would do is bathe him and then the thing that we ought to do is spank him." Notwithstanding all these good will missions we have taken, with all this maturity and experience we have had, and all these times that the Marines have had to get our Vice President home, I wondered the other day if Rockefeller could take him up in the Waldorf Astoria Towers, forty floors up, and make him rewrite his platform and make him sacrifice his convictions of a lifetime in one midnight conference, and wonder what Khrushchev could do that fellow if he got him in the bathroom all day. Now, I am not going to go into details on this phony Madison Avenue Hucksterism argument that they give you about maturity and experience. But I'll tell you how to answer in very short words—you just say what maturity and which experience. They reach out to neighboring nations which they insist they must have as a defense buffer against so-called external pressures. With each success they become bolder until the day arrives when they decide it is time to take on the whole world. We have seen that two times in our lifetime—the Kaiser, Hitler and Tojo. This is the path we have followed before, and Premier Khrushchev apparently has arrived at this stage in his development. He is standing at the summit with an atomic missile chip on his shoulder and he is daring anyone to knock it off. It is pointless to comfort ourselves with the losses that Khrushchev has sustained in the United Nations during the last few days. He is a man who counts not ballots or votes. He is less interested in winning arguments than he is winning a sale. The sale that he is out trying to make is that of Communism to the whole world. And he does a fine job of it by cramming it down our throats with a rifle. Already his forces in the Congo are regrouping and preparing for another assault on a new nation which has not even had the opportunity to get its feet on the ground. Already he has partnered with Fidel Castro in stripping the Marine base at Guantanamo Bay. Already the noose is tightening with fear around Berlin. If there ever was a time to unite America this is it. If there ever was a time for our people to resolve their differences so that they march forward as one country, this is it. Only yesterday, the Communists with their usual arrogance demanded that Billy Graham get out of West Berlin. Now I want to say this right now, the Communists have a much deeper understanding of this so-called religious issue than those who seek to inject it into this campaign. The Communists realize that the real issue of our time lies between those who believe in God and those who do not, those who are convinced of immortality and the human soul, and those who reduce mankind to the status of machinery. They know that the real issue is not between men who differ in their methods of worship. Isn't it about time, don't you think, that we wake up to the fact that those who seek to divide us are doing Nikita Khrushchev's work for him. Whether they are doing it willingly or not. And isn't it about time, don't you think, that we stop reacting to Mr. Khrushchev? And instead "get going," going forward, as Jack Kennedy says, to building a position of strength so that Mr. Khrushchev must react to us. Our next President is going to have a job cut out for him. I don't promise you that Jack Kennedy will give you a bed of roses. The road will be full of thorns and it will be hard going. I do promise that we will not react to the actions. They will start reacting to us.*[35]

Exhibit eighteen is an 8"x10" photograph taken September 30, 1960, on board an aircraft en route to Jackson, Tennessee. The photograph shows Lyndon Johnson sitting next to his close friend and confidant Tennessee Governor Buford Ellington. Frank Muto caught the future vice president with a very piercing look. This photograph can be found in the Lyndon B. Johnson Library and Museum, reference number 60-9-562FM.

**Exhibit #18**  ★  September 30, 1960, on board an aircraft en route to Jackson, Tennessee. Lyndon Johnson sitting next to his close friend and confidant Tennessee Governor Buford Ellington. ★ Photograph by Frank Muto

Exhibit nineteen is an 8"x10" photograph taken September 30, 1960, shortly after arriving at the Jackson airport in Jackson, Tennessee. The photo shows Lyndon Johnson kneeling down to show a youngster one of his beagle pups, most likely Little Beagle Johnson.

This photograph can be found in the Lyndon B. Johnson Library and Museum and has the Frank Muto reference number FM-CS-64-7. The library reference number is 60-9-567FM.

Lyndon Johnson was known to take his dogs along with him on official trips. LBJ's oldest dog was called Old Beagle Johnson, which was his first and most beloved beagle. He adored the dog so much that when Old Beagle died he had the dog cremated and kept the ashes on top of his refrigerator. Later, there was Little Beagle Johnson who sired the famous Him and Her beagles that resided at the White House.

**Exhibit #19** ★  September 30, 1960, shortly after arriving at the Jackson airport in Jackson, Tennessee. ★ Photograph by Frank Muto

# SENATOR LYNDON B. JOHNSON

## Transcript of Speech Delivered at Democratic Rally in Jackson, Tennessee, on September 30, 1960

*My beloved friend, Governor Ellington, my colleague and helpmate, Senator Gore, your very own able Congressman Bob Murray, Congressman Davis, and his gracious and charming wife who has contributed so much to the service of this country and particularly to my own public position, my friend Joseph Browning, whom I last saw in Nashville, Tip Taylor, the Democrats of Jackson and my fellow Americans. I think this is a wonderful thing for you to do to extend me an invitation to come to this great State that bears the name of the greatest Senator of them all—Senator Jackson. I think you should know there is recorded in my heart and my head a gratitude to the people of Tennessee that is second to none. So I am here today for a joint purpose. First, I want to thank you as much as I can for the fine leadership that the Governor of Tennessee and the delegation showed at the National Convention in support of my candidacy for President. And second, to come here and invite you to join with me in helping to restore the executive branch of the government and the White House to the people again by electing John Kennedy, President. As you already have heard in the last two days, the Republican candidate for President has tried to amend the Constitution of the United States all by himself. According to his new version, there is freedom of speech for everyone, except the Democrats. He says that when Khrushchev and Castro are in this country, Jack Kennedy and I ought to keep quiet about the record of the Republican Party and its candidates. I don't blame the Republican candidate for wanting to keep the issues out of sight until the election is over. If we had that kind of record, I would want to keep quiet about it too. This is the first time in history that an American political party has ever tried to hide behind a Communist dictator to escape a fair judgment by the people–and they aren't going to get away with it. So this morning here in Jackson, the home of one of the great ladies of our times, Pauline Gore, we would like to send the Republican candidate a message. I would advise the Republican candidate to take his political gag and see if he can use it on his old kitchen pal, Khrushchev, and not his fellow Americans. Our people are old enough, smart enough, and responsible enough to hear the truth. And I have absolute faith in their ability to choose the wisest course, if they know the truth. Americans want a stronger defense system. Americans want a more prosperous agriculture. Americans want and Tennessee wants, the way to a more productive economy. Americans want an expansion of business enterprise and the prudent development of the resources that God gave this land. And to support these things there is only one thing that can be done, and you people from Tennessee, as always, must lead the way with your chin up and your chest out, go to the polls and vote for the Democratic Ticket, from the Courthouse to the White House, on November 8th. That is what the Democratic Party stands for, and what this country will have when you have a President like Jack Kennedy to work with a Democratic Congress. The enemies of America are on the move–in Asia, in Latin America, and even into the outer reaches of space. In Cuba, they have reached our very doorstop. They are not smug, they are not fat, they are restless, and they are hungry. And they will not be satisfied until the whole world is theirs. So I ask you, if we in America who love God and who despise atheism, that we stand up and call the roll and ask our people to face up to the challenges. You can help here in Jackson to spread the message that Jack Kennedy and I are taking to the people from one end of America to the other. The message is one not of smug satisfaction with the past, it is a message of awakened hope, faith and confidence in the limitless future of America. You know where your future lies. Go and show it. Take with you your uncles and your cousins, and your aunts, and vote Democratic on November 8th for Jack Kennedy–the leader of the "New Frontier." I'll tell you that the road won't be easy—it will be no bed of roses. Your savings will be nibbled on. But, if you elect a Democratic President to work with a Democratic Congress we will face up to the problems. We will evaluate the situation that is running the farmers off the farm. We will try to find a solution to it. We will work with the farmers themselves instead of their enemies. We will come into these areas and try to get their advice and their judgment and their recommendations. We will seek the counsel of their spokesmen in*

Congress. I believe that under Jack Kennedy one of the first official acts will be to restore the Agriculture Department to the farmers of America and put at the head of it a friend of the farmers instead of an enemy of the farmer.

The Republican "half-way" approach is not good enough, it's not good enough for you, it's not good enough for me, and it's not good enough for Jack Kennedy, and it's not good enough for America. I urge you to listen to the candidates of this campaign because just two nights ago on that television debate you saw and you heard things that you haven't been able to read. And I haven't heard Mr. Nixon mention maturity since that recording went off the television. In Jack Kennedy you will see a forthright leader who has a program big enough for America's greatness—and who tells you what his program is. In the Republican candidate, you will see a debater who would just as soon prevent things from appearing as they really are. When you get to know them both, I don't think you will have much trouble making up your minds, and I am confident that you know what the answer will be. I am confident that when it comes November 8th you'll vote Democratic.

So, I say from the bottom of a grateful heart, thank you for coming this morning. Thank you for what you have done for the Democratic Party. Thank your Governor, your State officials, your Senator, and your Congressman, because they know where you interest is. They are the people that you have selected and trusted with your welfare. They are the folks who have helped develop your State. And under a Democratic Administration led by Jack Kennedy, I tell you that I am confident that no voice in the Union will be stronger than the voice of Tennessee.[36]

**Exhibit #20** ★ September 30, 1960, in Knoxville, Tennessee. Vice presidential candidate Lyndon Johnson standing on the back of a car waving to a crowd of supporters. ★ Photograph by Frank Muto

Exhibit twenty is an 8"x10" photograph taken by Frank Muto on September 30, 1960, in Knoxville, Tennessee. The photo shows vice presidential candidate Lyndon Johnson standing on the back of a car waving to a crowd of supporters. In the car with LBJ is Senator Albert Gore, Sr. of Tennessee, the father of another future vice president, Al Gore, Jr.

(1993–2001). This photograph can be found in the Lyndon B. Johnson Library and Museum and has the Frank Muto reference number FM-CS-46-7 written on back. The Lyndon B. Johnson Library reference number is 60-9-593FM.

The relationship between Al Gore, Sr., and LBJ was one of questionable but mutual respect, for both

were longtime Senate colleagues. Senator Gore and other senators had long criticized LBJ's management of the Democratic Caucus and their mutual respect would be strained even further on January 3, 1961, when the Democratic Caucus gathered in the Senate to formally elect Mike Mansfield to succeed LBJ as the majority leader. Several days earlier, LBJ had squared a deal with Mike Mansfield and Hubert Humphrey to continue presiding over the Senate Democratic caucus while he was vice president. LBJ figured that he could maintain his close ties to the Senate and assist the president in pushing forward his favored programs by having a continued role in the caucus. However, LBJ and Mike Mansfield had underestimated the backlash. The senators balked at the idea of having someone from the executive branch of government preside over Senate meetings. When Mike Mansfield stood up to accept his nomination as the new majority leader, he motioned to have the vice president preside over future Democratic caucuses. The senators lined up to speak their objections. All the while, LBJ sat quietly listening, but very red faced. When it was Senator Gore's turn to speak, he angrily stated, "We might as well ask Jack Kennedy to come back to the Senate and take his turn presiding." Mike Mansfield was so shocked by the comments that he threatened to resign as the majority leader right on the spot. The threat quieted the objections and the motion for the vice president to preside over future meetings was passed. However, LBJ took the hint from his fellow senators and never did preside over any caucus meetings.[37]

# SENATOR LYNDON B. JOHNSON

## Transcript of Speech Delivered at the Democratic Dinner in Knoxville, Tennessee, on September 30, 1960

*My beloved fellow Democrats. This is one of the most delightful days that I have ever spent in my life. I have come here to see the people that I wanted to know, in the land that I love, in the state that we hope so much. I just don't know how you could have done any better. Tonight I had greetings from Mr. And Mrs. Jim Lawson and the prettiest pair of beagles that I ever saw, except my own. Last night my old friend, Cliff Davis, his charming wife is with us tonight, Carrie, who did so much for me in the pre-convention campaign, and has been a source of help throughout the years. And in Memphis, as the bright shining star of all the Governors of the nation, Bufford Ellington, and if you want to know him, you better get busy because that kind of fellow is not going to stay around in Tennessee very long. He is going places, you watch that prediction. We met with a crowd of 1500 people at the airport, went and had a meeting with some loyal workers and then we went to Jackson today, then to Chattanooga and then to a wonderful university. They were so kind to us that in their enthusiasm they ran over my assistant, who just happens to be a Baptist preacher and knocked him down. His hand was bumped when the student body was trying to touch the Democrats in the car. I think those of us who have the great privilege of serving you in the Congress and other folks in public life, owe a great debt to you. Down in my country we would say, "You are what makes Sammy run", you get the job done. Without you, a lot of us wouldn't have the titles we have, and I want you to know how personally grateful I feel. Tennessee gave to the nation Andrew Jackson, and Tennessee gave to Texas, Sam Houston. A gift that changed the destiny of the nation. It was Tacqueville, the political philosopher, who said "Providence has not created mankind entirely independent or entirely free. It is true that around every man a fatal circle is traced beyond which he cannot pass, but within the wide verge of that circle he is powerful, he is free." Old Hickory and Old Sam were men who shaped the circle, and the results helped to ensure a better life and a glorious future for this country. The whole world is watching us as we approach this election, millions everywhere are weighing America's action in order to determine whether we really mean what we say, whether our high professions of democracy, our constitution, our sacred bill of rights, our sense of justice and liberty are merely pious phrases, or whether we really believe in them, really mean them, and if they are a reality. The world wants to know whether we are responsible enough and mature enough to assume the role of leadership in which destiny has cast a memory. The world is watching and waiting to know whether we will stretch out a sympathetic hand to those who are miserable, and who are distressed and oppressed. The world wants to know whether every American citizen stands on equal footing regardless of his creed or his race or his religion. The world wants to know whether we will protect the constitutional rights of all Americans without regard to the color of their eyes or the land of their ancestors or the color of their skin. The world is waiting and watching and wanting to know whether our leaders are truly national leaders, men who believe in protecting constitutional rights. The world wants to know whether we are a united people that know no north nor no south, nor no east nor no west. I want to say right now, here face to within the land that I love and to the people that I owe so much, that the administration of Jack Kennedy and Lyndon Johnson will be an administration that will protect the constitutional rights of all people.[38]*

## The 1960 Televised Debates

The first presidential campaign debates broadcast on public television occurred during the 1960 presidential campaign between John Kennedy and Richard Nixon. This was the first time that two opposing political candidates had appeared on the same stage at the same time before live television. There were a total of four debates. The first debate was broadcast on September 26, 1960. The remaining three debates were broadcast during the month of October each one a week apart.[39] The visual aspect of television soon challenged Nixon's confidence. Since television favors vertical lines, the taller John Kennedy appeared tanned, rested and freshly shaven. Kennedy also wore a dark blue suit that contrasted well with the gray background of the stage. Nixon's gray suit tended to blend into the background and the light accented his unshaven look. Nixon had lost about twenty pounds due to a recent illness, and he tended to perspire more under the hot lighting. Add all these issues to his tendency to rock back and forth, further reduced his visual presence on television. The television brought about a very different perspective for the candidates. Reports had indicated that radio listeners thought Nixon was a far better speaker, while those who watched the television debates favored Kennedy.[40] After the first debate, a Gallup poll indicated that 43 percent of respondents favored Kennedy, 23 percent favored Nixon, 29 percent considered it a tie, and 5 percent were undecided. After the last debate was over, the polls showed Kennedy being favored at 43 percent with Nixon favored at 30 percent. 23 percent of the polling considered the debates a tie with 5 percent undecided. Dr. Elmo Roper conducted a far more extensive survey for CBS. His survey indicated that 57 percent of the voting population said the television debates had greatly influenced their decisions. Another set of statistics showed that 6 percent of the voters had cast their vote based solely on the televised debates. On the Monday following the election, Kennedy had stated, "It was TV more than anything else that had turned the tide."[41]

**Exhibit #21** ★ October 4, 1960 in New Rochelle, New York. Lyndon Johnson at a podium greeting Mother Mary Peter Carthy, who was the president of the Catholic College of New Rochelle. ★ Photograph by Frank Muto

Exhibit twenty-one is an 8"x10" photograph taken October 4, 1960 in New Rochelle, New York. In this photo Frank Muto caught Lyndon Johnson at a podium greeting Mother Mary Peter Carthy, who was the president of the Catholic College of New Rochelle. This is an important and significant photograph because the issue of religion was a heated topic of debate in the 1960 election.

This photograph can be found in the Lyndon B. Johnson Library and Museum with reference number 60-10-66FM. On the back of this photograph is the hand written reference number FM-CS-75-4.

# SENATOR LYNDON B. JOHNSON
## Final Draft of Speech Delivered at New Rochelle College in New Rochelle, New York, on October 4, 1960

*This is the age of outer space. The headline voyages of our time are those that explore the regions of the moon and the other planets. But the inner man is still the measure of the outer man, and the most vital voyages of our time, as of any time, are those that occur in the inner space of the hearts and minds of men.*

*You know of these voyages. Here you are exploring the world of the mind, and are discovering, in the process, your own potentialities, the possibilities within yourselves and outside yourselves. Were I not a politician, I would rather be a teacher, as I once was. No experience is more wonderful to watch or to share than the one you are now undergoing. But I have foregone this privilege for another—the privilege of being a politician and of doing what I can to make certain that you, and all deserving young people like you, can have the opportunity you now have. As a politician, I am engaged in a national campaign that I believe crucial for a really young and growing America, and for a free and growing world.*

*I want to talk candidly, and I hope, responsibly about some of the issues in this campaign, and some of the realities that underlie the issues. We are a nation of mansions, and we cannot despise any of them. We cannot say, for example, that the welfare of an industrial worker is less than the welfare of a banker, or of a corporate president. Yet the spokesmen for the Republican Party tells us it is "normal" and "healthy" for four-million Americans to be unable to find work. One wonders what they would say if there were four million bankers or four million corporate presidents unable to find work. The issue is clear. Either we believe in real equality of opportunity or we don't. If we do believe in it, if we do believe that every American has a right to this kind of equality, then we must also believe that the first duty of government is to see to it that every American enjoys that right.*

*No man is exactly like another—one is brighter than another, one has a different interest than another, and one works harder than another. These are natural inequalities. The very purpose of a democratic society is to allow these inequalities free play. If allowed to flourish, these are the inequalities that move America forward and enrich its life. But there are other artificial inequalities that stifle these natural differences and abilities–the artificial barriers of race, of class, of religion, of economic position. These are the barriers that frustrate talent, that deny development, that withhold legitimate rewards. We are fallible and we are human. Never will we eliminate these barriers entirely. But as long as they exist we must struggle against them. For they increase in size and power to the exact degree that we relax our efforts against them. The business of government is to do what it can to remove these barriers, to encourage in our country a permanent climate of growth in which the only real and effective check to a man's opportunity are the inner checks of talent, of interest, and of effort.*

*Most people would agree with this in theory. Too many of them disagree with it in fact. The greatness of the Democratic Party is that it agrees in fact. That is why I am a Democrat, and that is why I am engaged in this campaign. For the underlying issue of this election is with which party, which candidate and with which program can best secure for all Americans real equality of opportunity.*

*No American believes that government is in any way the arbiter of a man's fate. This is what the Communists believe. But in a democracy, government must see to it that every man is free to be the arbiter of his own fate, and has the means to do it. The basic key to this freedom is education. And there is no good reason why every American should not have the education his talents deserve. Yet many Americans are now denied this kind of education. The Republican Secretary of Health, Education and Welfare tells us that the education of about 1 out of every 4 American children is being harmed by the present classroom shortage. To catch up with today's needs it will take us 13 years. In the meantime, elementary enrollment will be up 20% and high school enrollment will be up 50%. Our colleges alone will have to build more new buildings in the next 10 years than they built in the previous 200. How then can we justify the fact that in 1959 the national school construction rate was 3% less than it was in 1958? How then can we justify the fact that the present administration has frustrated every real Congressional attempt to help solve this problem?*

*If we are as incapable of meeting our problems at home, then it is no wonder we fail so often to meet them abroad. Even with the few facts I have given, are they enough to describe the large dimensions of our educational problem—and the need for urgent, adequate action? A crucial issue in this election is whether we will choose a President who will give us this kind of action.*

*But we cannot pigeonhole our areas of need. All the need programs for urban redevelopment and slum clearance, for an adequate minimum wage, for decent low and middle-income family housing, for aid to depressed area, for fair farm income—all of these programs are intimately related to each other, and to the need for real educational opportunity for all Americans. If a farmer or a laborer receives less than a decent wage, how can he provide his children with the education they need? The talented child of a department store worker may very well fail to receive the education he deserves, merely because his father hasn't got the money. The child of an individual banker may be much less talented, yet he is assured of the best education that money can buy. Is this equality of opportunity?*

*If a low or middle-income family cannot find a really decent home, how will this affect the up bringing of its children? Will this not tend to stifle, rather than encourage, their development? And what of slum neighborhoods and the slum environments? What of the many distressed areas throughout our nation, where men who want to work cannot find work? What of the children of these men? What of their wasted talents? I do not think we can be satisfied with an America where numbers of talented children find little or no opportunity to develop these talents—or even actual barriers to doing so. I do not think we can say this is none of the government's business, when the problem is increasing and quite obviously the local communities alone simply cannot handle it.*

*This is a public need which government cannot ignore—no matter how much or how loudly certain private privilege may take offense. Each of our talented children has a private privilege too. A privilege that must be protected, each having the opportunity to develop his talents. It is not governmental charity to try to save these talents from being wasted. This is governmental justice. It is not governmental domination or paternalism. It is responsible public action to promote private freedom and private opportunity.*

*If we do believe in equality of opportunity for all Americans, then we can honor that belief by making it a reality. Here, as in other things, faith without works is dead. Unless we achieve our works here in America, we cannot expect to win the faith and confidence of people outside of America. Here again, the inner man is the measure of the outer—and our success within America is the exact measure of our success abroad.*

*Our world is tri-partite. One-third is committed to freedom, one-third to the Communist tyranny, and the other one-third hangs in uncommitted balance. We cannot shift the balance unless we stand at full strength and bring that full strength to bear.*

*A policy merely of counter-attack and retreat, of rebuff and humiliation abroad—a policy merely of veto and hold-the-line, of squeezing money and forgetting people at home—these are unworthy of the United States, these are unnecessary and—in the long run—dangerous and wasteful. We have got to stop merely countering and reacting to Communist efforts towards world domination and put the Communists in the position of having to counter our efforts towards world freedom. We have got to remove, everywhere possible throughout the uncommitted world, the open invitations to Communism—the invitations of poverty, of ignorance, of fear, of backward social and economic conditions.*

We can only do these things with an affirmative leadership at home—a leadership that can call America to its feet. A leadership that can help America realize at home all the ideals that we would like those abroad to share with us. I know that Jack Kennedy will give us this kind of leadership.

The Republican candidate may utter charges—as he has recently done—of roads to surrender or to war, of "naïve" and "dangerous" policies. I think it is these charges themselves that are "naïve" and "dangerous."

What we need is a mounted and charging America—where the only charges are the ones that America makes against the ills at home and abroad.

This is the kind of America that Jack Kennedy will lead—if America will give him the chance.[42]

**Exhibit #22** ★ October 6, 1960 at the Richmond Arena in Richmond, Virginia during the 1960 presidential campaign. LBJ was caught doing what he enjoyed most, working a crowd. ★ Photograph by Frank Muto

Exhibit twenty-two is an 8"x10" photograph taken October 6, 1960 at the Richmond Arena in Richmond, Virginia during the 1960 presidential campaign. In this photograph, LBJ was caught doing what he enjoyed most, working a crowd. He took great pleasure in roaming through a crowd of supporters, meeting people face to face and shaking their hands. There was nothing phony about his delight in meeting the American public.

This photograph can be found in the Lyndon B. Johnson Library and Museum with reference number 60-10-182FM. The Frank Muto reference number has been hand written on the back and is FMCS-80-10.

The speech that Lyndon Johnson gave the evening of October 6, 1960, at the Commonwealth Club in Richmond, Virginia, provides a fascinating view on the 1960 campaign and some insight into his acceptance to be John F. Kennedy's running mate.

# SENATOR LYNDON B. JOHNSON

## Transcript of Recorded Remarks Delivered at the Dinner Held in His Honor at Commonwealth Club
## in Richmond, Virgini, on October 4, 1960

*You are here for a purpose and a principle, and that's primarily why I am on the Ticket. Now a lot of people in my own State don't understand it. Forty-one percent of them said in a poll, they thought I had made a mistake by agreeing to accept the nomination for Vice President. We in Texas have been in the Union for about 150 years, and we have had only one Vice President during that period, and they thought being Vice President this time would be a mistake—at least forty-one percent did. I sure do want to answer them, because I have been charged with everything from being a Benedict to a turncoat to a traitor and everything else. Of course, I didn't approach it that way. I never did see it that way. I had some grave doubts about whether or not I should take the offer. I considered it very carefully and resolved those doubts after I heard the evidence, and after I reached the conclusions. But to me, we had a fair shake of the dice. We did the best we could. We had hopes of winning the nomination and I think we would have won it if we could have convinced Dave Lawrence that his votes would do it. He wanted to vote for us in my opinion, but thought this would be a bad Ticket. He didn't think he could carry this Ticket to strangers. He never could quite see how we could get the votes. We had roughly 500 votes counting Florida and Mississippi. They never did go to it, so they didn't get too many votes. Florida and Mississippi, Montana, and Wyoming and one or two others didn't go with us. He finally just frankly told us what the situation was, and who was out. Now I had no earthly idea that I would be offered the Vice Presidency. As a matter of fact, I thought I would have been the last man, because we had fought pretty hard, pretty tough, given no quarters and asked for none. I had that debate with Jack and there had been a little feuding back and forth—pretty-high lofty approach—but still we were the only two men whose names went to the balloting. Mr. Rayburn called me about midnight and said now under no circumstances should I accept the Vice Presidency if it is offered. And I said, well it's not going to be offered, but why do you say that? And he said, he would like to discuss it with me and told me he thought it would be a mistake. And I went to bed. Next morning at about 8:30 Jack Kennedy called me. He came down about 9:30 or 10:00 and discussed it with me. At that time, he told me he had talked with various leaders of the Party and very frankly said that he would like to have my ideas on the Vice Presidency. I told him I thought he ought to make up his mind to which he wanted. Recommend him to the Convention, and we would try to help nominate him. Jack said, all right, I've made up my mind and I'm willing to recommend him if you can help me nominate him. Then we can get going. Jack said, I would like you to speak to my delegation. I asked Jack, who do you recommend, and he said you. Mr. Rayburn came around and said he had concluded that it was the only thing that could save the Party. He said we have no future with Nixon or Rockefeller or Lodge or any of them, and that if we are going to have a voice, the Party would have to exercise within the Party, a Chairmanship. Through leadership in Congress, and in his opinion, I could provide better leadership by being voted upon in the national election than to refuse and say no, I'm not going to run on the Ticket with you. If Kennedy lost, they'd very easily say to the Conference, they wouldn't support us, the South wouldn't join us, so let's elect our own leader. Or, if he wanted to say, I can't have those people leading us because they wouldn't help us. So, we all concluded that it was a wise thing to do. Whether it was or not, I don't know. We did it and we're in it. I have had a good many talks with the nominee. He seems to be very fair and reasonable. He knows the problems with different sections of the country. There are some parts of the platform that are very objectionable to, well, let's say the people of New England. There are a good many parts of it that are very objectionable to the South. Neither of us are in a position to repudiate it and say that I'm going to disown the platform. We don't think this would help the Ticket to do that, but we have been in about thirty States now and it looks to me like we've come to the bend in the road. I think the first television debate put us in high gear and if we have as much success tomorrow night as we had in the first, I rather think Nixon's going to be in trouble. He is acting like a feller who's cracking already. He's throwing them pretty wild. Nixon lashed out at the Democrats Civil Rights issue. His harshest attack came in an address to a crowd of about fifteen thousand at 38th Street and 7th Avenue in the garment district.*

*He said, do you want progress on Civil Rights he shouted, or do you want somebody that just talks about it? He charged that Kennedy had compromised on the issue by naming a southerner, Lyndon Johnson, to his Ticket. He accused him of refusing to talk about the same discrimination in the South as in the North. Do New Yorkers want this kind of man recommended or somebody who has the guts to talk about discrimination everywhere? Now with distortion and with no guts, with the unpatriotic stuff, we think Nixon is cracking like McCarthy, and if he goes on tomorrow night, and Jack takes him like I think he'll take him—pretty cool—and I've found out a little of what rattles Kennedy—I tried to rattle him some myself, but he's a pretty cool sort of feller and he doesn't lose his head very easily, I rather think he will give Nixon another one. If he does, we'll be in pretty good shape. I can't find a State that I know is positively Democratic, and I don't know one that I can positively say is Republican. I think that's the situation at this stage of the game. I believe we are better in the South than we have been since the Third Term. But I don't know that's conclusive at all. I think the principle issues are first the religious issue, and second is the platform issue.*

*All you know the religious issue can only be answered by the Constitution. For the platform issue, all you have to do is take our platform and compare their platform and see that the guy reads them both, but usually it's not the platform that keeps them from nominating either. Out of fifteen Committees, we have nineteen Senators that we can count on, lock stock and barrel. Of those nineteen, they are nineteen of sixty-six. Now, we are not going to like the control of the Executive Department during our lifetime unless we elect a Democratic President. We have had twelve Presidents succeed from the Vice Presidency and if I were Vice President, we might control the Executive Department. But the best chance I see of us having an effective voice in government is as Head of the House of Representatives and Head of the Senate. In the Senate, we have got fifteen Committees and we control ten of them, that is, as long as we control the majority. A majority of sixty-six can name the Senator, so it's customary for us to name the senior Senator on a Committee. The Republicans say we have the Appropriations Committee, the Space Sciences Committee with Lyndon Johnson, Foreign Relations with Bill Fullbright, Agriculture with Allen Ellender, Finance with Harry Byrd, and so forth. Now thirty-four men can take me out of Space Sciences, I'm the senior man on that Committee—and put in a junior man if they want to. But I don't think they'll ever do that as long as things are reasonably situated like they are now. I think as long as we control the Committees, maybe we can have a reasonably effective voice. I thought by going on this Ticket it would put us in a little better shape. We could help the Committees to help the President. I think that if I had turned Kennedy down and said hell no, I don't want on the Ticket with you—the South won't help you and we don't want you—you beat us, but we're going to pout, I think he would take the same position justifiably next January. And if he did, by God, we wouldn't have but nineteen Confederate votes—we wouldn't have the leadership, or anything. Now, first of all, I never said I would take the Vice Presidency—that's the first thing. As a matter of fact, when they asked me if I was offered the Vice Presidency, would I take it? My answer to this—which is in black and white—was, I was not a candidate for Vice President, that I was a candidate for President. I didn't anticipate this ever happening. I had no desire, quote "I had no desire to trade a vote for a gavel", but they pressed me a little further and I said, that I don't think that a man in public life has the right to determine solely himself the title that goes over his door. If I were convinced that my government needed my services, I would serve in any capacity from a Private to a General—that's the language of the verbatim transcript, which is available. I frankly did not look forward to doing what I am doing tonight—campaigning day and night all over this country. I had been nominated without opposition in Texas as Senator. I was Leader and had been unanimously elected Leader. I got a respectable vote for President—more than any other Southerner ever got. I am proud of my friends and I just like to go around by God kissing them the rest of my life and thanking them instead of going out and doing something else, but I had it put right in front of me and I was told you either come on and do this or you throw me into the jaws of something else. I evaluated it, my friends evaluated it, and we came to the conclusion that from the standpoint of the people who voted for me, the section I lived in, the friends I had, the people that I work with in the Congress, that this was the best thing to do under the circumstances. I asked them very frankly to talk to Senator Byrd*

*—he wasn't available. I asked them to talk to Senator Russell and they located him. He said, why hell no, I wouldn't do it. Then he said, well hell yes, I think you'd better. This was all in the same telephone conversation. Now that's the way it was. Mr. Rayburn went to bed at midnight and said under no circumstances should I accept the offer. The next morning, he called me up and said, goddamn it, don't you dare turn it down. So that's what was happening, and happening in fact. I had until 4 o'clock to make up my mind—I made it up—I'm not apologizing for it. I'm just explaining the reasons for it so all of you who were in on it and had an investment in it will know why I did it. I don't like for my wife to be running for Vice President and I don't like to be second to Mr. Kennedy. I'd rather be first, that's human nature, but I didn't want to be a poor sport. I don't think any of you will ever know—I'm going to say it once more and then I'm through. I don't think any of you will ever know how grateful I am to the State of Virginia—that means everybody in it by God. Texas—as proud as we are—didn't have as strong a resolution as Virginia and they didn't have any stronger Delegation, and they never stood any better. So I'll just try to be worthy of that and I'll try to be big enough for the grandkids one hundred years from now who can look back—and you don't have to apologize for Thomas Jefferson and Woodrow Wilson—and hope that I got that kind of record, but I'm going to try for it.*[43]

LYNDON B. JOHNSON
SENATE DEMOCRATIC LEADER

December 19, 1960

4500 3rd Street, S. E.
Washington, D. C.

Dear Bill:

The LBJ Victory Special has clickety-clacked into the past, but like Casey Jones' Number 97 and the Cannonball Express, its memory is a living thing with Lady Bird and me.

We'll always remember those 3,500 miles through eight states... our reporter friends working night and day.. the bands, balloons, and banners (including Lady Bird's "Kissing Cousins")... and above all, the people -- all kinds of people, working men, farmers, lawyers, homemakers -- all cheering us on to victory.

As part of the crew, you earned a lifelong membership in "The Whistlestop Club". So your grandchildren will know you made that famous ride, we are sending you a memento of the trip and a "badge" of membership, and we are both hoping the memories of that ride on the LBJ Victory Special will always mean as much to you as they do to us.

Merry Christmas and a Happy New Year.

Sincerely yours,

*Lady Bird Johnson*

Lady Bird and Lyndon Johnson

**Exhibit #23** ★ Letter relating to the 1960 whistle stop tour aboard the LBJ Victory Special.
This letter was sent to a personal friend and supporter who had participated in the campaign.

# The 1960 Whistle-Stop Tour

On October 10, 1960, Lyndon and Lady Bird Johnson began a fast-paced, five-day whistle-stop tour across eight southern states. The tour covered a total of 3500 miles. The train began in Virginia and went through the Carolinas, down through Georgia and Alabama, and finally ended in New Orleans.[44] The tour by train had actually been Harry Truman's suggestion. He had used the same strategy very effectively during his campaign. The train was made up of eleven cars and was called the LBJ Victory Special. However, some in the media had dubbed it the Cornpone Special. The aides to several Texas congressmen dressed in coveralls and positioned themselves throughout the crowd and led cheers for Johnson. An advance team of five women, led by the wife of Congressman Hale Boggs from Louisiana, all dressed in blue blazers, white pleated skirts, white blouses, and red hats flew ahead of the train to meet them at each city the train passed.[45] What was important on this trip, besides the speeches, were the visits with the state and local leaders who were being told they had better stay with the Democratic ticket. Johnson's back-slapping, in-your-face salesmanship, was in full swing.[46]

Exhibit #24 ★ Photograph by Frank Muto ★ October 18, 1960, LBJ never hesitated to jump into a crowd and meet the people.

Exhibit twenty-four is an 8"x10" photograph taken October 18, 1960, while campaigning through several small towns throughout Pennsylvania. LBJ never hesitated to jump into a crowd and meet the people. An interesting note should be made with this photograph. Notice the sign carried by a young lady in the crowd. The sign says "U.M.W. for Kennedy and Johnson." U.M.W. probably represents the United Methodist Women and not "United Mine Workers." Religion was an issue of heated discussion in the 1960 campaign because JFK was Catholic. LBJ, on the other hand, was a southerner who had a protestant upbringing. It is believed Johnson helped balance and temper the religion issue.

This photograph can be found in the Lyndon B. Johnson Library and Museum and has the Frank Muto reference number FMCS-100 written on the back. The LBJ Library reference number for this photo is 60-10-393FM.

# SENATOR LYNDON B. JOHNSON
## Final Draft of Speech Delivered in Allentown, Pennsylvania, on October 18, 1960

*I did not come here to tell the people of Allentown to relax and enjoy the declining days of American leadership and responsibility. I do not propose to soothe you with false illusions, or to suggest that our program for America will make no great demands on your hands and minds. I leave the lullabies and fairy tales to our Republican opponents, who do these things so well.*

*John Kennedy and I need and ask your help in our campaign to bring new strength, new vigor, and new ideas to the leadership of this nation. We ask you to join us in our fight to revive and expand the confidence of the world in the future of democracy under freedom. After we take office next January, we shall need you even more. All of your skills, all of your resources, all of your productive capacity will be required to fulfill America's need for growth, expansion and progress. We offer not ease but work, not complacency but opportunity, not platitudes, but performance. That is our challenge. That is our program.*

*The working people, the industries, and the enterprises of the Lehigh Valley must play a leading part in the attainment of our goals. You will be called upon to step up your production of the materials and tools needed to build America's future beyond any level you may have known in the past. These goals cannot be reached with part-time plants, unemployed workers and unused capacity. I want to see your great cement industry turning out all it can possibly produce—for we shall need that and more if the people of this country are to have the housing, the highways, the schools, the hospitals, the power and water resources, and the defense forces that we need. We shall need all the steel you can deliver and all the trucks you can make. If you want to work—if you want to produce—if you want to build a better and stronger America, then come along with us. That is the great mission of the Democratic Party and of John F. Kennedy and myself.*

*We do not believe in government for the sake of government. We believe in government for the sake of people. It is the people who count. It is they who are important. Their problems, their needs, and their hopes are riding on this election. Those are the issues at stake. And where do we find the Republican candidate for President, Mr. Nixon? What does he think is the vital burning issue of this campaign? Not the problems of millions of unemployed Americans. Not the crushing burden of medical costs borne by our aged. Not the poverty and economic decay of depressed areas. Not the repair of the dangerous gaps in our military defenses. Not the unmet housing and educational needs of American families. Not the farm depression. Not the economic recession. Not the Soviet missile threat and space lead. Not the surrender of the Monroe Doctrine and the rise of a new Communist menace on our very doorstop, 90 miles away, in Cuba.*

*Not any of those things, for they are far too close to home for his comfort. Each of these problems bears witness to his own party's failures and shortcomings. Like a drowning man, grasping as straws, he has reached for Quemoy and Matsu. Personally, I doubt if he can carry those precincts—not after what he said about their people. I have heard of candidates running away from the issues, but never quite that far. This must be a new record for distance, even for Nixon.*

*And why does he say that we should commit ourselves flatly and irrevocably in advance to these Chinese death traps, regardless of cost or circumstance? Not because of any strategic or real estate value. Not because of those little islands. According to Nixon, "They are not too important." That, by the way, is the most typical Republican remark of the entire campaign. No, he says it's for "principle". Well, if that is the reason, this is a new principle devised by*

*Richard Nixon—devised, I suspect to help him win an election. President Eisenhower has never announced any principle requiring us to go to war over Quemoy and Matsu. Neither has Congress. Neither have our generals and admirals. For all these authorities, the issue is not principle but common sense and strategy.*

*Principles are important, but so are people. We in the Democratic Party have strong principles and I would match our principles against Richard Nixon's any time, anywhere and on any issue—and spot him points to boot. But we also care very deeply about people. First and foremost, we care about the people of America.*

*On this and every other issue that this country faces today and tomorrow, we are not going to be governed by Mr. Nixon's unilateral commitments to a Chinese war or to anything else that suits his fancy.*

*We are going to be governed by one great principle—the best interests of the American people.*[47]

# SENATOR LYNDON B. JOHNSON

## Final Draft of Speech Delivered in Sunbury, Pennsylvania, on October 18, 1960

*I'm a man from the country, but I know something about your cities here in Pennsylvania, and I know something about you. Dave Lawrence has told me about you. In fact, that's all he wants to talk about—you and the wonderful progress you are making here in Sunbury, in Williamsport and other Pennsylvania communities.*

*I make you a promise—not a promise you have to take on faith, but a promise based on performance.*

*If on November the 8th you honor Jack Kennedy and me with the election, we are going to begin an "open door" policy for the American people. We are going to run a government whose doors will always be open to every American community. We want you to come in and see us. We want you to give us your advice and your thoughts. We want you to tell us your problems.*

*We have had for nearly eight years a government of closed doors—a government closed in upon itself like a bank vault. No matter how much you pounded on that door, nobody inside could hear you, because nobody inside wanted to hear you.*

*The Congress listened to you. We heard you when you told us about your problems.*

*When you told us you were concerned about low wage levels—we tried to pass a minimum-wage bill, but the administration closed the door on that. When you told us that unemployment was high, that factories were idle, that industries were going out rather than coming in—twice we passed distressed area bills. Twice the administration closed the doors on these. When you told us that your housing needs were fast outgrowing supply—we passed three housing bills. Twice the administration closed the doors on these. When you told us that millions of our elderly needed medical care—we tried to pass an adequate bill, but the administration closed the doors on that. When you told us that we needed many more schools and better paid teachers—we tried to pass an adequate bill, but the administration closed the doors on that. When you told us about the slums, about the air and water pollution—we tried to advance the progress for these, but the administration closed the doors on them. When you told us the highway program was not working as it ought to—we tried to see that it did, but the administration closed the doors on that.*

*Whatever your problems, we have opened our doors and let you in. We have listened to your ideas and we have acted. But it does no good for the Congress to let you in through one door if the administration will only lock you out by another. We cannot continue a house divided. Without the White House, the Congress can only partly succeed.*

*You are doing wonders here under David Lawrence. You know that all you need is the leadership to make progress.*

*Jack Kennedy will give you that kind of leadership nationally. With Jack Kennedy in the White House your efforts and David Lawrence's efforts will be twice as effective. With Jack Kennedy in the White House, you and all Americans will have a united government—a government united in itself and a government united with you in the common effort for a greater America.[48]*

**Exhibit #25** ★ Photographic proof sheet of six 120mm photographic negatives taken November 6, 1960, at a campaign rally in the Corpus Christi Airport in Texas ★ Photograph by Frank Muto

Exhibit twenty-five is an 8"x10" proof sheet of six 120mm photographic negatives taken November 6, 1960, at the Corpus Christi Airport in Corpus Christi, Texas. With only two days remaining before the November primary, LBJ remained fixed on the campaign trail.

This series of photographs shows several views of LBJ and Lady Bird Johnson at a podium set up in the Corpus Christi airport before a cheering crowd of supporters. People are carrying banners and streamers printed with "JFK," "Johnson for Vice President," "Let's Back the Team of Kennedy/Johnson," and many others. One interesting banner of note is shown condemning the Nixon/Lodge campaign that says "Down with Big D, those S.O.Bs (scared ole boys)."

This series of photographs can be found in the Lyndon B. Johnson Library and Museum; each photograph is referenced separately and has a reference number from 60-11-215FM through 60-11-220FM.

This original proof sheet has the Frank Muto reference number FM-230 written on the back.

# SENATOR LYNDON B. JOHNSON
## Transcript of Recorded Remarks Delivered at the Democratic Rally at the Corpus Christi Airport
## in Corpus Christi, Texas, on November 6, 1960

### Speaker—Congressman John Young

*Lady Bird, Lyndon, and you magnificent multitude of Democrats. It is with great privilege and honor to be here this evening and to greet and meet, and bring to you two of the finest first members of Texas families, Lyndon Johnson and Lady Bird Johnson. It makes me especially proud to have Lyndon here with us this evening because I think that there are a few people here in this area who know as well as I do how much Lyndon Johnson has meant to South Texas. I say to you Democrats, you Texans, 20,000 strong here and 10,000 more in their automobiles trying to get into this room, that we witnessed six months ago the most united action Texas has seen in its history, in the move to get Lyndon Johnson nominated for the Presidency of the United States. We did not succeed and we were disappointed, but we Texans don't give up easily. We're going to achieve our dream and our purpose, it may be eight years from now, but the first thing that we have to do is elect Lyndon Johnson Vice President and carry Texas Tuesday with the greatest majority ever given to a Democratic nominee in the State of Texas. It is now my high honor and real privilege to present to you, the greatest political gathering ever seen in South Texas, the next Vice President of the United States, Lyndon Johnson.*

### Speaker—Lady Bird Johnson

*Friends of Corpus Christi, friends of South Texas, I can see that you have been using some of those twelve days to put in some good Democratic work, and I do thank you. And now there is only one day left—only twenty-four hours—and I hope that all of you ladies are going to make good use of it. Call all your friends and ask them to go to the polls and vote Democratic, and then when Tuesday morning comes, be sure to take a full car yourself. Thank you and God bless you.*

### Speaker—Lyndon B. Johnson

*Como esta usted, amigos. I am back tonight where I started some thirty years ago, with the people that I know the best and the folks that I love the most. I have traveled more than 50,000 miles, I have visited more than forty states and have crossed both oceans several times. I have seen the sunrise on Mt. White, but the most beautiful vision these eyes have beheld was the friends that looked me in the face here in Corpus Christi. Are you going to vote Democratic? I think that I should tell you that I came back home the day before yesterday and I had a wonderful crowd of more that 20,000 people attend a luncheon in one of the great cities of our states. But it took forty minutes to get there because a Republican Congressman named Algar, and some nice looking ladies that one paper called the "Mink Coat Mob", carried Republican slogans and made it extremely difficult for me and my lady to get through the lobby of the hotel. Well, we are going to anchor them and their kind next Tuesday with a landslide, because we know something that they have forgotten. And that is—all people are equal on Election Day. What occurred in Dallas happened because the Republican Party in Texas and across the nation is frantic and panicky tonight. The Democratic ground swell through the nation has turned them to route, and they are resorting to the most desperate tactics imaginable in a last minute frenzy to carry at least one state. They went out and bought four hours of television yesterday. In doing so, the Republican Party has revealed its true face. It is not the face of Dr. Jeykle—it is the face of Mr. Hyde. I feel that you join me in feeling sorry for the people who took part in this demonstration in Dallas. I cannot believe that those well dressed and attractive women and teenagers really new what they were doing. They were only the actors, the script was written by a small band of Republicans who want Texas to become a puppet of the privileged few, the Republican Party. When I came to Corpus Christi in 1931, most of the homes that were mortgaged were being foreclosed. We had to bring in twenty-three federal farm appraisers to save the richest black land in Nueces County, because a Republican administration had been in office doing nothing too long. We saved some of those homes and some of those farmers. After our people were scarred from it, our boys were in the boxcars. Our women went to sewing rooms, our men worked with picks out on the highways on WPA and PWA because we had a Republican government that didn't care. Well, I'm telling you the administration of Jack Kennedy and Lyndon Johnson cares for all the people all the time. We care about educating our young. We care about providing adequate medical plans for our aged. We are determined to advance and protect the Constitutional rights of every living American regardless of his race or his religion or the region in which he lives. The administration of Jack Kennedy and Lyndon Johnson will say—we will be fair to all and special privilege to none. Every man that works in the petroleum industry in this state or has a farm with a little lawyer, knows that no one has been more fair than the Texas Delegation and myself have been. But we serve notices here and now to the oilmen of this state. You cannot buy this election and you can't frighten us in this election. We are going to win this election for all the people. I have worked with Jack Kennedy for fourteen years. I know him and I know him well. His record is clear. He has answered every question that has been asked. You had a right to ask them. He had a right to answer them, and you know the answer. The answer is that he is for the greatest good for the greatest number and he wears no man's collar. But you cannot overlook the fact that the religious question is in this campaign, and it is in every state, and particularly, it is evident in our state when we hear some of calls and some of the material we receive in the mail. So I want you to ask your conscience and ask your neighbor before you go vote, whether you are willing to vote to send all men to war to die for their country, but you won't let those who belong to a certain church serve in a civilian capacity. While we were in Jack Kennedy's plane a frail little lady walked up to the steps. Her husband was Wilford Wiley who had died with Jack Kennedy's brother, Joe Kennedy, in the European Theatre. She had with her, her little sixteen-year-old daughter who had never seen her father because he died before she was born. Wilford Wiley and Joe Kennedy were sitting in the operations room in the European Theatre when the Commanding Officer came in and said, "You boys have finished your missions and you can go back home to your families, the boat is about ready to go. But we have one more dangerous and hazardous mission that Uncle Sam has to fly, and I would like some volunteers." The first hand that went up was Captain Joe Kennedy, Jr., Jack's Brother, a pilot. The next hand to go up was Lieutenant Wilford Wiley, a co-pilot, a Texas boy, and a boy who was from Fort Worth. So they went down and took off into the clouds, never to return. Their plane was last seen with the Captain from Massachusetts holding the controls and Lieutenant Wiley in the co-pilot's seat. They died in order that you might be free; they died in order that you might live; and none of these folks had the nerve or audacity to ask either of them what church they belonged to or where they worshiped that morning.[49] The man whose religion is not questioned when he's dying for his country, oughtn't to have it questioned when he's trying to be President of his country.[50]*

## The 1960 Election Results

On November 8, 1960, John F. Kennedy and Lyndon Baines Johnson won the presidential election by one of the closest popular vote margins in United States history. A total of 68,836,385 votes were cast that day. Of the total, 34,227,096 votes for 49.7 percent were cast for JFK and Johnson, and 34,107,646 for 49.5 percent were cast for Nixon and Lodge. The JFK and LBJ ticket won by a margin where it counted, the electoral votes. They received 303 electoral votes with 56.43 percent, while Nixon and Lodge received 219 electoral votes at 40.78 percent.[51] The results of the election showed that Kennedy and LBJ had won the industrial states due to the support of the Catholics, and with the backing of blacks and labor. Nixon and Lodge did well in the southern states and in the west, with some of the votes coming from the farming states. Kennedy and LBJ took a total of twenty-two states to Nixon's twenty-six states. Had Illinois and Texas voted for Nixon, Nixon would have been elected president. However, when Illinois voted for Kennedy and LBJ, the electoral vote swung in their favor. Ultimately, the Democrats lost some of their strength in Congress due to Kennedy and LBJ winning the election. However, the new administration maintained a sixty-four-seat to thirty-six-seat advantage in the U.S. Senate. They lost twenty seats in the House of Representatives, but still maintained a majority of 263 Democratic seats to the 174 Republican seats. The voters had spoken in this election. They were tired of the stalemates on bills offered in both houses of Congress, and they wanted a president with a party majority who could overcome the issues.[52]

# The Vice Presidency
# 1961–1963

It was LBJ's friend and mentor Sam Rayburn who swore LBJ into office as the thirty-seventh vice president of the United States on January 20, 1961. This was the first time a Speaker of the House of Representatives had ever sworn in a vice president.[1] Much controversy and speculation still exists over Johnson's acceptance as John Kennedy's vice president. For Lyndon Johnson, choosing to accept the vice presidency was not an easy decision. LBJ was leaving behind the powerful position of Senate majority leader with many years of seniority in both the Congress and the Senate. Nonetheless, LBJ accepted the second place position and performed his duties with much resolve. By mid-1962, much of his fellow constituents were wondering what the vice president was even doing. When LBJ was the Senate majority leader, he was well publicized. In June 1962, William McGaffin wrote a story in *The Dallas Times Herald* called "The Quiet Man — Capitol Hill Wondering: What's Johnson Up To?"[2] Lyndon Johnson was not a headliner anymore and that was very difficult for him. He was accustomed to being approached for his opinion and having reporters seek him out for comments. The vice presidency became one of the most difficult times in his political career. Lyndon Johnson was warned several times before making the decision to accept the role of vice president. There had been plenty of vice presidents in the past who had less-than-favorable opinions about the position. John Garner, who was vice president under Franklin Roosevelt, said, "The Vice Presidency isn't worth a pitcher of spit!"[3] Johnson also knew that Bobby Kennedy and Kenny O'Donnell, Kennedy's special assistant and chief

organizer during the campaign, had opposed the choice. This created an ongoing animosity between them and Johnson. Although Johnson was invited to all the important meetings at the White House, he usually just kept to himself.[4] Lady Bird had a much different perspective on the vice presidency. In an interview with Merle Miller, she said, "When he became vice president, I had a ball. I loved it. I had a great time. We bought a beautiful home and took a sizeable share of entertaining visitors. And we did a lot of traveling—all the things I enjoy doing and had done very little of before. But I would not say Lyndon shared the same feeling. It was a life that was not nearly as pleasant for him as it was for me."[5] John Kennedy recognized the leadership qualities of his vice president and leveraged those qualities by handing him some very important assignments. Johnson was assigned four important positions; 1) chairman of the National Aeronautics and Space Council, 2) head of the President's Committee on Equal Employment Opportunity, 3) chairman for the Advisory Committee of the Peace Corps, and 4) a member of the National Security Council. The chairmanship of the National Aeronautics and Space Council was a new position for the vice presidency. The position had previously been reserved for the president. However, Kennedy had the law changed for Lyndon Johnson.[6] As vice president, he and Mrs. Johnson played very important roles as foreign ambassadors. In April 1961, the Johnsons, along with a staff of advisors and diplomats, set off on a round-the-world trip that included Hong Kong, the Philippines, Formosa, South Vietnam, Thailand, India, and Pakistan. The most important part of the

1961 trip was to South Vietnam, where they offered a show of support to President Diem. Later that year, Kennedy would send LBJ to Germany where the communists would build the Berlin Wall. LBJ met with Konrad Adenaur and Berlin's mayor, Willi Brandt, to ensure them of U.S. support. The next major overseas trip for LBJ would not come until late 1962. That trip would take them to Turkey, Greece, and Italy.[7] By 1963, the Johnsons had traveled to more than thirty countries in eleven separate trips that logged over 120,000 miles.[8] A trust and confidence had grown between John Kennedy and Lyndon Johnson. Johnson had remained true to his pledge to "be the kind of vice president I would want if I were president." He always responded with vigor to any Kennedy suggestions or requests. He performed overseas errands, made political speeches for Kennedy when he requested them, and attended many White House conferences for the president—Lyndon Johnson always made himself available.[9] Many years later, Lyndon Johnson would reflect, "The vice presidency was filled with trips around the world, chauffeurs, men saluting, people clapping, chairmanships of councils, but in the end, it was nothing. I detested every minute of it."[10]

## The German Chancellor

Exhibit twenty-six is an 8"x10" proof sheet of six large/medium-format photographic negatives taken April 17, 1961, during the Texas visit of Konrad Adenauer, the chancellor of West Germany. These six photographs are a series of shots taken shortly after the chancellor had arrived in Austin by helicopter. Of particular note is the presence of Admiral Chester Nimitz who can be seen in the boardroom photos. Admiral Nimitz, participated in the Adenauer visit because the admiral's hometown is Fredericksburg, Texas, which still has the largest population of German immigrants in the state. The people of Fredericksburg provided a very old German-style welcome for the Chancellor.

Chancellor Adenauer spent the weekend in Texas after visiting with President Kennedy in Washington a few days before. The presidential meeting was the first of the new administration. Chancellor Adenauer and President Eisenhower had already created a good relationship; however, Adenauer was concerned about the support and "resolve under NATO to use nuclear weapons to defend Western Europe against a Russian attack." The worry was quickly dispelled after meeting with President Kennedy. After meeting with Kennedy, Adenauer felt that he had established a "great spirit of friendship" with the new president.[11] The chancellor arrived at Bergstrom Air Force Base in Texas on Sunday April 16, 1961, with an official party of sixteen German dignitaries that included the German minister of foreign affairs

Dr. Frederick von Brentano and his daughter along with about thirty German newsmen. They all had arrived aboard a Lufthansa Boeing 707 airliner and were greeted by Vice President Johnson and Texas Governor Price Daniels. After a short reception at Bergstrom Air Force Base, they boarded helicopters that took them to the LBJ Ranch in Stonewall, Texas. At the ranch, a crowd of over one-thousand people greeted them. The festivities at the ranch included a Texas style barbeque and other activities. Later that afternoon, the chancellor and the vice president along with Admiral Nimitz, attended a reception and parade in Fredericksburg. There in Fredericksburg, Vice President Johnson said in a speech, "Where you stand to resist communism, the United States will stand by your side."[12]

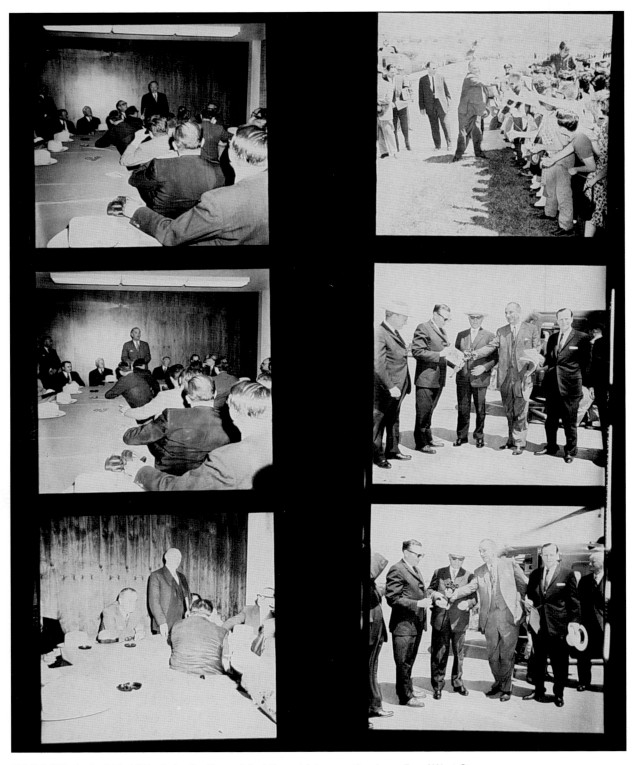

**Exhibit #26** ★ April 17, 1961, during the Texas visit of Konrad Adenauer, the chancellor of West Germany.

★ Photograph by Frank Muto

## The Failed Invasion of Cuba

On this same day, Monday April 17, 1961, while Lyndon Johnson was entertaining Chancellor Konrad Adenauer, President Kennedy and his inner circle were overseeing an invasion to overthrow the regime of Fidel Castro in Cuba. This invasion would prove to be an embarrassing failure. The United States denied any role in the invasion, although it would later be determined that the plan had been in the works since President Eisenhower. "Richard Nixon had proposed it, Eisenhower had planned it, Robert Kennedy championed it, John F. Kennedy approved it, and the CIA had carried it out. This controversial and most embarrassing of missions was called 'The Bay of Pigs.'"[13] Robert Dallek, in his book *Flawed Giant*, takes a very different view of the JFK/LBJ relationship and discusses Kennedy's impulse to keep Johnson at arm's length in the management of foreign affairs. "During the Bay of Pigs crisis in April 1961, when the CIA-supported anti-Castro Cubans staged an abortive invasion of their homeland, Johnson, at JFK's request, had entertained West German Chancellor Konrad Adenauer at his Texas ranch. Moreover, Kennedy had systematically excluded Johnson from any part in the operation. Johnson was so frustrated at being ignored in these deliberations that he had a secretary ask a Kennedy friend to lobby the president for a larger role in foreign policy. When the friend asked JFK why he didn't lean more on Lyndon, Kennedy replied: 'You know, it's awfully hard because once you get into one of these crunches you don't really think of calling Lyndon because he hasn't read the cables . . . . You want to talk to the people who are most involved, and your mind does not turn to Lyndon because he isn't following the flow of cables.' Of course, Kennedy could have arranged to make it otherwise, but he obviously had no desire to give Johnson a more central part in shaping foreign policy."[14]

Exhibit twenty-seven is another 8"x10" proof sheet of large-format photographic negatives taken Monday April 17, 1961, in Austin, Texas, during the visit of Konrad Adenauer. On this Monday morning, the chancellor awakened at the LBJ ranch and discussed foreign policy with the vice president. After the morning discussions, LBJ and the chancellor boarded a helicopter for a short tour of Highland Lakes before heading to Austin. Once in Austin, they took part in a parade up Congress Avenue that took them to the State Capitol for an address before a special joint session of the Texas Legislature. All six photographs on this proof sheet were taken during the Chancellor's address before the Texas Legislature. Both Chancellor Adenauer and the vice president spoke to a full house of representatives that day and after the event they had lunch at the governor's mansion. Tickets were made available for the public to attend this special joint session of the Texas Legislature through their state representatives. One Texas senator had said he alone had more than fifty or sixty calls for his three tickets. There were only 470 seats available in the Senate gallery and thousands of requests were made. The event was televised nationally with local schools and universities being dismissed early so students could attend the historic occasion.[15]

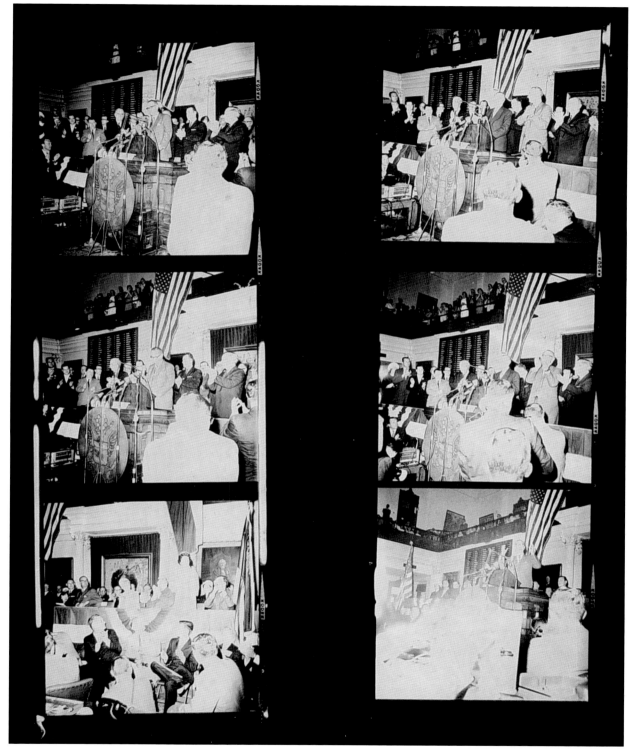

**Exhibit #27** ★ Photographer's proof sheet of large/medium format photographic negatives taken April 17, 1961, during a visit to Texas by Konrad Adenauer, the Chancellor of West Germany ★ Photograph by Frank Muto

Recorded addresses by Vice President Lyndon Johnson and the chancellor of the Federal Republic of Germany, Dr. Konrad Adenauer, on Monday, April 17, 1961, at a joint session of the Texas Legislature at the State Capitol building in Austin, Texas.

# VICE PRESIDENT LYNDON B. JOHNSON
## Address to the Joint Session of the Texas Legislature

*Mr. Chancellor and his charming daughter and members of his party, Governor, Mr. President, Mr. Speaker, members of the Senate, members of the House, my fellow countrymen, I am glad to have the privilege to return here to the House Chamber, a scene of my childhood. In this Chamber, my grandfather labored. In this House, my father gave his happiest service to his country for six terms. This is a proud moment for me and my family and the people of Texas.*

*Our State—like our Nation—is a land of many heritages. Men of many tongues have come here. They have lived together, worked together, and together they have learned to speak the language of freedom. In our world today, no man speaks that language of freedom with greater clarity or greater force or greater inspiration than the man who does us the great honor of his presence today, the Chancellor of the Federal republic of Germany, Dr. Konrad Adenauer.*

*Standing in the jaws of grave danger at the edge of the Free World, he has shown a personal courage and unfailing resolution, which will be honored so long as men are free anywhere on this earth. And I should like for the entire world to know that all Americans admire this man, but we in the Lone Star State of Texas feel a special affinity for him.*

*More than a hundred years ago—in the 1830s—there began coming to Texas the first of what was to be a great tide of families from Germany. Throughout the years, as Texas became a Republic and then as Texas became one of the States of the Union, these fine people have made a contribution to our region, to our nation, and to the cause we support in concert with free men everywhere.*

*The German people who have meant so much to Texas came here seeking freedom—and seeking peace. What led those early families to our State more than a hundred years ago is the same thing that leads our guest to Texas today—the support of freedom throughout the world and the quest for peace for all the peoples of the world. I speak for our own President when I say that the United States of America will not hesitate to walk the last mile—to go more than half way—to assure peace with honor throughout the world.*

*I can say that with equal resolve that until such peace is assured, the United States will not retreat one inch—will not move an eyelash—will not hesitate a fraction of a moment in maintaining whatever strength is necessary to preserve freedom throughout the world. So, I would say to you, my most treasured friends of Texas today, and to my good and long-time friend, Dr. Adenauer, that the people of the United States have a man of courage, have a man of wisdom and vigor equal to his grave responsibilities as their President; the brilliant John F. Kennedy, President of the United States.*

*At our President's request, I have just completed a 13,000-mile mission into the world—to Africa, to Geneva, to France, to NATO. That was a mission of freedom for peace—and there will be many more. The leadership of America understands its responsibilities, today that leadership welcomes its opportunities, and that administration is now ready to go wherever and whenever duty calls to assure the success of the cause of freedom. The security of Free Germany and Free Berlin is America's security. The freedom of all men and all women wherever they live is the concern of all the people of the United States of America. The betterment and the improvement of the lives of all human beings of all races of all religions and of all regions of the earth is the objective of the United States of America. We recognize the perils but we have faith in our prayers. Keeping our faith we shall overcome those perils, and so today it gives me great pleasure and great honor to present to you, my beloved homefolks, a man who has kept great faith, a man who has overcome great perils—a man who is really an authentic giant of our times, the Chancellor of the Federal Republic of Germany, Dr. Konrad Adenauer.*

# CHANCELLOR KONRAD ADENAUER
## Address to the Joint Session of the Texas Legislature

*Mr. Governor, Presiding officers, Ladies and Gentlemen of both Houses of Texas.*

*I have looked forward with great pleasure to this day on which I am to speak to you. What I have experienced here on my trip surpasses by far all my wildest dreams. So much friendliness, so much joy, among the young and the old, as I experienced among you in Texas—yesterday in Fredericksburg, today here in your capital city—remains unique, I believe, in the life of a man.*

*Now my honored Ladies and Gentlemen, for us in Europe, Texas is still considered the embodiment of the expanse and diversity of America, of its vitality, it's abundance and its generosity. Although the previous speakers have already done so, I believe that I may once again call to memory our many fellow countrymen who came to this country a hundred years ago or more, in order to find for themselves a new home. Just yesterday in Fredericksburg I was witness to the fact that, although the spirit and vitality of the United States have long ago covered over these beginnings of the immigration, yet precisely there the German spirit spoke to me. And in this I saw the fulfillment of a task, which the United States has. They have in my opinion the task to create among all of the European peoples a certain order and a certain unity, which however will leave to every individual that which belongs to him, his own way of life. This the United States has done splendidly in their land. And I hope, they now by means of their strength—not only their material strength but also their spiritual strength—have become the champions of liberty and peace, that they will carry out the same mission in the uniting of Europe.*

*Vice President Johnson, with whom I am bound by long-standing personal and political ties, has spoken similarly, also in the words of President Kennedy, with words of very great, indeed of decisive significance. May I thank President Kennedy and Vice President Johnson for this clear, this unmistakable language, which will be greeted warmly not only in Germany, but also by all people in the free world, especially among the partners in our common alliance. And it will also be heard and understood—of this I am persuaded—far beyond the circle of the free peoples.*

*Here in Texas we have always found understanding for our problems, for the fate of our divided country, and its capital Berlin, which is cut off and isolated from the free West. In spite of the geographic distance thoroughly aware of the significance of this outpost of the free world. I hope, through my visit here, to have strengthened the ties between you and us. I would be especially happy if as many members as possible of both the House of Texas would visit us in our German home as soon as possible.*

*Let me add some words, which arise from the experience of this day. I would like to convey to you in a few sentences what pleased me so hugely about Texas. We flew about considerably in our helicopter yesterday, and today too, here from the ranch of Vice President Johnson. How here in Texas the difficulties of the soil have been overcome is unparalleled. These huge irrigation works, this care of the soil is indeed exemplary.*

*And what further touches a chord, that is the freshness and the vitality of the people, especially also of the children. I believe the saying was just spoken: if one looks into someone's eyes, then one knows what one has before oneself. Now believe me, I must indeed look into the eyes of people very frequently. But so many happy, so many bright, so many shining eyes as I have seen here yesterday and today, I have for many a long day not seen in one place. And therefore the people of Texas, whose individuality, power and strength will, I hope, continue to be maintained in the United States, has moved me to the depths of my heart.*

*I thank you, the Representatives of the people of Texas, with all my heart for this, and express the wish that God will continue to protect your people and your land.[16]*

Just four months later, on August 13, 1961, Russia began the construction of the Berlin Wall, separating West Germany from the communist-held East. It took the communist workers only four days to complete the twenty-five mile construction.[17] It would take more than twenty-eight years to bring it down.

**Exhibit #28** ★ August 2, 1961, at the Sheraton Park Hotel during the official luncheon honoring the vice president and the premier of Nationalist China, Chen Cheng. ★ Photograph by Frank Muto

## The Chinese Premier

Exhibit twenty-eight is an 8"x10" proof sheet of six 120mm photographic negatives taken August 2, 1961, at the Sheraton Park Hotel during the official luncheon honoring the vice president and the premier of Nationalist China, Chen Cheng. This series of photographs shows Vice President Lyndon Johnson introducing Chen Cheng to members of the United States Senate. From top left to right, the first photograph shows the premier being introduced to John Connally. The next series of photographs shows the vice president making introductions to the Chinese representatives. The final two photographs

show Senator Everett Dirksen from Illinois and Senator Thomas Dodd from Connecticut being introduced.

While LBJ wined and dined the Chinese dignitaries, there were two days of serious discussions between Chen Cheng and President Kennedy. These discussions were centered on the issue of admitting Nationalist China to the United Nations. During the discussions, President Kennedy made it very clear that the United States opposed the admission of Communist China, but was supportive of Nationalist China. The president "welcomed the opportunity to reaffirm the close ties between their governments and the people of the United States with

those of the Republic of China. Both men ended their talks recognizing the importance of strengthening the close cooperation of both countries in matters affecting their common security interests." Kennedy pledged to continue the military and economic aid to Taiwan, but expressed concern about China's possible veto to admit communist Outer Mongolia to the U.N. Other countries in the U.N. had said that if China vetoed Outer Mongolia, they would veto the newly formed country of Mauritania. President Kennedy was concerned that these veto threats would cause a chain reaction of dissent between countries.[18]

·.★Dwayne Bridges★·.

# Toasts of President John F. Kennedy and Vice President Chen Cheng of the Republic of China That Were Given at the State Luncheon Held in the East Room of the White House on July 31, 1961

## Toast by President John F. Kennedy

*I want to express our great pleasure at being honored by the visit of the Vice President of the Republic of China and his wife, the Foreign Minister, and the members of his party who are here with our good friend, their Ambassador and his wife.*

*We are delighted to have him for several reasons. First, because he represents a distinguished country, a leader with whom this country of ours is most intimately associated in very difficult times and also because in his own right, his own character, his own qualities of leadership in good times and bad in his country's fortunes have won him the admiration and respect of all of my countrymen who have seen him. His own military leadership on the mainland, the efforts he has made to maintain the life of his country during recent years, the great contribution which he has made, which was described to me by our Vice President on his recent trip there to rebuild the economy of the island, all these things have won for him a special position in the minds and hearts of all of us.*

*So we are glad to have him for what he is himself, and we are glad to have him also because he represents and has the complete confidence of the President of his country.*

*His country and ours are intimately associated. I believe that the visit of the Vice President can do much to make sure that both his country and ours move on parallel lines in the difficult days and months and years ahead. So for every reason, Mr. Vice President, we are very proud to have you here. You are surrounded by friends. Some Members of the Congress had to leave, though they are coming back. But they left to vote for a cause in which all of us are committed, and therefore they serve us better on the Hill than they would here.*

*The Vice President informed me that Congressman Judd came from a part China which is known for its tight hold on the dollar, where some of the most famous financiers of China come from, which illuminates the scene you have here today.*

*So we are glad to have you, Mr. Vice President, and I know that all the people here today are devoted to you and your country. You have also sent to us three of your children who have come before you who are, I think, the most obvious indication of your regard for us.*

*I know that you will all join with me in drinking a toast to the President of the Republic of China who has sent us this fine emissary.*

## Toast by Vice President Chen Cheng of China

*"Mr. President, it is my great honor to be invited to visit the United States. This is the high point in my personal life, especially this morning in the conversation with Your Excellency, that left me with a very deep impression that this will be a great contribution to our national policy so determined to fight against international communism.*

*"I am very much impressed by the remarks you made, but I would like to say at this time that whatever progress the Republic of China, my country, has achieved, an important factor is the encouragement and the aid given by the Government and the people of the United States.*

*"With our two countries together, we can march toward our common goal, and with your leadership over the entire free world, Mr. President, I am sure that the future of the world will be greatly benefited.*

*"All actions taken by our country will be coordinated with the leadership of you, Mr. President.*

*"Last May, Mr. President, when you sent the able Vice President to Asia, it was a very important and lasting event in Asia, because it not only constituted a stabilizing force so far as Asia was concerned, but it gave tremendous encouragement to the people of Asia.*

*"I would like to propose a toast at this time to your health, and to the continued prosperity of the United States of America."[19]*

## Neiman Marcus

The Johnson family had a fine relationship with the Neiman Marcus store in Dallas, Texas, that dates back to their days in the Congress and Senate. As Lynda and Luci grew, they too established a wonderful relationship with the store. The following photographs and correspondence came from the estate of a former Neiman Marcus employee and typifies this relationship.

Exhibit twenty-nine is an original 8x10 photograph of Lynda and Luci Johnson taken at the Johnson's residence, called The Elms, on the day of the 1961 Inauguration. The young ladies are dressed in their Inauguration gowns, which most likely came from Neiman Marcus of Dallas, Texas. This photograph originated from the estate of a former employee of Neiman Marcus.

**Exhibit #29** ★ Lynda and Luci Johnson taken at the Johnson's residence, called The Elms, on the day of the 1961 Inauguration.

★ U.S. Army Photo - Series #61-1-111 thru 115

THE WHITE HOUSE

WASHINGTON

December 17, 1963

Each time I go to my closet I am always
grateful for all the hours you spend helping me
organize my wardrobe.

Enclosed is a photograph taken in the green
velvet suit I enjoy so much.  It was taken with the
Grand Duchess Charlotte in the Royal Palace in
Luxembourg.

With all best wishes,

Sincerely, *and affectionately*

*Lady Bird*

Mrs. Lyndon B. Johnson

Neiman Marcus
Dallas 1, Texas

**Exhibit #30**

Lyndon and Lady Bird Johnson traveled to over thirty countries during the vice presidential years. One of those countries was Luxembourg. Exhibit thirty is a letter that was written by Lady Bird Johnson to an employee of Neiman Marcus who had assisted the first lady in selecting her wardrobe for the trip.

A photograph was sent with the letter, but is not available here. The letter mentions that Lady Bird was wearing a green velvet suit for her visit to Luxembourg.

Interesting to note, the letter was written only a few weeks after the death of President Kennedy. This obviously was an extremely difficult period of time for the Johnson's, but Lady Bird Johnson still took the time to remember a friend. This thoughtful effort was very typical of the Johnson family, even during the worst of times.

KTBC
AM · FM · TV

RADIO 59 · CBS NETWORK
TV CHANNEL 7 · CBS, NBC, ABC
FM RADIO 93.7 MEGACYCLES

10TH & BRAZOS ST.      TELEPHONE GR 2-2424      P. O. BOX 1155      AUSTIN, TEXAS

Exhibit thirty-one is a letter from Lady Bird Johnson as she was planning her wardrobe for the overseas trips. Lady Bird speaks of a white and tan reversible coat and some shoes that she determines will not suffice for the trip.

This vice presidential period letter was written on Lady Bird Johnson's radio station KTBC letterhead and is considered extremely rare. When Mrs. Johnson became the first lady in November 1963, she had to relinquish her interests in the station, along with other properties.[20]

4040 52nd Street, N.W.
Washington, D. C. 20016
August 29, 1963

On going over the schedule and on hearing more about the climate in every country, I realize the adorable tan and white reversible coat will not suffice as my one standard coat -- especially in Iceland, Greenland and northern parts of Norway. I am returning the coat for credit, and hope to get it in the mail today.

I am also returning for credit the shoes, since other accessories made it necessary that I use plain black.

Everything is working out beautifully with the rest of my clothes. Thanks so much          for all your wonderful help.

Sincerely,

Lady Bird Johnson
Mrs. Lyndon B. Johnson

Neiman-Marcus
Dallas 1, Texas

**Exhibit #31**

·*· Dwayne Bridges ·*·

**Exhibit #32** ★ Photograph of Bernard Rosenbach and Lynda

Johnson taken December 27, 1963. LBJ Library #W-278-31

★ Photograph by Yoichi Okamoto

While Lyndon and Lady Bird Johnson were busy traveling and performing their role as foreign ambassadors, their eldest daughter Lynda became engaged to a young naval officer named Bernard (Bernie) Rosenbach.[21]

Exhibit thirty-two is a photograph of Lynda Johnson with her fiancé Bernie Rosenbach, along with a letter on the following page that Lynda Johnson had sent thanking a Neiman Marcus employee for clothing she had received.

The romance between Lynda and Bernard Rosenbach was short lived. By April 1964, they had decided to call the engagement off. It was difficult for the family. Lady Bird Johnson mentioned the breakup in her memoirs, ". . . it was painful, because I liked him and I respected him so much, . . . he is going back to that cold, gray ship, all steel and loneliness, and Lynda Bird will stay here surrounded by warmth and family and excitement. My heart ached for him."[22] By late April 1964, the press had heard of the breakup and had published a photo of Lynda and Bernie; the newspaper headlines read 'The Last Dance.'"[23]

A few years later, Lynda would meet another handsome man, this time a young Marine Corps captain assigned to the White House Guard. His name was Charles Robb. They would marry in 1967.

**OFFICE OF THE VICE PRESIDENT**

WASHINGTON

*August 29, 1963*

     *After I talked to you today I found this picture taken after I got engaged. I thought you might like it.*

     *I know I will love all the clothes I got and you can be sure that they will get alot of wear.*

     *I will see you when I get back. Stay well. Tell Mrs. Marcus hello for me.*

*Love,*

*Lynda*

*Lynda*

Letter from Lynda Johnson to an employee of Neiman Marcus, sent August 29, 1963, thanking them for clothing that was received. This letter was likely typed by Lynda herself, as a White House secretary would never have allowed this letter to be sent with two over-typed words. Lynda was only nineteen at the time she wrote this letter.

Exhibit thirty-three is a lovely 7.5"x9.25" color photograph of Lady Bird Johnson in her 1965 inaugural gown, which was purchased from Neiman Marcus. This photograph was signed and sent to a Neiman Marcus employee who had assisted Lady Bird Johnson with much of her wardrobe over the years. The photograph was taken January 6, 1965, and was personally signed for an employee of Neiman Marcus. Lady Bird Johnson signed on the lower portion of the mat, "—with happy memories and affection, Lady Bird Johnson."

**Exhibit #33** ★ LBJ Library Reference #D-369-9110 — White House Staff Photo ★ Lady Bird Johnson in her 1965 inaugural gown, which was purchased from Neiman Marcus.

# The Space Program

## National Aeronautics and Space Council

One of Lyndon Johnson's greatest accomplishments as vice president was his work as chairman of the National Aeronautics and Space Council. Johnson's interest and support in the space program dates back to his early years as Senate majority leader.

On October 4, 1957, the Russians successfully placed into orbit the first man-made satellite. This single event launched man's quest for outer space. Not until several months later, on January 31, 1958, did the United States launch their first satellite, Explorer I. This very year and during the Democratic caucus of 1958, Lyndon Johnson spoke passionately about the space program. Johnson said, "Control of space means the control of the world. There is something more important than the ultimate weapon. That is the ultimate position—the position of total control over earth lies somewhere in outer space. If there is this ultimate position, then our national goal and the goal of all free men must be to win and hold that position."[24] To better secure that position, on October 1, 1958, the National Aeronautics and Space Administration (NASA) was formed.

During the next few years, the Mercury and Apollo projects would get underway. Unfortunately, the Russians would beat the United States once again. On April 12, 1961, Russian cosmonaut Yuri Gagarin became the first man to orbit the earth. With this second loss in the undeclared challenge for outer space, President Kennedy and Vice President Johnson effected measures necessary to accelerate the American space program.

On May 25, 1961, President Kennedy prepared a special State of the Union message that was presented to a joint session of Congress. That speech addressed such topics as the economy, the social progress of the nation, civil defense, arms disarmament, and the space program.

In his speech, President Kennedy laid the groundwork for what would ultimately be realized as some of the greatest accomplishments in science and technology ever achieved by mankind.

# Special Message to the Congress on Urgent National Needs
## John F. Kennedy ★ May 25, 1961

*Mr. Speaker, Mr. Vice President, my copartners in Government, gentlemen—and ladies:*

*The Constitution imposes upon me the obligation to "from time to time give to the Congress information of the State of the Union." While this has traditionally been interpreted as an annual affair, this tradition has been broken in extraordinary times. These are extraordinary times. And we face an extraordinary challenge. Our strength as well as our convictions has imposed upon this nation the role of leader in freedom's cause. No role in history could be more difficult or more important. We stand for freedom. That is our conviction for ourselves—that is our only commitment to others. No friend, no neutral and no adversary should think otherwise. We are not against any man—or any nation—or any system—except as it is hostile to freedom. Nor am I here to present a new military doctrine, bearing any one name or aimed at any one area. I am here to promote the freedom doctrine.*

### *Space*

*If we are to win the battle that is now going on around the world between freedom and tyranny, the dramatic achievements in space which occurred in recent weeks should have made clear to us all, as did the Sputnik in 1957, the impact of this adventure on the minds of men everywhere, who are attempting to make a determination of which road they should take. Since early in my term, our efforts in space have been under review. With the advice of the Vice President, who is Chairman of the National Space Council, we have examined where we are strong and where we are not, where we may succeed and where we may not. Now it is time to take longer strides—time for a great new American enterprise—time for this nation to take a clearly leading role in space achievement, which in many ways may hold the key to our future on earth.*

*I believe we possess all the resources and talents necessary. But the facts of the matter are that we have never made the national decisions or marshaled the national resources required for such leadership. We have never specified long-range goals on an urgent time schedule, or managed our resources and our time so as to insure their fulfillment.*

*Recognizing the head start obtained by the Soviets with their large rocket engines, which gives them many months of lead-time, and recognizing the likelihood that they will exploit this lead for some time to come in still more impressive successes, we nevertheless are required to make new efforts on our own. For while we cannot guarantee that we shall one day be first, we can guarantee that any failure to make this effort will make us last. We take an additional risk by making it in full view of the world, but as shown by the feat of astronaut Shepard, this very risk enhances our stature when we are successful. But this is not merely a race. Space is open to us now; and our eagerness to share it's meaning is not governed by the efforts of others. We go into space because whatever mankind must undertake, free men must fully share.*

*I therefore ask the Congress, above and beyond the increases I have earlier requested for space activities, to provide the funds, which are needed to meet the following national goals:*

*First, I believe that this nation should commit itself to achieving the goal, before this decade is out, of landing a man on the moon and returning him safely to the earth. No single space project in this period will be more impressive to mankind, or more important for the long-range exploration of space; and none will be so difficult or expensive to accomplish. We propose to accelerate the development of the appropriate lunar spacecraft. We propose to develop alternate liquid and solid fuel boosters, much larger than any now being developed, until certain which is superior. We propose additional funds for other engine development and for unmanned explorations—explorations which are particularly important for one purpose which this nation will never overlook: the survival of the man who first makes this daring flight. But in a very real sense, it will not be one man going to the moon—if we make this judgment affirmatively, it will be an entire nation. For all of us must work to put him there.*

*Secondly, an additional 23 million dollars, together with 7 million dollars already available, will accelerate development of the Rover nuclear rocket. This gives promise of some day providing a means for even more exciting and ambitious exploration of space, perhaps beyond the moon, perhaps to the very end of the solar system itself.*

*Third, an additional 50 million dollars will make the most of our present leadership, by accelerating the use of space satellites for worldwide communications.*

*Fourth, an additional 75 million dollars-of which 53 million dollars is for the Weather Bureau—will help give us at the earliest possible time a satellite system for world-wide weather observation.*

*Let it be clear—and this is a judgment which the Members of the Congress must finally make—let it be clear that I am asking the Congress and the country to accept a firm commitment to a new course of action-a course which will last for many years and carry very heavy costs: 531 million dollars in fiscal '62—an estimated seven to nine billion dollars additional over the next five years. If we were to go only half way, or reduce our sights in the face of difficulty, in my judgment it would be better not to go at all.*

*Now this is a choice which this country must make, and I am confident that under the leadership of the Space Committees of the Congress, and the Appropriating Committees, that you will consider the matter carefully.*

*It is a most important decision that we make as a nation. But all of you have lived through the last four years and have seen the significance of space and the adventures in space, and no one can predict with certainty what the ultimate meaning will be of mastery of space.*

*I believe we should go to the moon. But I think every citizen of this country as well as the Members of the Congress should consider the matter carefully in making their judgment, to which we have given attention over many weeks and months, because it is a heavy burden, and there is no sense in agreeing or desiring that the United States take an affirmative position in outer space, unless we are prepared to do the work and bear the burdens to make it successful. If we are not, we should decide today and this year.*

*This decision demands a major national commitment of scientific and technical manpower, materiel and facilities, and the possibility of their diversion from other important activities where they are already thinly spread. It means a degree of dedication, organization and discipline, which have not always characterized our research and development efforts. It means we cannot afford undue work stoppages, inflated costs of material or talent, wasteful interagency rivalries, or a high turnover of key personnel.*

*New objectives and new money cannot solve these problems. They could in fact, aggravate them further—unless every scientist, every engineer, every serviceman, every technician, contractor, and civil servant gives his personal pledge that this nation will move forward, with the full speed of freedom, in the exciting adventure of space.*[25]

## First American Manned Orbital Flight

On February 20, 1962, the first and single most important event of the American space program was accomplished. On that day, Lt. Colonel John H. Glenn, Jr., aboard the Mercury-Atlas capsule *Friendship 7*, successfully orbited the Earth three times and returned safely to a very enthusiastic and grateful nation.

The scheduled launch of *Friendship 7* was initially set for December 20, 1961, but was rescheduled to January 27, 1962, after project officials determined that the mounting pressures from the public surrounding the launch were hampering technicians in readying the Atlas for a safe flight.[26] With all the mechanical issues resolved, on January 27, 1962, the official countdown for the first American manned orbit began. There would be several more launch cancellations during the following weeks, but most were due to weather conditions.

Finally, on the morning of February 20, 1962, at 9:47 a.m. John Glenn, aboard the Mercury capsule *Friendship 7* powered atop an Atlas rocket, flew into the history book. *Friendship 7* completed three orbits of the earth at an altitude of 162 miles, traveling at a speed of 17,500 miles per hour. The total time of the mission from launch to landing was just under five hours.

The Mercury capsule landed about 800 miles southeast of Bermuda, near Grand Turk Island, and was recovered by the United States destroyer *USS Noa*. Once the Mercury capsule was sighted, it took the *USS Noa* about twenty–one minutes to recover it from the ocean.[27]

"Expectations in the United States were high as NASA attempted to place the first American in orbit. In keeping with NASA's policy of openness, the launch of John Glenn aboard *Friendship 7* was broadcast live on television to millions of people around the world. Thousands of people gathered in spots around Cape Canaveral to witness the launch in person, while in New York City an estimated crowd of 5,000 people paused during their daily commute to view the launch on a large monitor set up in Grand Central Station. The success of the *Friendship 7* space flight sent the nation into a patriotic fervor and made the mission's astronaut an instant hero. During the two weeks following Glenn's space flight, the nation celebrated on a scale not seen since Charles Lindbergh's solo trans-Atlantic flight in 1927.

"Immediately after his mission Glenn flew from the aircraft carrier *USS Randolph* to Grand Turk Island in the Bahamas for two days of debriefing and medical tests. On February 23, 1962, Vice President Lyndon Johnson flew to the island to escort Glenn on the flight back to Patrick Air Force Base in Florida. At the air force base, Glenn was reunited with his family, including his mother Clara and his father, the senior John H. Glenn. The Glenn family, accompanied by Vice President Johnson and other *Mercury 7* astronauts, proceeded by automobile to Cape Canaveral where they were scheduled to meet with President Kennedy. The eighteen-mile trip between the air force base and the NASA facility turned into a parade route as thousands of people from around Cocoa Beach stood along the highway to greet the returned astronaut. Later that day, with ceremonies held at Cape Canaveral, President Kennedy presented John Glenn with NASA's Distinguished Service Medal. "[28]

The previous excerpt came from the Ohio State University library Web site titled the *Celebration of the Flight of Friendship 7*. Upon John Glenn's retirement as U.S. Senator in 1998, he donated his papers to the university where the John Glenn Insitutue for Public Service and Public Policy was established.

The following sets of exhibits are original photographs taken February 23, 1962, by White House photographer Robert L. Knudsen. These photographs were taken during the historic celebration of John Glenn's return from space.

Exhibit thirty-four is an original 8"x10" color photograph taken February 23, 1962, by White House photographer and Navy Petty Officer Robert L. Knudsen, celebrating the return of astronaut John Glenn from the first U.S. manned space orbit. The photograph shows Vice President Lyndon Johnson being introduced to John Glenn's mother and father just outside of *Air Force Two*. John Glenn's wife Annie, his son Dave, and his daughter Lyn are also in the photograph. This was John Glenn's first meeting with his family since the Mercury launch.

In his autobiography, *John Glenn—A Memoir,* he describes this very moment captured in Robert Knudsen's photograph. "Vice President Johnson flew to Grand Turk to accompany me back to Patrick Air Force Base, south of Cape Canaveral, on February 23. Annie, Dave, and Lyn were waiting, along with a crowd that sent up a loud cheer. I hugged Lyn and Dave, and then hugged and kissed Annie. She was gorgeous, wearing a choker necklace, an orchid corsage, and a pillbox hat. I couldn't hold back the tears. Annie, most of all, had been at the back of my mind the entire flight. Vice President Johnson told the crowd, 'It's a great pleasure to welcome home a great pioneer of history.' I quickly learned that his accolade was only a prelude to a tidal wave of attention."[29]

---

**Exhibit #34** ★ U.S. Navy Photo number #20230 stamped on the reverse "February 23, 1962, by R. L. Knudsen PHC, USN, Office of the Naval Aid to the President." ★ Provenance — From the estate of Robert L. Knudsen. Acquired at public auction, Guernsey's, New York, November 16, 2002.

·٠★Dwayne Bridges★٠·

John Glenn recalls, "The drive twenty miles to the Cape along highway A1A through Cocoa Beach turned into a parade that I found out later Henri Landworth and city officials had helped organize. Each of the other astronauts and his family were in a separate car. Bands were playing. Thousands of people lined the route, waving and clapping. A sign over the road said, 'Welcome Back, John.' Another said, 'Our Prayers Have Been Answered.' Johnson saw a boy wearing a toy space helmet riding on his father's shoulders. He asked the driver to stop, and beckoned the man over. People surged around the car, asking for autographs. They were saying things like, 'Thank you,' and 'God bless you.' Dave and Lyn looked at each other, their mouths open and eyes wide and shining with astonishment. When the motorcade approached the guard gate at the Cape, I took my NASA identification card out of my wallet. Johnson thought I was serious. He leaned over and gave me an amused look from underneath his eyebrows, 'I think they know who you are,' he said. The motorcade went to the Cape landing strip where President Kennedy was to arrive aboard *Air Force One*. When President Kennedy landed, we toured the NASA facilities, including Launch Complex 14 and Hanger S where *Friendship 7* was on display. Somebody told me a decision had been made to send it on an around-the-world tour—the fourth orbit of *Friendship 7*—and then to the Smithsonian for permanent display alongside the Wright brothers' first plane and Lindbergh's *Spirit of St. Louis*."[30]

**Exhibit #35** ★ Original 8"x10" color photograph taken February 23, 1962, at Cape Canaveral in Florida by White House Photographer Robert L. Knudsen, celebrating the return of astronaut John Glenn from the first American manned orbit in space. On the reverse of photograph is the photographer's reference number #20234 and is stamped "February 23, 1962, by R. L. Knudsen PHC, USN, Office of the Naval Aid to the President." ★ Provenance—From the estate of Robert L. Knudsen. Acquired at public auction, Guernsey's, New York, November 16, 2002.

* * Dwayne Bridges * *

**Exhibit #36 (on left)** ★ Original 8"x10" color photograph taken February 23, 1962, at Cape Canaveral in Florida, by White House Photographer Robert L. Knudsen, celebrating the return of astronaut John Glenn from the first American manned orbit in space. This picture shows President Kennedy and Lt. Colonel John Glenn in the back seat of a car en route to NASA for a tour and ceremony. On the reverse of photograph is the photographer's reference number #20259 and is stamped "February 23, 1962 By R. L. Knudsen PHC, USN, Office of the Naval Aid to the President."

★ Provenance—From the estate of Robert L. Knudsen. Acquired at public auction, Guernsey's, New York, November 16, 2002.

**Exhibit #37 (on right)** ★ Original 8"x10" color photograph taken February 23, 1962, at Cape Canaveral in Florida by White House Photographer Robert L. Knudsen. The photograph shows President Kennedy and astronaut John Glenn walking through the entranceway of the Mercury Control Center at Cape Canaveral. On the reverse of the photograph is the photographer's reference number #20243 and is stamped "February 23, 1962 By R. L. Knudsen PHC, USN, Office of the Naval Aid to the President."

★ Provenance—From the estate of Robert L. Knudsen. Acquired at public auction, Guernsey's, New York, November 16, 2002.

**Exhibit #38** ★ Original 8"x10" color photograph taken February 23, 1962, at Cape Canaveral in Florida by White House Photographer Robert L. Knudsen. The photograph shows President Kennedy, astronaut John Glenn, and Director of Flight Operations Christopher Kraft discussing the mission while touring the Mercury Control Room at Cape Canaveral. On the reverse of the photograph is the photographer's reference number #20242 and is stamped "February 23, 1962 By R. L. Knudsen PHC, USN, Office of the Naval Aid to the President."

★ Provenance — From the estate of Robert L. Knudsen. Acquired at public auction, Guernsey's, New York, November 16, 2002.

**Exhibit #39** ★ Original 8"x10" color photograph taken February 23, 1962, at Cape Canaveral in Florida by White House Photographer Robert L. Knudsen. The photograph shows President Kennedy speaking at Cape Canaveral during the ceremony honoring John Glenn's return from space. President Kennedy awarded NASA's Distinguished Service Medal to Glenn during this ceremony. On the reverse of the photograph is the photographer's reference number #20248 and is stamped "February 23, 1962 By R. L. Knudsen PHC, USN, Office of the Naval Aid to the President."

★ Provenance—From the estate of Robert L. Knudsen. Acquired at public auction, Guernsey's, New York, November 16, 2002.

John Glenn said, "The president awarded me and Bob Gilruth NASA's Distinguished Service Medal." He talked about going to the moon and said, "Our boosters may not be as large as some others, but our men and women are."[31]

Over the next couple of weeks, John Glenn would be invited to a private White House reception, take part in four separate parades, and deliver a speech to a joint session of Congress. John Glenn eventually returned to work on the Mercury project and became a goodwill ambassador for NASA by traveling the world and meeting with world leaders. He worked diligently to return to the space program and wanted to take part in the Gemini and Apollo programs. However, President Kennedy considered him too valuable a national treasure to risk him with another space flight.[32]

John Glenn's speech to a joint session of Congress on February 26, 1962, has content that is still relevant today as we continue our venture into space. John Glenn said in his speech, "*Questions are sometimes raised regarding the immediate payoffs for our efforts. What benefits are we gaining from the money spent? The real benefits we probably cannot even detail. They are probably not even known to man today. But exploration and the pursuit of knowledge have always paid dividends in the long run—usually far greater than anything expected at the outset.*

*Experimenters with common green mold, little dreamed what effect their discovery of penicillin would have. The story has been told of Disraeli, Prime Minister of England at the time, visiting the laboratory of Faraday, one of the early experimenters with basic electrical phenomena. Disraeli asked, "But of what possible use is it?" Faraday replied, "Mister Prime Minister, what good is a baby?"*

*That is the stage of development in our program today—in its infancy. And it indicates a much broader potential impact, of course, than even the discovery of electricity did. We are just probing the surface of the greatest advancements in man's knowledge of his surroundings that has ever been made. There are benefits to science across the board. Any major effort such as this results in research by so many different specialties that it is hard to even envision the benefits that will accrue in many fields . . . Knowledge begets knowledge . . . We are on the verge of a new era.*"[33]

From 1962 to 1963, NASA continued to realize great accomplishments in the space program. On May 24, 1962, astronaut Scott Carpenter confirmed the success of the Mercury-Atlas 6 Project by duplicating John Glenn's orbit. On October 3, 1962, astronaut Walter Schirra successfully doubled the time in space by orbiting six times and on May 15, 1963, astronaut Gordon Cooper completed twenty-two orbits, which tested man's ability to withstand the dynamics of space.

President Kennedy and Vice President Johnson continued their support of the space program with a goal to place a man on the moon. President Kennedy delivered a monumental speech at Rice University in Houston, Texas, on September 13, 1962. In that historic speech, Kennedy said, "*We choose to go to the moon in this decade, and do the other things—not because they are easy; but because they are hard; because that goal will serve to organize and measure the best of our energies and skills; because that challenge is one that we're willing to accept; one we are unwilling to postpone,*

*and one we intend to win.*

*It is for these reasons that I regard the decision last year to shift our efforts in space from low to high gear as among the most important decisions that will be made during my incumbency in the office of the Presidency.*

*We have given this program a high national priority, even though I realize that this is in some measure an act of faith and vision, for we do not know what benefits await us.*

*However, I think we're going to do it, and I think that we must pay what needs to be paid. I don't think we ought to waste any money, but I think we ought to do the job—and this will be done in the decade of the sixties.*

*Many years ago the great British explorer, George Mallory, who was to die on Mount Everest, was asked why did he want to climb it. He said, "Because it is there."*

*Well, space is there, and we're going to climb it. And the moon and the planets are there, and new hope for knowledge and peace are there. And therefore, as we set sail, we ask God's blessing on the most hazardous and dangerous and greatest adventure on which man has ever embarked.*"[34]

## Final Visit to NASA

On November 16, 1963, President Kennedy made a final visit to Cape Canaveral and Merritt Island, where NASA had just purchased 80,000 acres to expand the launch facilities. This new area was called the NASA Launch Operations Center.[35] When President Kennedy arrived at NASA, he was greeted by NASA Administrator James Webb, Dr. Kurt Debus, and Major General Leighton Davis. Kennedy was first taken to Launch Complex 37 where he was briefed on the Saturn program. He then toured Merritt Island by helicopter to view the new facilities and later watched the successful launching of a Polaris missile from the nuclear submarine *Andrew Jackson*.[36] President Kennedy was extremely pleased with the progress being made in the space program. After the tour, he returned to his family's home in Palm Beach, Florida. Over the next few days, President Kennedy would travel to Tampa and Miami before finalizing his plans for the trip to Texas.

Exhibit forty is an original 8"x10" color photograph taken November 16, 1963, by White House photographer Robert L. Knudsen at Cape Canaveral, Florida. This stunning photograph shows President Kennedy standing on the launch pad looking up at the new Saturn V rocket. Standing next to President Kennedy is Senator George Smathers of Florida. This would be President Kennedy's final visit to NASA. In just seven days from the time this photograph was taken, President Kennedy would be assassinated while traveling in a motorcade through Dallas, Texas.

**Exhibit #40** ★ U.S. Navy Photograph reference number #30544 dated November 1963.

★ Provenance — From the estate of Robert L. Knudsen. Acquired at public auction, Guernsey's, New York, November 16, 2002.

# The Trip to Texas
# November 1963

# Chronology

President Kennedy's November schedule in 1963 was a busy one. On Saturday November 16, 1963 President Kennedy, along with Vice President Johnson, visited Cape Canaveral and watched the launch of a Polaris missile. On Sunday, November 17, the president traveled to his Palm Beach residence for a day of relaxation *where* the president's trip to Texas was being formalized. On Monday, November 18, 1963, the president went to Miami and gave a speech before the Inter-American Press Association. He then returned to the White House where on Tuesday morning, November 19, he met and had breakfast with several members of Congress. On this day he began his preparations for the trip to Texas. The next day, Wednesday, November 20, was Robert Kennedy's birthday. He spent that evening with his family, celebrating his brother's birthday.[1]

At 11a.m. on Thursday morning, November 21, President Kennedy departed Andrews Air Force Base for San Antonio, Texas. When he arrived in Texas, the president and his entourage visited Brooks Medical Center and Kelly Air Field before heading to Houston. In Houston, they addressed a Latin-American citizens' group at the Rice Hotel and later attended a dinner honoring Congressman Albert Thomas. By late evening, President Kennedy boarded *Air Force One* with Vice President Johnson aboard *Air Force Two*, and flew to Carswell Air Force Base in Fort Worth. There they would spend the night at the Hotel Texas. The next morning on Friday, November 22, 1963, the president awakened to a crowd of supporters who he addressed in the parking lot across from the hotel. After his speech, he returned to the hotel where he and Mrs. Kennedy, along with the vice president and Mrs. Johnson, had breakfast with members of the chamber of commerce. After breakfast, and at about 10:30 a.m., the president traveled by motorcade through downtown Fort Worth to Carswell Air Force Base for the short flight to Dallas.[2]

The flight time to Dallas Love Field was only about thirteen minutes. Once they arrived, the president and Mrs. Kennedy were greeted by the mayor of Dallas and his wife,—Mr. And Mrs. Earle Cabell. At approximately 11:55 a.m., after the formal greetings, they took some time to shake hands with supporters who had gathered along a fence line. The president and his party then got into their cars for the trip through downtown Dallas. The next destination was the Dallas Trade Mart, where a luncheon was scheduled in honor of the president.[3]

As history dictates, the president did not make it to the Dallas Trade Mart. At approximately 12:30 p.m. CST, when the president's limousine turned left on Main Street just in front of the Texas School Book Depository, three shots were fired, striking President Kennedy and wounding Governor Connally.

Both were rushed to Parkland Hospital. At 1 p.m. CST, Dr. Kemp Clark of Parkland Hospital declared that President Kennedy was dead.[4]

## The Motorcade

On the right is the specific order of cars and the officials that were in the motorcade during President Kennedy's visit to Dallas on Friday November 22, 1963.

The remaining cars in the procession (not listed), followed shortly behind the motorcade and contained other officials and various members of the press.

***Unless otherwise noted, the motorcade information was compiled from the book*** Pictures of the Pain—Photography and the Assassination of President Kennedy, ***by Richard B. Trask.***

**Car #1**

President John F. Kennedy and Mrs. Kennedy,
Governor John Connally and Mrs. Connally

**Car #2**

President's Secret Service follow-up car with agents,
Assistants to the president, Kenneth O'Donnel and David Powers

**Car #3**

Vice President Lyndon Johnson and Lady Bird Johnson
Senator Ralph Yarborough

**Car #4**

Vice president's Secret Service follow-up car with agents

**Car #5**

City officials' car
Dallas Mayor Earl Cabell and Mrs. Cabell, Congressman Raymond Roberts

**Car #6**

Press pool car
UPI, Associated Press, ABC, and *Dallas Morning News* representatives,
Press Secretary Malcolm Kilduff

**Car #7**

Camera car
NBC and CBS cameramen and White House movie photographer, Thomas Atkins

**Car #8**

Camera car
White House photographer Cecil Stoughton, *LIFE* photographer Arthur Rickerby,
Associated Press photographer Henry Burroughs, *Dallas Morning News* photographer
Clint Grant, UPI photographer Frank Cancellare

**Car #9**

Camera car
KRLD cameraman James Underwood, *Dallas Morning News* photographer Thomas Dillard,
WBAP cameraman Jimmy Darnell, WFAA cameraman Malcom Couch,
*Dallas Times Herald* cameraman Robert Jackson

**Car #10**

Texas Congressional car[5]
Congressman George Mahon, Congressman Homer Thornberry,
Walter Rogers, and special assistant to the president Larry O'Brien

⋆⋆ Dwayne Bridges ⋆⋆

## A New President

At 1:30 p.m. CST, when the official announcement came that President Kennedy was dead, Lyndon Johnson and Mrs. Johnson had already left Parkland Hospital and were on their way to Love Field to board *Air Force One*.

Before they took off from Dallas, Lyndon Johnson wanted to be formally sworn into office. Federal Judge Sarah T. Hughes was called to administer the oath of office. At 2:38 p.m. CST, Lyndon B. Johnson, aboard *Air Force One,* became the thirty-sixth President of the United States.

The famous photograph taken by White House photographer Cecil W. Stoughton, shows Lyndon Johnson being sworn into office aboard *Air Force One*. Cecil Stoughton had actually taken several pictures of this event with both a 35mm camera and a Hasselblad camera. In order to capture this historic event, Mr. Stoughton had to stand on a sofa with his back against the wall in the corner of the state room of *Air Force One*. This particular photograph was taken with a wide-angle lens and his Hasselblad.[6] In an interview with the LBJ Library in 1971, Cecil Stoughton recalls that he was so close that he could have reached out and touched Jackie Kennedy.[7]

I do solemnly swear that I will faithfully execute the office of President of the United States, and will to the best of my ability, preserve, protect and defend the Constitution of the United States. So help me God.

— Lyndon B. Johnson, November 22, 1963

Lyndon B. Johnson being sworn into office by Judge Sarah T. Hughes on board *Air Force One*, ★ Photograph by Cecil W. Stoughton ★ Lyndon Baines Johnson Library Photo# 1A-1-WH63, November 22, 1963

# RECOLLECTIONS OF TEXAS CONGRESSMAN GEORGE MAHON

As mentioned before, Texas congressman George Mahon was part of the presidential entourage that fateful day in Dallas. The LBJ Library and Museum interviewed Congressman Mahon on August 16, 1972. In that interview, the congressman recalled his experiences that dreadful day in November.

**Interview with Congressman George Mahon by Joe B. Frantz representing the LBJ Library. Interview conducted August 16, 1972 at Congressman Mahon's office located in Washington, D.C.**

JF = Joe B. Frantz          GM = George Mahon

**JF**    *You went to Texas at the time Kennedy came down there?*

**GM**    *I went on the plane with President Kennedy from Andrews Airport….we took off from here and we went to San Antonio and then I believe I didn't ride with the President from San Antonio. I believe I rode with the Vice President from San Antonio to Houston where they had the party that night for Albert Thomas. Then that night after the party in Houston I rode with the President and visited with him considerably on the way to Carswell AFB in Fort Worth. And then the next day which was the day Kennedy was killed, assassinated, I rode in plane number two (Air Force Two) with Johnson and Lady Bird into Dallas. Then I was about four or five cars (actually 10th car) behind at the time of the shooting.*

**JF**    *Everything seemed to be going fine on the trip as far as Love Field?*

**GM**    *Yes, I think so, but even so Albert Thomas was interested in bringing Yarborough and all these factions together and he was talking about these things and so forth as the trip progressed and wanting Yarborough and somebody, I forget who now, to ride in the same car.*

**JF**    *Must have been Connally.*

**GM**    *Albert Thomas was trying to be the man to help cement relationships. He looked upon this as being the object of the trip. I had not considered it to that same extent.*

**JF**    *I've got several views of this trip. What was your reaction in the motorcade? Did you have some idea of what happened? You went on to Parkland, didn't you?*

**GM**    *Yes, well, I was a little unhappy with Dallas because they had been so bitter against Kennedy prior to the visit.*

**JF**     *Of course, to Johnson too.*

**GM**    *Yes. I was riding in the back seat of a car, top down of course, with Homer Thornberry, it seems to me, and Walter Rogers. Sitting in the front seat with the driver was Larry O'Brien, and we commented that we thought the people looked a little antagonistic and unfriendly. They didn't act like they had at Fort Worth and that wholesome "Hurrah, Hurrah" encountered in San Antonio and in Houston. This cold atmosphere—it may have been imagination, but I don't think so—was a little upsetting. And then we went down a certain street and turned to the right and shortly after we turned we were facing the building from which the shot was fired we later learned, we heard these shots fired. I remember I had a coat, a raincoat or a light topcoat, I held it over my head. I don't know why I thought that would protect me from anything.*

**JF**     *Kind of like pulling the cover over your head? (Laughter) A reaction.*

**GM**    *Yes. It sort of shocked us. We just didn't know what had happened. But then we saw the cars at the corner and then we saw them race off. We were I'd say four or five cars behind and Secret Service men were falling on cars and, you know, all that kind of business. We dashed off to the Trade Mart and they said they had gone on to Parkland and we followed as fast as we could to the hospital. There we went to the car and we saw the blood and brains in the car and we knew it had been a terrible thing. And I went inside.*

**JF**     *Were things fairly clear-cut? Did you know who had been shot?*

**GM**    *Oh, I think so, yes. Connally and the President. So we went inside and I know I went to the door in the corridor which leads more or less into the inter-sanctum where this business of the President was, not in the very room, but in that area. I remember there was some conflict that arose at the time between the FBI agents and the Secret Service. One of them challenged the other and they wrestled and went to the floor.*

**JF**     *Over who got jurisdiction?*

**GM**    *Who got jurisdiction. This was a little upsetting. I never heard anything about this and if the press had seen it I think they would have played it up. But we stayed outside and talked and wondered and so on. And then finally I believe Thornberry and Brooks and somebody went inside. It wasn't long before Johnson left the hospital along with Brooks and the fellows who came back with him. We followed shortly after that.*

**JF**     *You didn't get to talk with Johnson personally?*

**GM**    *No, I didn't talk with Johnson personally after the shot was fired. And then we talked with Cabell who I believe then was Mayor of Dallas at the airport.*

**JF**     *Earle?*

**GM**    *Earle Cabell. And then we took off in Air Force Two and landed in Washington that evening.*

## Helen Mahon
## Remembers That Day

Helen Mahon did not accompany her husband on the trip to Dallas. She had stayed home and was playing bridge with some of the other congressional wives when the news started coming in that the president had been shot.

"I knew that George was supposed to be in car number three, and for about an hour, I don't know who could have been more frantic than I was. Of course, all the news was coming in."

"We turned the television on in one room and the radio on in the other room and there was nothing said about anybody having been shot except the president and the governor and then, of course, the next report was that Lyndon had been hit and that he had suffered a heart attack and all these dreadful things.

"I realized after about an hour that George was bound to be all right because the news would have gotten to us by that time. And I also realized that there wouldn't be a line out of Dallas and there would be no way for him to call me."

"Later, the Air Force called and said that he was on his way home in the second plane. He came back in the vice president's plane.

"George arrived here at the apartment about eight o'clock. They had called me from Andrews Air Force Base when they landed and told me that he was on his way home in an Air Force car. The whole experience was most nerve-wracking to him and we stayed up until 2:30 that morning watching the news, and then he couldn't sleep and we got up about six o'clock and started watching again on Saturday morning."[8]

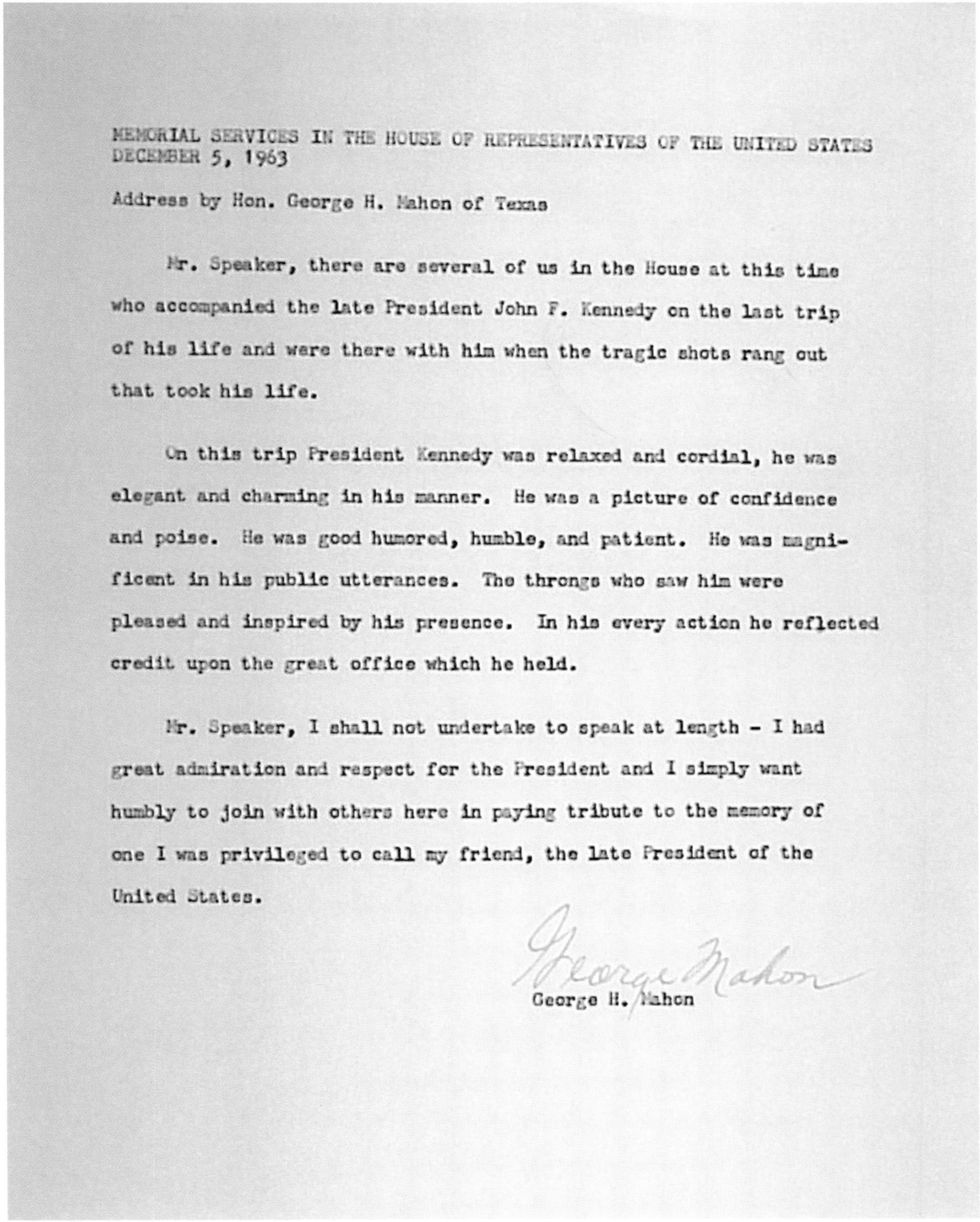

## Memorial Address

MEMORIAL SERVICES IN THE HOUSE OF REPRESENTATIVES OF THE UNITED STATES
DECEMBER 5, 1963

Address by Hon. George H. Mahon of Texas

Mr. Speaker, there are several of us in the House at this time
who accompanied the late President John F. Kennedy on the last trip
of his life and were there with him when the tragic shots rang out
that took his life.

On this trip President Kennedy was relaxed and cordial, he was
elegant and charming in his manner. He was a picture of confidence
and poise. He was good humored, humble, and patient. He was magnificent in his public utterances. The throngs who saw him were
pleased and inspired by his presence. In his every action he reflected
credit upon the great office which he held.

Mr. Speaker, I shall not undertake to speak at length - I had
great admiration and respect for the President and I simply want
humbly to join with others here in paying tribute to the memory of
one I was privileged to call my friend, the late President of the
United States.

George H. Mahon

In both the House of Representatives and in the Senate, our nation's elected officials held memorial services and public addresses in honor of the fallen president. Congressman George Mahon contributed his own address in the House of Representatives, made poignant by the fact he was in the motorcade that day when President Kennedy was shot.

**Exhibit #41** ★ Exhibit forty-one is an original signed copy of Congressman Mahon's memorial address that was delivered before Congress in the House of Representatives on December 5, 1963, in honor of the late President John F. Kennedy.

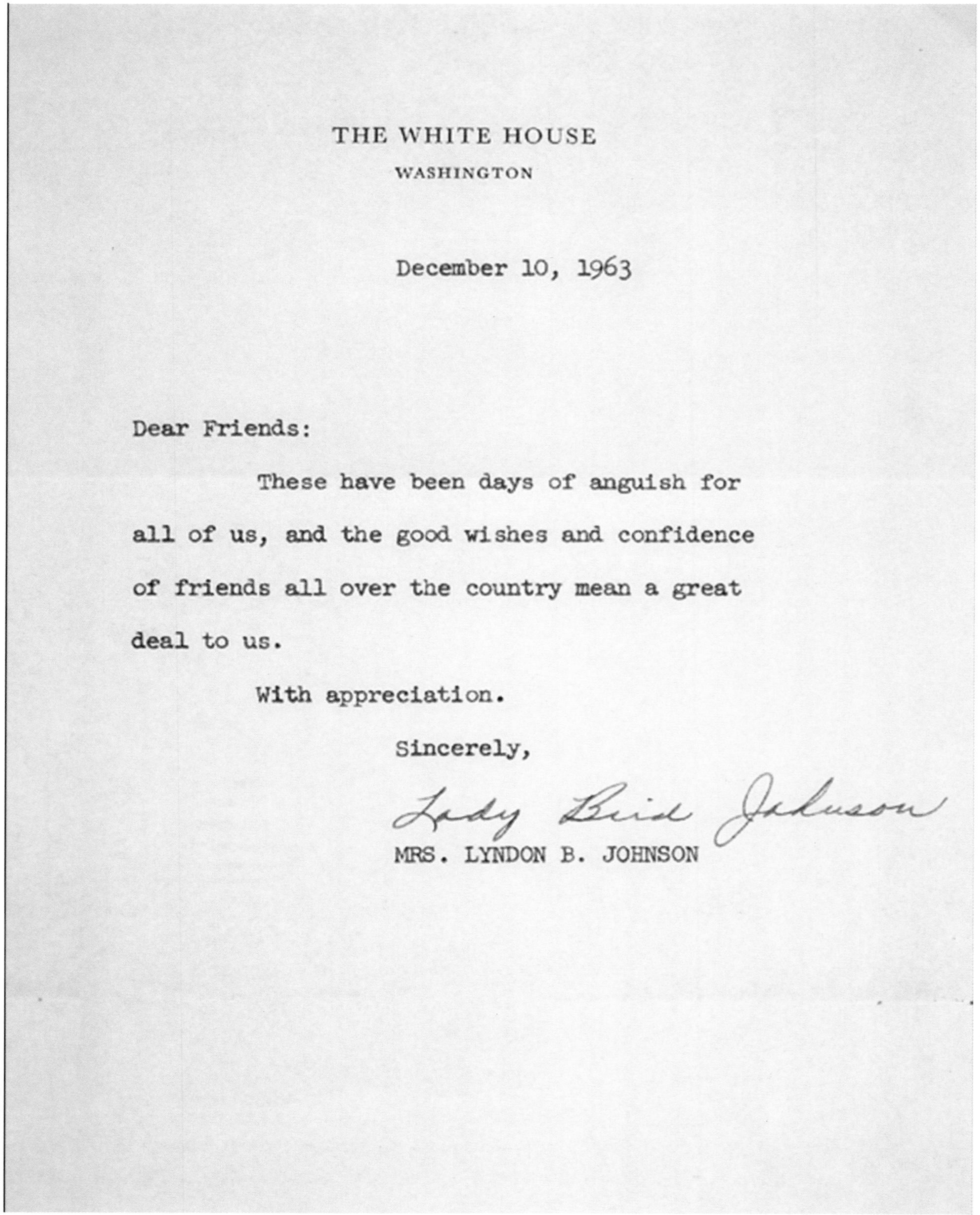

THE WHITE HOUSE

WASHINGTON

December 10, 1963

Dear Friends:

These have been days of anguish for
all of us, and the good wishes and confidence
of friends all over the country mean a great
deal to us.

With appreciation.

Sincerely,

*Lady Bird Johnson*

MRS. LYNDON B. JOHNSON

## Citizens Respond

The outpouring of sympathy from the nation was overwhelming. President Johnson had to focus on the responsibilities of the office during this time of transition while Lady Bird Johnson took up the charge of moving from their residence at The Elms to the White House.

In order to respond to all of the letters arriving at the White House, Lady Bird Johnson set up a temporary office at The Elms. It was there where secretaries and many of Lady Bird's friends, including such ladies as Mrs. Eugene McCarthy and Mrs. Hale Boggs, assisted in responding to the multitude of letters.[9]

**Exhibit #42** ★ Exhibit forty-two is one of the first pieces of correspondence sent by Lady Bird Johnson as first lady. It is a letter that was sent just three weeks after the assassination in response to letters from the public expressing their support for the Johnsons as well as their sympathy concerning the death of President Kennedy.

## Christmas 1963

The Christmas holiday season for 1963 was a solemn one. Shortly after returning to Washington, D.C., from Texas, President Johnson announced an official thirty days of mourning for the country. After the thirty-day period, it was time for the nation to move forward. On December 22, 1963, the new president and his family led the way with a candlelight memorial service for the fallen president and his family at the Lincoln Memorial with the lighting of the national Christmas tree.

## Lighting of the National Christmas Tree

Exhibit forty-three is an original 4.5"x7.5" color photograph of President Lyndon Johnson with Lady Bird and Luci Johnson taken at the lighting of the National Christmas tree on December 22, 1963. This photograph was taken by photographer Robert Knudsen and came from the estate of Sanford L. Fox.

**Exhibit #43** ★ President Lyndon Johnson with Lady Bird and Luci Johnson taken at the lighting of the National Christmas tree on December 22, 1963. ★ Photograph by Robert L. Knudsen

# PAGEANT OF THE PEACE
## Speech presented by Lyndon B. Johnson during the Pageant of the Peace ceremony
## that was held on December 22, 1963

*"Tonight we come to the end of the season of great national sorrow, and the beginning of the season of great eternal joy. We mourn our great President, John F. Kennedy, but he would have us go on. While our spirits cannot be high, our hearts need not be heavy.*

*We were taught by Him whose birth we commemorate that after death there is life. We can believe, and we do believe, that from the death of our national leader will come a rebirth of the finest qualities of our national life.*

*On this same occasion 30 years ago, at the close of another troubled year in our Nation's history, a great President, Franklin D. Roosevelt, said to his countrymen, "To more and more of us the words 'Thou shalt love thy neighbor as thyself' have taken on a meaning that is showing itself and proving itself in our purposes and in our daily lives. I believe that this is no less true for all of us in all of our regions of our land today.*

*There is a turning away from things which we are false and things which are small, and things which are shallow. There is a turning toward those things which are true, those things which are profound, and those things which are eternal. We can, we do, and live tonight in a new hope and new confidence and new faith in ourselves and in what we can do together through the future.*

*Our need for such faith was never greater, for we are heirs of a great trust. In these last 200 years we have guided the building of our Nation and our society by those principles and precepts brought to earth nearly 2,000 years ago on that first Christmas.*

*We have our faults and we have our failings, as any mortal society must. But when sorrow befell us, we learned anew how great is the trust and how close is the kinship that mankind feels for us, and most of all, that we feel for each other. We must remember, and we must never forget, that the hopes and the fears of all the years rest with us, as with no other people in history. We shall keep that trust working, as always we have worked, for peace on earth and good will among men.*

*On this occasion one year ago, our beloved President John F. Kennedy reminded us that Christmas is the day when all of us dedicate our thoughts to others, when we are all reminded that mercy and compassion are the really enduring virtues, when all of us show, by small deeds and by large, that it is more blessed to give than to receive.*

*So in that spirit tonight, let me express to you as your President that one wish that I have as we gather here. It is a wish that we not lose the closeness and the sense of sharing, and the spirit of mercy and compassion, which these last few days have brought for all of us.*

*Between tonight and Christmas Eve, let each American family, whatever their station, whatever their race or their region—let each American family devote time to sharing with others something of themselves; yes, something of their own. Let us, if we can do no more, lend a hand and share an hour, and say a prayer—and find some way with which to make this Christmas a prouder memory for what we gave instead of what we receive.*

*And now here, as we have done so many years, we turn on in your Capitol City, the lights of our National Christmas Tree, and say that we hope that the world will not narrow into a neighborhood before it has broadened into a brotherhood."*[10]

# The Presidency
# 1963–1969

# The 1964 Presidential Campaign

The 1964 Democratic National Convention was held August 24–26 in Atlantic City, New Jersey. Both Lyndon Johnson and Hubert Humphrey were successful on the first ballot as the Democratic candidates for president and vice president. The Johnson and Humphrey campaign was run on "Kennedy's plan for civil-rights legislation, federal aid to education, and medical care for the elderly. President Johnson was eager to put Kennedy's New Frontier proposals into effect and build a 'Great Society' in which the quality of life would be raised for everyone."[1] The Republican National Convention was held July 13–16 in San Francisco, California. Barry Goldwater and William Miller were selected as the Republican presidential and vice presidential candidates. The 1964 Republican platform was one of ultra conservatism. "Barry Goldwater linked the welfare state with 'softness' on Communism and 'crime in the streets.' He promised moral as well as economic salvation by returning to the pre-New Deal past."[2] One particular issue that alarmed people, including members of his own party, was his advocacy to use nuclear weapons in order to win "total victory" over communism.[3] It was these extreme ideals and a divided party that virtually eliminated any chance for a Republican presidential victory. "Some men were born to campaign, and Lyndon was," Lady Bird Johnson once remarked. In late September of 1964, Lyndon Johnson hit the campaign trail. He went on a forty-two-day, 60,000-mile campaign stump that delivered speeches in the nearly two hundred towns and municipalities that he landed in. He would stop his motorcade and give impromptu speeches with a bullhorn, then leave the car to shake hands with the people. Many times his hand would be swollen and bleeding from so much hand shaking. When people would gather he would discuss his Great Society in down-home language, talk about his family and tell jokes about politics.[4] Lyndon Johnson loved speaking to people. However, he disliked speaking on television where his audience was removed. It was the up-close-and-personal venue that LBJ liked best. In 1964, the population of the United States had grown to almost 192 million people. There were about 114 million eligible voters and of those eligible voters, nearly 62 percent of them showed up to vote. Lyndon Johnson received 486 electoral votes with a staggering 61.1 percent of the popular votes. Barry Goldwater received only fifty-two electoral votes and only 38.5 percent of the popular votes. Lyndon Johnson finally got what he had always wanted. He became president by a majority vote and by his own right.[5]

**Exhibit #44** ★ LBJ Library and Museum photo #355-28-WH64 ★ Photograph by Cecil Stoughton

Exhibit forty-four is an original 8"x10" black-and-white photograph taken the first day of the Democratic National Convention on August 24, 1964. President and Democratic Candidate Lyndon Johnson with Governor John Connally are shown leading the way to the podium. Vice Presidential Candidate Hubert Humphrey is following directly behind them. The Democratic National Convention was one of Cecil Stoughton's final assignments before he retired from the White House.

## The Lady Bird Special

On October 6, 1964, Lady Bird Johnson embarked on a four-day, 1,628-mile campaign trip aboard a train called the Lady Bird Special. The campaign would take her through eight southern states during a time when many of the southern states opposed the president's civil rights agenda. President Johnson had just passed the Civil Rights Act a few months earlier, which abolished the old "Jim Crow" laws and afforded blacks fair access to public buildings and equal employment. Because of the potential danger of violent protest, President Johnson did not join Lady Bird on this trip. The president did board the train initially for a fifteen-minute ride to Alexandria, Virginia. When the train pulled into the Alexandria terminal, President Johnson gave the public a short speech with a rousing sendoff for his wife.

The Lady Bird Special whistle-stop campaign was well orchestrated. Since Lady Bird Johnson was from the South, it was thought that she could defend the civil rights issue without offending the southern voters. She met with some jeers and heckling along the way, but she handled the situations with grace and charm that afforded a southern belle respect, and she got it.

The trip proved to be successful not only for the president, but for Lady Bird Johnson as well. Within those four days, Lady Bird gave a total of forty-seven speeches to approximately 500,000 people. She proved that a first lady had a political influence worthy of great respect.[6]

Exhibit forty-five is an original 8"x10" black-and-white photograph of the Lady Bird Special train pulling into the terminal at Alexandria, Virginia, on October 6, 1964. Aides can be seen crowded at the back of the train as it inches toward the Presidential podium. Note the "LBJ for the USA" posters in the train windows.

Exhibit forty-six is an original 8"x10" black-and-white photograph of President Lyndon Johnson making a speech before a crowd that had gathered to see Lady Bird Johnson off on her whistle-stop campaign through the south. In this photograph by Abbie Rowe, President Johnson can be seen at the podium with Lady Bird and daughter Lynda standing close behind.

**Exhibit #45** ★ White House Photo #8862-A ★ Photograph by Abbie Rowe

**Exhibit #46** ★ White House Photo #8862-H ★ Photograph by Abbie Rowe

# LADY BIRD JOHNSON
## Remarks at the Station in Alexandria, Virginia, at the Start of Mrs. Johnson's Trip through the South
### 8:30 a.m. October 6, 1964

*Friends: Sunshine and lots of friends! What could be a better way to start the Whistlestop? Right here in Alexandria, in view of the monument to one of your first and foremost citizens, George Washington. I am delighted to be on this platform with several Johnson's, two of who are candidates for office. This is a campaign trip, and I would like to ask you for your vote for both Johnson's. And because this is the beginning of a 4-day trip that will take us down the railroad track 1,682 miles to New Orleans, I would like to tell you some of the reasons I am going. For me, this trip has been a source of both anxiety and anticipation – anxiety because I am not used to whistle stopping without my husband; anticipation because I feel that I am returning to familiar territory and heading into a region that I call home. I wanted to make this trip because I am proud of the South and I am proud that I am part of the South. I love the South. I am fond of the old customs, of keeping up with your kinfolks, all your uncles, your cousins, and your aunts, right down to the fifth cousin; of long Sunday dinners after church; of a special brand of gentility and courtesy. I am even more proud of the new South, the glistening new skylines of the cities, the spirit of growth, the signs of prosperity, both in the factory and on the farm. There are so many advances in the South, in its economy, in its interest in the arts, in its progress and education. I am proud of what the South has contributed to our national life. I am proud of the valor with which southerners have served their country in every war in which we have been engaged. Even before we were a nation, southerners were supplying learning and leadership to the task of building our great country. We can all recite the record of our Southern statesmen through the many years of our Nation's trials and triumphs—12 Presidents, 15 signers of the Constitution, 15 Secretaries of State, from Thomas Jefferson to Dean Rusk. Yet in recent times we recognize the strain in the*

*South from the national life as a whole. I have shared with many of you the concern that has come with this strain. I share the irritation when unthinking people make snide jokes about the South as if the history and tradition of our region could be dismissed with ridicule. None of this is right. None of this is good for the future of our country. We must search for the ties that bind us together, not settle for the tensions that divide us. A great southerner, Robert E. Lee, said it best when he advised his fellow southerners, 'Abandon all these local animosities and make your sons Americans. So these are the main reasons I wanted to make this trip. I wanted to tell you from Alexandria to New Orleans that to this President and his wife the South is a respected and valued and beloved part of this country. We are a Nation of laws, not men. And our greatness is our ability to adjust to the national consensus. The law to assure equal rights passed by Congress last July with three-fourths of the Republicans joining two-thirds of the Democrats has been received by the South for the most part in a way that is great credit to local leadership, to mayors and ministers, to white citizens and Negro leaders, to all the Mr. And Mrs. John Citizens who live in our communities. This convinces me of something I have always believed, that there is in the Southland more love than hate. I have, as you have, I am sure, thrilled to see Southern legislatures put education as their top priority; to watch city councils make headway with community conflict. Certainly there are problems ahead, but my husband has always felt that problems are there to be solved, not just deplored. I think we all understand that the hard duty of assuring equal rights to all Americans falls not only on the President of the United States, but upon all who love this land. I am sure we will rise to that duty. I asked for this assignment for many reasons. This trip takes me not only to the queen like cities of the South, but to the small towns and rural areas. I was born in such an area and I am at home there. I believe it is well for the people of the crossroads and the backcountry, in the timberlands and the mountain coves, and the sand hills where the pavement runs out and the city people don't often go, to have a personal part in this election. They all have equal share in the Government. To me, as to you, the South is not a place of geography, but a place of the heart. And so it is with great joy I undertake what is for me in every sense a journey of the heart. And now I yield to the speaker in my family, my husband, and the President of the United States.*

# PRESIDENT JOHNSON

## Remarks at the Station in Alexandria, Virginia, at the Start of Mrs. Johnson's Trip through the South
### 8:30 a.m. October 6, 1964

*Governor, Mr. Chairman, ladies and gentlemen, boys and girls: Alexandria has been chosen as the first stop for one of the greatest campaigners in America, and I am very proud to announce that I am her husband. Tonight I am going to catch up with her in Raleigh, N.C., although I know I will never really overtake her. I plan to use the jet Air Force One tomorrow to try and meet her in New Orleans, but Lady Bird on her train will probably beat me there. She always does. Since I don't dare try to compete with her too much, we are going separate ways tomorrow. Tomorrow I am going out to the Midwest, heartland of America. I am going to report to the American people. I am going to talk about the proud record of our administration, the Kennedy-Johnson administration of the last 4 years. I am going to present the overwhelming and the urgent issues of this campaign, and I am not going to tear down any person or any group in doing that. Never before within the memory of any person here have the American people been asked to make a basic and radical departure from the beliefs and values, which are the source of our economic health and our hopes for peace. I do not believe they are going to choose to keep and build on the careful work of the men of both parties, the hard, patient work that has been going on for more than 30 years now. They are going to choose to look ahead to the new problems which are rushing in upon us, our overcrowded cities, our inadequate schools, the growing mastery of the machine, the need to use our leisure time wisely and creatively. They are going to choose to, I think, continue the search, the quest, for peace, with reason and restraint—and, I hope, with constructive imagination. From now until election day we are going to talk about the problems of the future, for this should be a campaign in which we explore the different ways to meet the new challenges of America in the turbulent sixties. Instead, the gauntlet has been thrown down, not to the future, but to the proved and tested values and solutions of the past. This is far less related to the real needs of our present day world. But it is a more fundamental challenge. We have no choice but to meet it, to crush it, to discard it, and then to get on with the tangible and difficult work of this fast-moving decade that we live in. I want to ask each of you to pledge yourselves this morning to go out for the next 4 weeks, for the next 30 days, and contribute your time and your talents and your energy to your country by supporting Gus Johnson for Congress and Lyndon Johnson and Hubert Humphrey for the Presidency and the Vice Presidency.*

*This is a wonderful crowd. We thank you so much for coming out.[7]*

**Exhibit #47** ★ LBJ Library Photo #415-181-WH64 ★ Photograph by Cecil Stoughton

Exhibit forty-seven is an original 11"x14" black and white photograph of Lyndon Johnson, dated October 15, 1964, on a campaign trip to Brooklyn, New York. This is a wonderful perspective shot of LBJ standing and waving to a large crowd that had gathered in Albee Square to hear him speak. Cecil Stoughton called these shots the "Hail Mary;" a camera up overhead pointing down with a wide-angle format, so that you have him (the president) in the foreground and the deployed thousands in the background.[8]

**Exhibit #48** ★ Los Angeles, California October 28, 1964, LBJ Library Photo #432-130-WH64 ★ Photograph by Cecil Stoughton

Lyndon Johnson doing what he loved best, but his security men feared most—venturing into a crowd.

Exhibit forty-eight is an original 11"x14" black-and-white photograph showing Lyndon Johnson walking through a crowd of supporters in Los Angeles, California, during the 1964 campaign. Nobody could greet a crowd and extend a friendly hand better than Lyndon Johnson.

# THE PRESIDENT'S INAUGURAL ADDRESS
## January 20, 1965

*My fellow countrymen:*

*On this occasion the oath I have taken before you and before God is not mine alone, but ours together. We are one nation and one people. Our fate as a nation and our future as a people, rest not upon one citizen but upon all citizens. That is the majesty and the meaning of this moment. For every generation there is a destiny. For some, history decides. For this generation the choice must be our own. Even now, a rocket moves toward Mars. It reminds us that the world will not be the same for our children, or even for ourselves in a short span of years. The next man to stand here will look out on a scene that is different from our own. Ours is a time of change—rapid and fantastic change—bearing the secrets of nature, multiplying the nations, placing in uncertain hands new weapons for mastery and destruction, shaking old values and uprooting old ways. Our destiny in the midst of change will rest on the unchanged character of our people and on their faith.*

## THE AMERICAN COVENANT

*They came here—the exile and the stranger, brave but frightened—to find a place where a man could be his own man. They made a covenant with this land. Conceived in justice, written in liberty, bound in union, it was meant one day to inspire the hopes of all mankind. And it binds us still. If we keep its terms we shall flourish.*

## JUSTICE AND CHANGE

*First, justice was the promise that all who made the journey would share in the fruits of the land. In a land of great wealth, families must not live in hopeless poverty. In a land rich in harvest, children just must not go hungry. In a land of healing miracles, neighbors must not suffer and die untended. In a great land of learning and scholars, young people must be taught to read and write. For more than 30 years that I have served this Nation I have believed that this injustice to our people, this waste of our resources, was our real enemy. For 30 years or more, with the resources I have had, I have vigilantly fought against it. I have learned and I know that it will not surrender easily. But change has given us new weapons. Before this generation of Americans is finished, this enemy will not only retreat, it will be conquered. Justice requires us to remember: when any citizen denies his fellow, saying: "His color is not mine or his beliefs are strange and different," in that moment he betrays America, though his forebears created this Nation.*

## LIBERTY AND CHANGE

*Liberty was the second article of our covenant. It was self-government. It was our Bill of Rights. But it was more. America would be a place where each man could be proud to be himself: stretching his talents, rejoicing in his work, important in the life of his neighbors and his nation. This has become more difficult in a world where change and growth seem to tower beyond the control and even the judgment of men. We must work to provide the knowledge and the surroundings, which can enlarge the possibilities of every citizen.*

## THE WORLD AND CHANGE

*The American covenant called on us to help show the way for the liberation of man. And that is today our goal. Thus, if as a nation, there is much outside our control, as a people no stranger is outside our hope. Change has brought new meaning to that old mission. We can never again stand aside, prideful in isolation. Terrific dangers and troubles that we once called "foreign" now constantly live among us. If American lives must end, and American treasure be spilled, in countries that we barely know, then that is the price that change has demanded of conviction and of our enduring covenant. Think of our world as it looks from that rocket that is heading toward Mars. It is like a child's globe, hanging in space, the continent stuck to its side like colored maps. We are all fellow passengers* on a dot of earth. And each of us, in the span of time, has really only a moment among our companions. How incredible it is that in this fragile existence we should hate and destroy one another. There are possibilities enough for all who will abandon mastery over others to pursue mastery over nature. There is world enough for all to seek their happiness in their own way. Our Nation's course is abundantly clear. We aspire to nothing that belongs to others. We seek no dominion over our fellow man, but man's dominion over tyranny and misery. But more is required. Men want to be part of a common enterprise, a cause greater than themselves. And each of us must find a way to advance the purpose of the Nation, thus finding new purpose for ourselves. Without this, we will simply become a nation of strangers.

## UNION AND CHANGE

The third article is union. To those who were small and few against the wilderness, the success of liberty demanded the strength of union. Two centuries of change have made this true again. No longer need capitalist and worker, farmer and clerk, city and countryside, struggle to divide our bounty. By working shoulder to shoulder together we can increase the bounty of all. We have discovered that every child who learns, and every man who finds work, and every sick body that is made whole—like a candle added to an altar—brightens the hope of all the faithful. So let us reject any among us who seek to reopen old wounds and rekindle old hatreds. They stand in the way of a seeking nation. Let us now join reason to faith and action to experience, to transform our unity of interest into a unity of purpose. For the hour and the day and the time are here to achieve progress without strife, to achieve change without hatred; not without difference of opinion but without the deep and abiding divisions which scar the union for generations.

## THE AMERICAN BELIEF

Under this covenant of justice, liberty, and union we have become a nation—prosperous, great, and mighty. And we have kept our freedom. But we have no promise from God that our greatness will endure. We have been allowed by Him to seek greatness with the sweat of our hands and the strength of our spirit. I do not believe that the Great Society is the ordered, changeless, and sterile battalion of the ants. It is the excitement of becoming—always becoming, trying, probing, falling, resting, and trying again—but always trying and always gaining. In each generation, with toil and tears, we have had to earn our heritage again. If we fail now then we will have forgotten in abundance what we learned in hardship: that democracy rests on faith, that freedom asks more than it gives, and the judgment of God is harshest on those who are most favored. If we succeed it will not be because of what we have, but it will be because of what we are; not because of what we own, but rather because of what we believe. For we are a nation of believers. Underneath the clamor of building and the rush of our day's pursuits, we are believers in justice and liberty and in our own union. We believe that every man must some day be free. And we believe in ourselves.

And that is the mistake that our enemies have always made. In my lifetime, in depression and in war they have awaited our defeat. Each time, from the secret places of the American heart, came forth the faith that they could not see or that they could not even imagine. And it brought us victory. And it will again.

For this is what America is all about. It is the uncrossed desert and the unclimbed ridge. It is the star that is not reached and the harvest that is sleeping in the unplowed ground. Is our world gone? We say farewell. Is a new world coming? We welcome it, and we will bend it to the hopes of man.

And to these trusted public servants and to my family, and those close friends of mine who have followed me down a long winding road, and to all the people of this Union and the world, I will repeat today what I said on that sorrowful day in November last year: I will lead and I will do the best I can.

But you, you must look within your own hearts to the old promises and to the old dreams. They will lead you best of all.

For myself, I ask only in the words of an ancient leader: "Give me now wisdom and knowledge, that I may go out and come in before this people: for who can judge this thy people that is so great?" [9]

# Presidential Pets

Exhibit forty-nine is an 8"x10" color photograph taken in February of 1964, shortly before LBJ got in big trouble with his dogs. During a tour of the White House rose garden, the president had been entertaining some visiting financial experts and had taken them on a traditional walk around the White House lawn. When the president encountered his beagles, he lifted them up by their ears to show how they would yelp. The president said laughingly, "You see what a dog will do when he gets into a crowd of bankers!"[10] A photograph of the incident appeared in worldwide publications. Liz Carpenter, Lady Bird's staff director and press secretary called it "the yap heard around the world."[11] "The ASPCA was outraged. Scores of bitter editorials and cartoons appeared in papers throughout the world, and the White House switchboard became clogged with messages about the horrible way the president treats his dogs."[12]

The truth of the matter, Lyndon Johnson absolutely loved his dogs. Traphes Bryant, the White House dog keeper said, "President Johnson was the greatest pet lover I had ever known—and possibly the greatest pet lover of all our presidents."[13] Mr. Bryant would know, his career spanned the White House years from Truman to Nixon. As the controversy over the subject of ear pulling raged on in the tabloids, the president maintained that the dogs actually enjoyed the ear pulling.

Johnson attempted to cool the controversy through photographs with his dogs. Exhibit forty-nine on the following page is a photograph that was signed and given to Congressman George Mahon. The president added a very thoughtful and personal inscription at the bottom that reads, "To George Mahon, my friend who always champions popular causes," signed Lyndon B. Johnson.

Although his dogs, named Him and Her, were always considered the president's dogs, they were equally loved and shared by the president's daughter Luci. The president and Luci were the true animal lovers in the family.

President Johnson had several dogs during his administration and only one during his retirement. The President's first Beagle was named Old Beagle. Then came Little Beagle Johnson, who was the sire of Him and Her. A short time after LBJ became president, a schoolgirl in Illinois sent the president a white collie. The Johnsons named him Blanco. Blanco was a very high-strung dog and was given sedatives at times just to keep him calm. Although a more difficult pet, LBJ loved and respected Blanco equally. In November 1964, Her met an untimely death when she swallowed a large stone and died during surgery in an attempt to remove it. In June 1966, Him was struck by a car driven by Luci's driver. It was a most tragic and difficult day for Lyndon and Luci. "LBJ was the saddest I had ever seen him, and the angriest," said Traphes Bryant. LBJ called Mr. Bryant and screamed at him saying, "Can't you make those guys control their speed?" Mr. Bryant knew that LBJ was screaming just to keep from crying.[14]

On Thanksgiving Day in 1966, and just a few months after Him's death, Luci was driving to the LBJ Ranch for dinner and picked up a stray white dog she found along the way. Luci gave the dog to her father, and that evening named him Yuki, which means snow in Japanese. Yuki and LBJ became inseparable from that moment on. In fact, Yuki became one of his all-time favorite companions.

When LBJ retired, Yuki and Luci's Beagles went with the president to the LBJ ranch. The remaining Beagle offspring of Him and Her went to several friends, while Blanco retired to a doctor's ranch in Corbin, Kentucky. Shortly after LBJ left the White House, he wrote a letter to Traphes Bryant, who had taken care of his dogs.[15]

---

*Dear Mr. Bryant,*

*The companionship of my dogs has brought comfort through all my time at the White House. I am grateful to you for making that companionship possible, at whatever hour of the day or night you were called upon, and for caring for the dogs so devotedly. You have been their faithful friend and master as well.*

*Sincerely, Lyndon Johnson*

---

Letter written to Traphes Bryant from Lyndon B. Johnson during the closing days of the presidency. From the book *Dog Days at the White House* by Traphes Bryant and Frances Spatz Leighton.

Original 8"x10" White House photograph dated February 20, 1964, showing President Lyndon Johnson playing with his two pet beagles named Him and Her, on the White House lawn. It is signed, "To George Mahon, my friend who always champions popular causes, Lyndon B. Johnson."

**Exhibit #49** ★ LBJ Library Reference #CA96-8-WH64 ★ Photograph by Cecil Stoughton

★ ★ Dwayne Bridges ★ ★ ★

**Exhibit #50** ★ Photograph by Michael Geissinger ★ LBJ Library Reference #8116-13

Exhibit fifty is an 8"x10" color photo of LBJ with his faithful companion Yuki taken on December 29, 1967. Luci had found the dog on her way to Thanksgiving dinner at the Ranch in 1966. This photograph was taken the following year during Christmas vacation at the LBJ Ranch. The photograph was signed and sent to a friend. The sentiment reads, ". . . with gratitude for your friendship—Lyndon. B. Johnson."

To Dr. Travell, with affectionate best wishes, [signature: Lyndon B. Johnson]    Lady Bird Johnson Christmas, 1964

**Exhibit #51** ★ LBJ Library Reference #C251-2-WH64 ★ Photograph by Cecil Stoughton

Exhibit fifty-one is a 5″x6.5″ color photo showing the Johnson family gathered on the White House lawn. The photo was taken April 17, 1964, and was personally signed by the president and first lady and given as the first family's 1964 Christmas gift to close friends and family. This particular photograph was intended for Dr. Janet Travell, who had been President Kennedy's personal physician. Lady Bird Johnson wrote in the lower margin of the photograph, "To Dr. Travell, with affectionate best wishes, Lady Bird Johnson, Christmas 1964." It was then signed separately and in different pen by LBJ.

Interesting to note, the LBJ Library and Museum has a copy print of this photograph on file, but no original negative, thus making these original prints scarcer than others. Dr. Travell's daughter, Virginia Travell Street, notes that this same photograph was sent to her mother, but was signed with a slightly different sentiment. The signed photograph shown here may have been withheld because the Johnsons had decided on a more personal sentiment or for a number of other possible reasons.[16]

## Luci's Wedding Day
## August 6, 1966

The wedding of Luci Baines Johnson to Patrick John Nugent was the eighth presidential wedding to occur during an administration. Pat Nugent was twenty-three and Luci just nineteen when they exchanged their vows. The ceremony was not held at the White House, but at the National Shrine of the Immaculate Conception, the largest Catholic Church in the United States. This was the first time in U.S. history that a president's daughter was married somewhere other than the White House, and she was the first to be married by Catholic ceremony.

Exhibit fifty-two is a 6"x9" color photograph of Luci Johnson and her fiancé Pat Nugent taking a walk on the south lawn of the White House. The photograph was signed and dated to Sanford Fox just three days before their wedding. The inscription reads to "Alias Santa Claus" because Mr. Fox would play Santa Claus for underprivileged children, during Christmastime at the White House.

**Exhibit #52** ★ LBJ Library reference a#C2087-33 ★ Photograph by Robert Knudsen

To Lucille and Sandy Fox — on a happy day —
with all our thanks for so many things
Lady Bird Johnson    [signature: Lyndon B. Johnson]

Christmas 1966

**Exhibit #53** ★ LBJ Library Reference #C2706-11 ★ Photograph by Frank Wolfe

Exhibit fifty-three is an 8"x10" color photograph of Luci and Pat Nugent with both their families standing on the balcony of the White House on their wedding day, August 6, 1966. Although the wedding had taken place at the National Shrine of the Immaculate Conception, the wedding reception was held at the White House.

This photograph was given to Lucille and Sanford Fox as a Christmas gift that year. The photograph was custom mounted and framed with a personal sentiment from the president and first lady. Signed on the mat below the photograph, Lady Bird Johnson wrote, "To Lucille and Sandy Fox—on a happy day—with all our thanks for so many things," signed Lady Bird Johnson and Lyndon B. Johnson, Christmas 1966.

★ Dwayne Bridges ★

Exhibit fifty-four is a 6.5"x9.5" black-and-white photograph of Lynda Bird Johnson taken the evening of February 17, 1967, in formal gown when she was hosting a dinner and dance in honor of Princess Irene of Greece. This lovely photograph was sent to an admirer along with a written letter of thanks. Signed letters and signed photographs of Lynda Johnson before she became Mrs. Charles Robb are scarce.

**Exhibit #54** ★ LBJ Library Photo #17FE67C-4583-02A ★ Photograph by Robert Knudsen

## Charles S. Robb

Charles Spittal Robb was born June 26, 1939, in Phoenix, Arizona. He graduated from the University of Wisconsin in 1961 and joined the Marine Corps that same year. He served in the United States Marines from 1961–1970. After leaving the Marine Corps, he received his law degree from the University of Virginia in 1973. With several years of private practice, he successfully ran and served his first public office as the lieutenant governor of Virginia from 1978–1982. He then became the Governor of Virginia and served in that capacity from 1982–1986. He also served as U.S. Senator from Virginia from 1989–2001.[17]

This exhibit is an original 11"x14" color photograph taken November 9, 1967, with Lyndon Johnson standing in the background alongside Crown Prince Vong Savang of Laos. In the foreground is marine captain Charles (Chuck) Robb. Captain Robb was engaged to the president's daughter, Lynda Johnson when this photo was taken. They would be married at the White House on December 9, 1967—exactly thirty days from the date of this photo.

**Exhibit #55** ★ LBJ Library and Museum Reference #7357-25A ★ White House Staff Photo

To Helen and George
From all of us including Arturio
with all our love,
The LBJs

**Exhibit #56** ★ LBJ Library and Museum Reference #C-7547-31 ★ Photograph by Robert Knudsen

Exhibit fifty-six is an 11"x14" color photograph that was sent with thanks to Congressman George and Helen Mahon from the president and Mrs. Johnson. The photograph was taken during a party hosted by Lynda Bird Johnson and Charles Robb in honor of the president and Mrs. Johnson's thirty-third wedding anniversary. The painting entitled "Arturio and the Doves" by Henriette Wyeth was a gift to the president and Mrs. Johnson from Congressman George Mahon and others of the Texas delegation.

The small plaque on the painting says "Lady Bird—who has given me thirty-three years of devotion and love—Lyndon, Nov. 17, 1967."

The photograph is signed by President Lyndon Johnson at the bottom margin with a most personal sentiment, "To Helen and George from all of us including Arturio, with all our love, The LBJs."

**Exhibit #57**

Exhibit fifty-seven is an official 10"x14" Flight Certificate dated November 21, 1967, signed by President Lyndon Johnson and was presented to Helen Mahon as a gift to certify she had flown aboard *Air Force One*. Liz Carpenter speaks of this practice by President Johnson in her book, *Ruffles and Flourishes*. "Johnson would give out a memento of each flight—a special paper certificate which stated that you had flown on *Air Force One* at such and such time. It papers the walls of many a Congressman and friend."[18] Although these certificates may have at one time hung on the walls of many a friend, very few of these are ever seen on the public market and are considered quite rare.

President Johnson, having spent many years as a congressman and as a senator, appreciated the difficulties associated with travel on a tight budget. Congressmen and senators were typically reimbursed at twenty cents a mile for one round trip between their hometowns and Washington, D.C. They were then reimbursed for the actual amount for only two more trips in the same year. Most congressmen and senators would make numerous trips in a year, and those expenses would come out of their own pockets.[19] Understanding this, President Johnson would always lend a ride on *Air Force One* to members of Congress and their families, whenever it was possible or appropriate.

Exhibit #58 ★ Photograph by Kevin Smith ★ LBJ Library and Museum Reference #7858-16A

## Lynda's Wedding Day, December 9, 1967

Exhibit fifty-eight is an original 11"x14" White House photograph of the receiving line at the wedding of Lynda Johnson and Charles Robb on December 9, 1967. The photograph was sent to Congressman George and Helen Mahon, and shows them being greeted by the president and the newly married couple. "Only fourteen senators and their wives—especially close ones—had been invited."[20] Lady Bird does not mention in her memoirs how many congressman were invited, but it would be safe to assume that there were very few with the exception of those who were close friends to the president and Mrs. Johnson. Mrs. Johnson described the wedding as a "setting in the grandest manner. She had never seen a lovelier ceremony. Her heart was a roaring tumult of pride, of desire to wring from this wonderful time every second of pleasure, living to the fullest this milestone of their lives."[21] This was a joyous occasion for the entire Johnson and Robb family. However, there was controversy brewing over Charles Robb being a U.S. Marine and if he would be considered for duty in Vietnam like other soldiers, now that he had married into the first family. Charles emphatically stated publicly that he was not being offered any special privileges and that he would be deployed to Vietnam like any other soldier. Captain Robb

was deployed to Vietnam a few months later. The Johnson's youngest daughter Luci had just been married the year before in August, and the White House staff was still recuperating from that wedding. To add to the stress, the time span for preparing for Lynda and Charles Robb's wedding was only three months. Liz Carpenter describes in her book how she received the word of Lynda's wedding engagement: "A phone call came in from the LBJ ranch, which caught me just as I was between bath and evening gown, preparing to attend a party for the King of Greece in Newport." "Liz, " said Mrs. Johnson on the phone. "Are you ready for another wedding?" "No," I replied, ungraciously but honestly. "Well, take a firm grip on both sides of your chair," continued Mrs. Johnson cheerfully, "and I'll put Lynda and Chuck on the phone." The Johnson family wanted the engagement to be released to the press quickly to fend off any potential rumors. The news of the wedding announcement was on the airwaves within an hour. The week before the wedding, some five hundred reporters descended on the White House to cover the event.[22] There had not been a White House wedding since July 30, 1942, when one of FDR's advisors, Harry Hopkins, married Louise Macy. The only previous presidential family wedding had occurred on August 7, 1918, when the niece of President Woodrow Wilson, Alice Wilson, married Isaac McElroy in a small and uneventful White House wedding.[23]

# Closing Days
of the Presidency

1968–1969

Exhibits fifty-nine through sixty-one are original 11"x14" White House photographs taken September 13, 1968, during the last dinner reception at the White House for Texas constituents and close friends.

On March 31, 1968, the president made his Address to the Nation and said in part:

*Tonight I want to speak to you of peace in Vietnam and Southeast Asia. No other question so preoccupies our people. No other dream so absorbs the 250 million human beings who live in that part of the world. I renew the offer I made last August—to stop the bombardment of North Vietnam. We ask that talks begin promptly, that they be serious talks on the substance of peace. In the hope that this action will lead to early talks, I am taking the first step to deescalate the conflict. We are reducing—substantially reducing—the present level of hostilities. And we are doing so unilaterally, and at once. With America's sons in the fields far away, with America's future under challenge right here at home, with our hopes and the world's hopes for peace in the balance every day, I do not believe that I should devote an hour or a day of my time to any personal partisan causes or to any duties other than the awesome duties of this office—the presidency of your country. Accordingly, I shall not seek, and I will not accept, the nomination of my party for another term as your president.*

President Johnson stated in his memoirs, "I felt deep satisfaction in the knowledge that by refusing to be a candidate for the presidency, I might have hastened the day when peace would come to Vietnam." But satisfaction turned to grief, when on April 4 Martin Luther King, Jr., was slain and then on June 5 when Senator Robert Kennedy was shot and killed in Los Angeles.[24]

Liz Carpenter stated that after LBJ announced he would not run again for president, he wanted to have his close friends and supporters from Texas back to the White House one more time before he retired from office. They held a final gathering and dinner the evening of September 13, 1968, on the White House lawn. Liz Carpenter states that this was "the most sentimental gathering of his administration."[25]

**Exhibit #59** ★ LBJ Library and Museum Reference #B1704-33 ★ Photograph by Michael Geissinger

Photograph taken September 13, 1968, during the dinner reception for close friends of the President and Mrs. Johnson. The photos show President Johnson greeting and shaking hands with Congressman George Mahon of Texas.

**Exhibit #60** ★ LBJ Library and Museum Reference #B1704-34 ★ Photograph by Michael Geissinger

Original 11"x14" White House photograph taken September 13, 1968, showing President Johnson greeting
and shaking hands with Helen Mahon, the wife of Congressman George Mahon of Texas

**Exhibit #61** ★ LBJ Library and Museum Reference #D1691-37 ★ Photograph by Yoichi Okamoto

This is a photograph taken September 13, 1968, during the dinner reception for close friends of President and Mrs. Johnson that was held on the White House lawn. The photo shows Helen Mahon at the far end of the table and her husband Congressman George Mahon at the lower right.

From left to right at the table: Harry Middleton, Mrs. Harry Middleton, Mrs. Eldon Mahon, Mr. Eldon Mahon, Helen Mahon, Mr. William McMillan, Mrs. William McMillan, Mr. Grandville, Mrs. Grandville, Mr. John Criswell, Congressman George Mahon, Miss Marie Fehmer.

**Exhibit #62** ★ LBJ Library and Museum Reference #A7416-10 ★ Photograph by Yoichi Okamoto

Exhibit sixty-two is a White House photograph taken December 11, 1968, during the state dinner and reception in honor of the amir of Kuwait. Shown in the photo is the Amir of Kuwait standing next to President Johnson, who is shaking hands with Congressman Mahon.

This was one of the last state dinners held during the Johnson administration.

After the state dinner, the president and the amir of Kuwait held a private meeting in the Oval Office. White House photographer Kevin Smith was sent up to the Oval Office to take photographs. He was supposed to take only a few snapshots and leave, but when he arrived, he made the decision to sit down behind a couch in order to be less conspicuous. As he was taking photos of the meeting, he realized the president and the amir were totally engaged in conversation through the help of an interpreter. Kevin knew that if he got up to leave he would disrupt the conversation. So, he decided to stay where he was and not move. Kevin said, "This was the best meeting I ever witnessed while serving at the White House. You could tell the two men were truly enjoying their conversation." When the president and the amir finished their meeting, the president stood up and said, "I have really enjoyed speaking with you this evening, and if you ever return to Washington I would love to speak with you again." Before the interpreter could translate the president's words, the amir quickly said in perfect unbroken English, "Mr. President, I too have thoroughly enjoyed our conversation and when I visit Washington again I too would enjoy meeting with you." The president's eyes popped open and his jaw dropped. The interpreter stood there looking stunned. By that time, they had been speaking through the interpreter for nearly an hour. The president took a moment, then smiled and said, "By damned you speak better English than I do!" They both chuckled and shook hands again. Kevin took a few more shots and went back to the White House photographer's office, where Oke was waiting for him.[26]

Exhibit sixty-three shows the staff of the White House Social Entertainment Office with Lady Bird Johnson, taken January 16, 1969.

The remaining few days of the presidency were spent meeting and thanking those who had served the president and first family while at the White House. The following photograph was taken just four days before the president's retirement. This photograph was taken in the White House Social Entertainment Office and shows Sanford Fox, chief of the White House Social Entertainment Office, seated at his desk, surrounded by his staff that had gathered to meet with Mrs. Johnson. The LBJ Library and Museum cannot identify all of the staff members seen in this photo, but the staff consisted of the following: Miss Jan Ingersol, Mrs. Margaret Deeb, Mrs. Myra Boland, Mr. John Scarfone, Mr. Paul M. Breeder, Mr. Alexander Schiaroni, and Ms. Ruth E. Johnston.

Lady Bird Johnson has signed this photograph for Mr. Fox with personal sentiment, "For Sandy Fox—What great days they were!—With my fond appreciation for your talent and your dedication—Lady Bird Johnson." Mr. Fox added to the lower left portion of the photograph the date of January 16, 1969—The White House.

Sanford Fox and his staff managed and oversaw all of the official White House functions, state dinners, and most notably, the weddings of both Luci and Lynda Johnson.

**Exhibit #63** ★ LBJ Library and Museum Reference #B3080-17 ★ Photograph by Robert Knudsen

Christmas Greetings

The next sets of exhibits are from the estate of Congressman George Mahon. They are Christmas cards that were sent to the congressman and his wife during the holiday season from the president and first family. Congressman Mahon and his wife apparently kept all of the White House Christmas cards they had received. The congressman had been in office for many years and had served under eight presidents. The George Mahon collection of White House Christmas cards begins with President Eisenhower, and ends with President Ford. The exhibits here will show only the cards from the Kennedy and Johnson administration beginning with the 1962 card that was sent from Mr. and Mrs. John F. Kennedy. This particular card was a very special memento that came from a young president and his lovely wife, which I am sure the Mahon family treasured with kind regard and pleasant memories.

Exhibit sixty-four is the official White House Christmas card from the Kennedys that was sent to Congressman George Mahon and his family during the 1962 holiday season. The card was signed by a secretary for the president and then personally signed by the first lady, Jacqueline Kennedy. Based on Charles Hamilton's important work on John F. Kennedy's handwriting, "The Robot that Helped Make a President—A Reconnaissance into the Mysteries of John F. Kennedy's Signature," the president's secretarial signature can be attributed to secretary one, who was prominent during the timeframe of 1962–1963. Charles Hamilton believes this particular secretary was Ms. Priscilla Wear.[27]

"The 1962 White House Christmas card was produced by Hallmark. One thousand of the cards were printed with facsimile signatures and had the greeting 'Christmas Greetings and Best Wishes for a Happy New Year.' There were only 700 cards produced (like the one shown here in Exhibit number sixty-four) without printed signatures. These blank cards were intended for personal signature and were sent to special friends, family, and important constituents."[28]

This was the second official White House Christmas card sent by the Kennedys and sadly, it was to be their last. Mrs. Kennedy selected the 1962 Christmas card from a photograph that was taken earlier that year by staff photographer Cecil Stoughton. The card shows Jacqueline Kennedy taking Caroline and John Jr. for a sleigh ride on the south lawn of the White House.

In an interview with Cecil Stoughton, the question was asked, "How did you come about capturing this photograph, which was selected for the 1962 Christmas card?" Mr. Stoughton replied, "Well I saw them out there while up by Mrs. Lincoln's office, just outside of the president's office. I could see out the window from there. It was a snowy day and it was rumored that there was going to be some activity, so I made myself available. I went outside to take some photographs and as it turned out, I captured this tremendous moment."[29]

Exhibits sixty-five through sixty-nine are the official White House Christmas cards that were sent to Congressman George and Helen Mahon from the president and Mrs. Johnson. The only card missing in this collection is the 1963 card, which is considered the Johnsons' first presidential card. "The Johnsons' 1963 Christmas card was made in very limited quantity and on very short notice following the tragic death of John F. Kennedy. The 1963 card was not even known to exist until a collector had come across an example nearly thirty years later. Through the assistance of a senior archivist at the LBJ Library and Museum, the Library confirmed the existence of the 1963 Christmas card, but not until the year 1995."[30]

The White House Christmas cards in the George Mahon collection cover the complete years of the Lyndon Johnson administration from 1964 to 1968, excluding the year 1963. It is not known if a 1963 card was sent to the Mahon family.

These White House Christmas cards are representative of the president and first lady's love of the outdoors and their high regard of natural beauty. On February 8, 1965, President Johnson delivered a message to Congress concerning the preservation of natural beauty. "We must protect the countryside and save it from destruction; we must restore what has been destroyed and salvage the beauty and charm of our cities."[31] With this speech, the Johnson administration launched a bipartisan beautification initiative. Lady Bird Johnson promoted many of the beautification programs herself. The following Christmas cards are very symbolic of Mrs. Johnson's love of nature and reflect that lovely charm and character she liked to express during the holiday season.

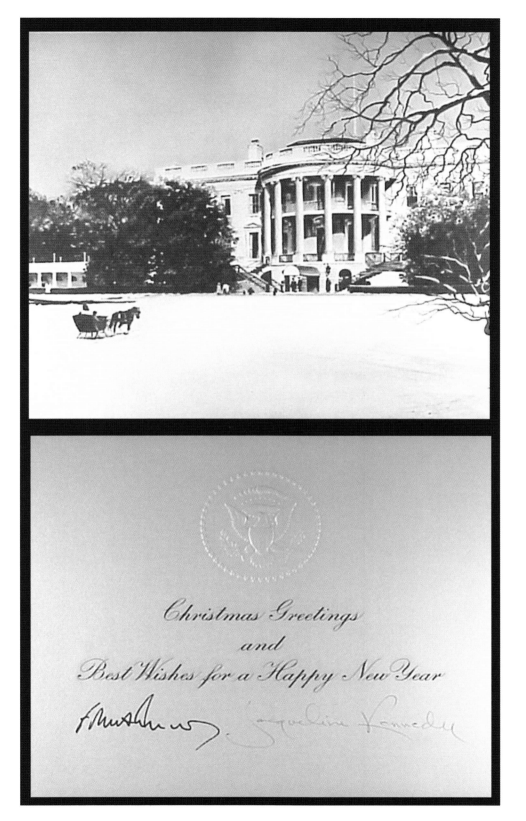

**Exhibit #64** ★ 1962 White House Christmas card

**Exhibit #65**

Exhibit sixty-five is the official 1964 White House Christmas card. This same year, President Johnson awarded a contract to American Greetings Corporation to produce White House Christmas cards. All previous cards had been produced by Hallmark, which had been the status quo since the Eisenhower administration. However, American Greetings and Hallmark both would later create cards for many future presidents.

"The 1964 Christmas card shows a black-and-white illustration of the willow oak from a painting by Robert Laessig. It just so happened, the Johnson family had planted this willow oak themselves on the lawn of the White House. The greeting inside the card says 'With our wishes for a joyous Christmas and a Happy New Year' with facsimile signatures of the president and first lady. The American Greeting Corporation indicates that 2,904 of these cards were printed that year."[32]

**Exhibit #66**

"The 1965 official White House Christmas card, as the year before, came from a Robert Laessig painting. This year, Robert Laessig had chosen to characterize the South Lawn of the White House. The illustration shows a winter scene with tree-covered mounds, near the White House. In the picture, the president's dogs can be seen being taken for a walk. The picture was titled "Winter at the White House." American Greetings issued 2000 of these cards with the greeting, "With our wishes for a joyous Christmas and a Happy New Year" with facsimile signatures of the president and first lady."[33]

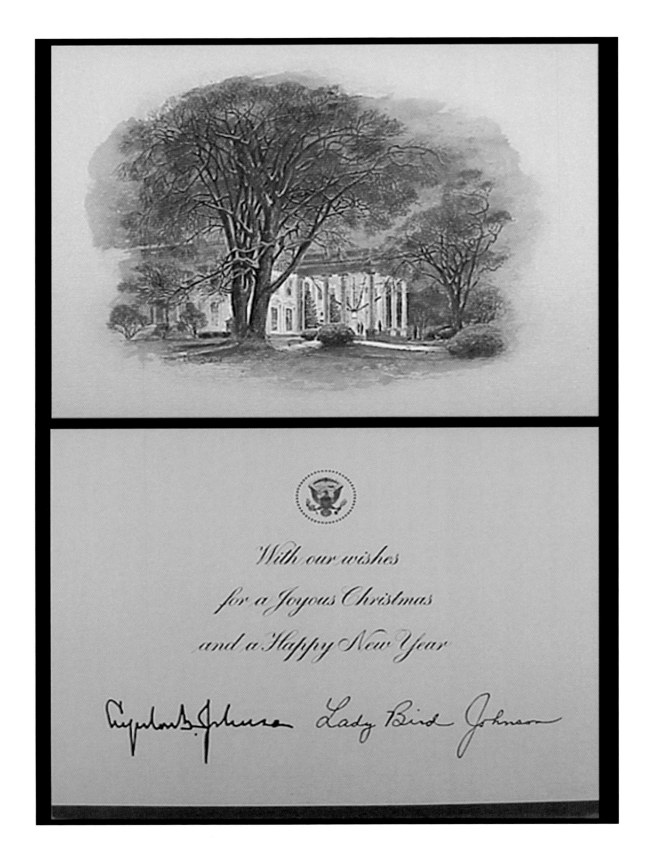

**Exhibit #67**

Exhibit sixty-seven shows the 1966 White House Christmas card. "The 1966 card presents an evening view of the North Portico of the White House with the American elm tree that was planted by President Woodrow Wilson in 1913. American Greetings Corporation printed 2,400 of these official White House Christmas cards for the Johnsons. The greeting inside was the same sentiment as previous cards."[34]

With our wishes

for a Joyous Christmas

and a Happy New Year

*Lyndon B. Johnson*　*Lady Bird Johnson*

Exhibit #68

For their 1967 White House Christmas card, the Johnsons chose a card that depicted the Christmas tree in the Blue Room of the White House. This particular theme varied from previous Christmas cards, primarily due to Lynda Johnson's upcoming wedding to Captain Charles (Chuck) Robb on December 9, 1967.

"For the official 1967 White House Christmas card, 2,600 cards were ordered from American Greetings."[35]

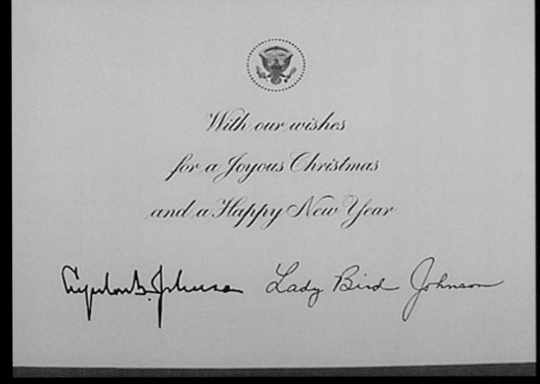

With our wishes
for a Joyous Christmas
and a Happy New Year

*Lyndon B. Johnson*    *Lady Bird Johnson*

Exhibit #69

The final White House Christmas card sent out by the Johnson family was in 1968. "This card represented another painting by Robert Laessig and shows a winter scene from the South Portico of the White House. American Greetings printed 2,300 of these cards for the first family. As shown, Robert Laessig had designed each of the White House Christmas cards during the Johnson administration. No previous artist had ever been given this opportunity. Robert Laessig reflected on this honor by saying, I'm pleased that I was chosen to do it, but so much depended on where you were at the time. I wasn't always satisfied with my paintings, but I painted to try to please the first lady.'"[36]

Lady Bird Johnson wrote in her diary on this last holiday at the White House, "Christmas Eve was the nicest day of the Christmas season to me. I spent the morning winding up the endless list of pictures, books, and engravings that I was autographing for friends and family and staff. The house was beautiful. I love to stop by the entrance to the Yellow Room and look through that great central window framing the nation's Christmas tree. And if you move a little bit to the side, there is the Washington Monument. The fragrance of evergreens filled the halls and holly was everywhere throughout the house."[37] "Deep within me—and millions of others, I think—there was a feeling that at the end of this most awful year, there had been some things that had come out right. Unemployment was at a fifteen-year low; the men on the ship Pueblo were brought home; and there was the glory of achievement for the three astronauts who had flown around the moon."[38]

# Back at the Ranch
# The Retirement Years
# 1969–1973

For Katy and Pat
whose son is sharing the hard work and
excitement of our Nation's Capital —
Lady Bird Johnson

**Exhibit #70** ★ LBJ Library Reference #D1504-3 ★ Photograph by Yoichi Okamoto

After President Johnson retired from office in 1969, he returned to his ranch and to the rural life that he loved so very much. He spent the remaining years writing his memoirs while enjoying his ranch and family. With his health rapidly in decline, he slowed his pace. He became more mellow and lived his retirement years in complete contrast to the fast pace life that he maintained while in politics.

Exhibit seventy is a color photo of Lady Bird Johnson taken on the front lawn of the LBJ ranch in Stonewall, Texas. The photograph was taken August 30, 1968, by Yoichi Okamoto, and was sent to the parents of a young schoolboy who had visited Washington, D.C., along with a letter from Mrs. Johnson's secretary, Helene Lindow. The photograph was signed by Lady Bird Johnson and says, "For Katy and Pat—whose son is sharing the hard work and excitement of our Nation's Capital—Lady Bird Johnson."

**Exhibit #71** ★ LBJ Library and Museum Reference #D3966-14A ★ Photograph by Frank Wolfe

Exhibit seventy-one is an original 4.5"x 6.5" photograph dated December 26, 1970. The photograph was taken during the 1970 Christmas holiday and shows the Johnson family on the front porch of the LBJ Ranch house. From left to right are Charles and Lynda Robb with their children, Lady Bird and Lyndon Johnson, and then Luci and Pat Nugent with their children. The photograph is mounted and signed "To Helen and George Mahon, with the love and gratitude of <u>all</u> of us, the Lyndon B. Johnson's."

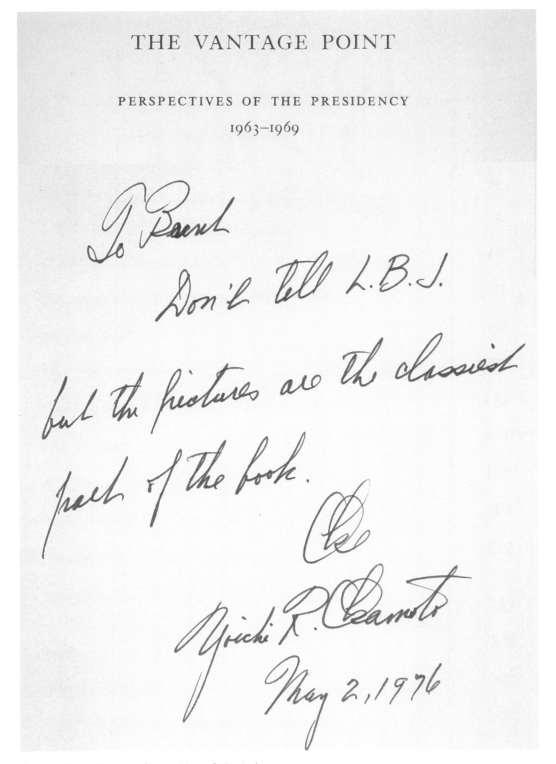

THE VANTAGE POINT

PERSPECTIVES OF THE PRESIDENCY

1963–1969

*To Brent*

*Don't tell L.B.J.*

*but the pictures are the classiest*

*part of the book.*

*Oke*

*Yoichi R. Okamoto*

*May 2, 1976*

**Exhibit #72** ★ (From the George Meyer Collection)

## The Presidential Memoirs

Shortly after retiring to the ranch, LBJ, along with several staff members, quickly began compiling and writing his presidential memoirs. The book was published in 1971 and was called *The Vantage Point: Perspectives of the Presidency, 1963–1969*. Many people assisted LBJ with the documentation, research, and writing of the book. Several were former White House staff members, such as Robert Hardesty, William Jordan, Harry Middleton, Walt Rostow, Tom Johnson, and Doris Kearns.[1] However, there is one important name missing in that list of people who had assisted in documenting the presidency. Those are the names of the White House photographers, and in particular, Yoichi Okamoto. Within the *The Vantage Point*, there are 130 photographs. Of those 130 photographs, Yoichi Okamoto took eighty-three. That is more than half, and just shy of two-thirds of the total photographs chosen for use in the memoirs. I believe this was an honor bestowed upon Yoichi Okamoto for his contribution to history and service to the president. This does not overshadow the contributions made by all the other White House photographers. I am sure that Oke himself would have said it took a dedicated team effort to cover the presidency.

Exhibit seventy-two is a rare if not unique memento from Yoichi Okamoto. It is a first edition copy of *The Vantage Point* that has been inscribed, signed and dated by Yoichi Okamoto to a friend. Yoichi Okamoto offers a bit of humor in his sentiment. He writes, "To Brent, Don't tell LBJ, but the pictures are the classiest part of the book. (signed) Oke, Yoichi R. Okamoto, May 2, 1976."

Exhibit seventy-three is an original 8"x10" color photograph of Lyndon B. Johnson and Lady Bird Johnson, taken December 31, 1972, by photographer Frank Wolfe. Twenty-three days later, Lyndon Johnson would suffer his final heart attack. President Johnson passed away on January 22, 1973.

This photograph was matted and signed later at the bottom by Lady Bird Johnson. The sentiment reads, "To Clarence—this picture of long ago comes with my best wishes for the New Year—Lady Bird Johnson."

**Exhibit #73** ★ LBJ Library Reference #D4826-6 ★ Photograph by Frank Wolfe

# Memorial Tributes

Lyndon Baines Johnson died on January 22, 1973, around 3:50 p.m., from a heart attack while resting in bed at the LBJ ranch. During his heart attack, President Johnson was able to contact the ranch switchboard, which sent Secret Service agents to assist, but their attempts to revive him were futile. He was taken to Brook Army Medical Center in San Antonio, Texas, where they certified his death. Lady Bird Johnson took his body to the Lyndon Baines Johnson Library where he lay in state for the first day.[2] The next day, on January 24, 1973, the former president was taken to the rotunda of the United States Capitol in Washington, D.C., to lie in state. Remarks and tributes were made at the rotunda while funeral services were held at the National City Christian Church in Washington, D.C. On January 25, 1973, Lyndon Johnson's body was flown back to his ranch where he was buried in the family cemetery along the Pedernales River. The Reverend Billy Graham and Reverend Wunibald Schneider officiated the graveside services. John Connally provided the eulogy, and singer Anita Bryant sang the "Battle Hymn of the Republic."[3] Both the House of Representatives and the United States Senate paid honor to the late president with speeches and remarks before Congress and the nation.

## MEMORIAL TRIBUTE DELIVERED BEFORE THE HOUSE OF REPRESENTATIVES
### by Congressman George H. Mahon • January 23, 1973

*Mr. Speaker, I have been pleased to observe the deep feeling which has been apparent in the remarks made here today about Lyndon Johnson. This is not hard to understand. It is all because Lyndon Johnson meant so much to so many of us personally, aside from what he meant to the Nation and to the world. It is hard to know what one should say about this warm and devoted friend who has left us—this great American. I shall not speak at length. Others will recount many things about this man but we all have so many cherished memories of our association with him over so many years we know not where to start or what to say. Lyndon Johnson was much beloved but he was much criticized in certain quarters prior to his departure from the White House and*

*thereafter. All Presidents receive a full measure of criticism. It is often not easy for a public official to deal with criticism. All public officials long to be loved by the people, and certainly Lyndon Johnson yearned for the support and good will, and shall I say, the love of his fellow man. And I must say he had it in large measure.*

*Mr. Speaker, Mrs. Mahon and I spent a couple of days and nights at the Johnson ranch with the Johnson's in late October of last year. At that time I talked to him about the criticism he suffered and as we talked it became obvious to me that he considered this to be a matter of little consequence. He was not disturbed or embittered. He was most tolerant. It was clear to me that Lyndon Johnson was so convinced he had done the right thing, insofar as he knew the right, that he could not be bothered by the criticisms which were made of him. Furthermore, Mr. Speaker, Lyndon Johnson knew that he had a place in history. I feel certain that the Members of Congress agree with me that Lyndon Johnson's place in history is secure. He earned it. None of the critics can ever take away from him his shining record of achievement. Lyndon Johnson had great respect for our institutions and for our system of government. This was nowhere more evident than in the great respect he showed for the Office of the President.*

*The relations between the Republican Party and the Democratic Party are naturally characterized at times by spirited partisanship. That is our system. But, when President Johnson laid down the responsibility of the Presidency, he did everything he could to provide for a smooth transition and to remove stumbling blocks from the path of his successor. He felt his successor should have the fullest opportunity to address himself to the awesome responsibilities of the Presidency—and no one was as acutely aware of the responsibilities and problems confronting Richard Nixon as was President Johnson. President Johnson was most considerate of his successor and President Nixon extended to him great respect and friendship.*

*I have heard President Johnson say many times we cannot have but one President at a time. In office President Johnson conducted himself in an exemplary way. When he departed from the Presidency he conducted himself in the most commendatory and gracious manner as a former President.*

*With pride I join in the salute being given today to his memory. My wife Helen joins me in sentiments of warmest affection for Lady Bird and for his wonderful and talented daughters and loved ones who meant so much to him. They all have our deepest sympathy.[4]*

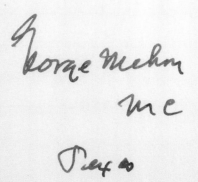

3

With pride I join in the salute being given today to his memory. My wife Helen joins me in sentiments of warmest affection for Lady Bird and for his wonderful and talented daughters and loved ones who meant so much to him. They all have our deepest sympathy.

George Mahon
MC
Tex

**Exhibit #74**

Shown here is an original typewritten page of the final remarks and tribute presented in honor of Lyndon Baines Johnson and delivered before the House of Representatives by Congressman George Mahon. January 23, 1973.

*Stonewall, Texas*

March 7, 1973

Dear Mrs. Dwyer:

Thank you so much for your kind letter
and your generous words about Lyndon.  He had
a special place in his heart for those who had
made the Hill their home for awhile, and I
know he would be grateful for your fine tribute.

I am quite sure that at some time in the
future his loss will come crushing down on me
in deep sadness, but for now, my thought is one
of gratitude for the thirty-eight years we
shared.

Sincerely,

*Lady Bird Johnson*

A few short months after Lyndon Johnson had passed away, Lady Bird Johnson responded to a friend's letter. In this letter, Lady Bird Johnson reflects upon the great loss both she and others had yet to realize.

**Exhibit #75**

Exhibit #76 ★ LBJ Library Reference #D8682 ★ Photograph by Frank Wolfe

## Lady Bird Johnson

Exhibit seventy-six is an original 5"x7" black-and-white photograph of Lady Bird Johnson from a series of photographs taken January 8, 1988, by photographer Frank Wolfe.

Mrs. Johnson would cease responding to autograph requests and began reducing her personal correspondence around this time.

Signature Study

This final section is provided as an overview and short analysis of the handwriting and autographs of the Johnson family. The study and collecting of autographs is referred to as the science of philography. The autographs and signatures represented within this text have come primarily from my own collection or have passed through my hands at some time. This section by no means can be considered a final interpretation of Johnson family autographs but will hopefully supplement the many fine works that have been completed to date.

Compared to all of the United States presidents, authenticating and attributing the handwriting of Lyndon Johnson is extremely difficult, second only to the handwriting of President John F. Kennedy. Fortunately for the collector, the handwriting of JFK has been widely studied and published, but very few publications exist that focus on Lyndon Johnson.

All signatures provided in this section have been reproduced to scale for accuracy and presented by date to help show transition of handwriting style over time.

## LBJ Signature Study Analysis

### Secretarial Signatures

Over the years, I have looked at many forms of Lyndon Johnson signatures. After a while, some very distinct features of his signature begin to appear. I have researched and spent a good deal of time interviewing experts in the field of presidential autographs. Interestingly enough, many of my own observations about LBJ signatures began to correspond to what many of the experts had noticed as well.

I had often thought, without any actual proof, that Lyndon Johnson's secretary, Mary Rather, had signed for Johnson over the years. The Universal Autograph Collectors Club (UACC) issues a periodic publication called *The Pen and Quill*, which offers signature examples from time to time. In their Jan/Feb 1998 issue, a long-time and respected collector, George Meyer, featured a 1956 memorandum that confirmed the theory about Mary Rather **(See Diagram #1)**.[1] Mr. Meyer discovered this memorandum while conducting his own research at the LBJ Library.

Other LBJ staff members besides Mary Rather were also given authorization to sign for Johnson. During the very early years when Lyndon Johnson was a congressman, Gene Latimer and Warren Woodward had authorization to sign for him. Gene Latimer has mentioned that his signature rendition was not very good and would be easily recognized as secretarial. He also said that Johnson signed most of the mail himself during those early years, but when he did not have time, Warren Woodward usually signed for him.[2] In later years, there was John Connally and Walter Jenkins. There are no indications or records that show John Connally had ever signed for Lyndon Johnson, but Walter Jenkins did on occasion.

During the presidential years, both Walter Jenkins and Bruce Thomas signed for the president, but primarily it was Bruce Thomas.

### Autopen Signatures

There have been debates among collectors about whether the autopen machine could place the all-important dot in the signature of Lyndon B. Johnson. This debate can be put to rest. On December 14, 1999, an oral request was placed with the LBJ Library from an undisclosed researcher. That oral request was documented with a response that can be seen in Diagram #2.[3] Claudia Anderson was the LBJ Library Archivist who had processed the request and responded that the autopen machine had signature templates with and without the dot. An example of an autopen signature "with" the dot can be seen on the 1968 White House Card on page 210 as well as autopen signatures displayed on page 204. An example of an autopen signature "without" the dot can be seen on the 1968 Christmas card on pages 211–212.

Charles Hamilton identifies three LBJ autopen pattern types in his book *American Autographs*.[4] The autopen signatures discovered and offered within this text would constitute additional patterns.

There are no definitive records indicating a date when Lyndon Johnson began using the autopen machine. However, a small handful of records indicate that the machine did not exist before 1951. An LBJ Senatorial memo discovered at the LBJ Library does place the Autopen machine into practice around 1953 **(See Diagram #3)**.[5] Although there are no records substantiating the purchase of the autopen machine in 1953, an internal LBJ Library memo from Tina Houston to Harry Middleton and Charles Corkran dated 11/22/88 does indicate that the machine was purchased and used beginning in the Senate years **(See Diagram #4)**.[6] The statement made in this memorandum that the autopen was not used during the White House period is simply incorrect. Take note that the autopen signatures within this text are dated and confirmed to be from 1968. This is not to say that the autopen was not used throughout the White House years, but simply to say that it appears to have been used on many fewer occasions during the early years. Documentation indicates that the administration was afraid to use the autopen for fear that someone might say LBJ had not really signed a piece of legislation **(See Diagram #5)**.[7]

Lady Bird Johnson had commented to her assistant, Betty Tilson, on her husband's signing practices and briefly discussed the use of the autopen machine in a letter dated October 27, 1983. **(See Diagram #6)**.[8]

## Identifying Autopen Signatures

The best and most foolproof method for identifying autopen signatures is through typology. In other words, by matching identical signatures from two or more original documents. There have been claims that autopen signatures can be forensically identified through patterns that can only be created by mechanical means. I am skeptical of this practice. For the future this will be even truer. The next generation of autopen machines will be based on technology that will have the ability to replicate signatures with more human characteristics than ever before.

Typology is far from being the easiest and most expedient means for identifying autopen signatures. However, for now it remains the most accurate.

## Authentic Signatures

As mentioned previously, most of Lyndon B. Johnson's later signatures have a dot placed below the middle initial and usually to the left of the "J" in Johnson. However, his early signatures did not always have this dot. There is no clear time when Johnson began this practice other than it was sometime during his Senate years when the placement of the dot became more evident.

Respected autograph experts John Reznikoff and Stuart Lutz introduced an observation in 1997 that Johnson did not take the time to form his middle initial "B"; he never moved it back left, but continued his writing stroke straight into the "J" of his last name.[9] This observation appears to be true for the most part, especially for his later signatures beginning around the vice-presidential period. Some early authentic congressional and senatorial signatures do have the backtracking strokes that can be prominently seen in the middle initial.

During the short post-presidential years of 1969–1973, Lyndon Johnson signed most of his correspondence himself. When he did, he generally signed with his initials only. Full signatures of President Johnson's handwriting from his retirement years, outside of his memoirs and bookplates, are very scarce.

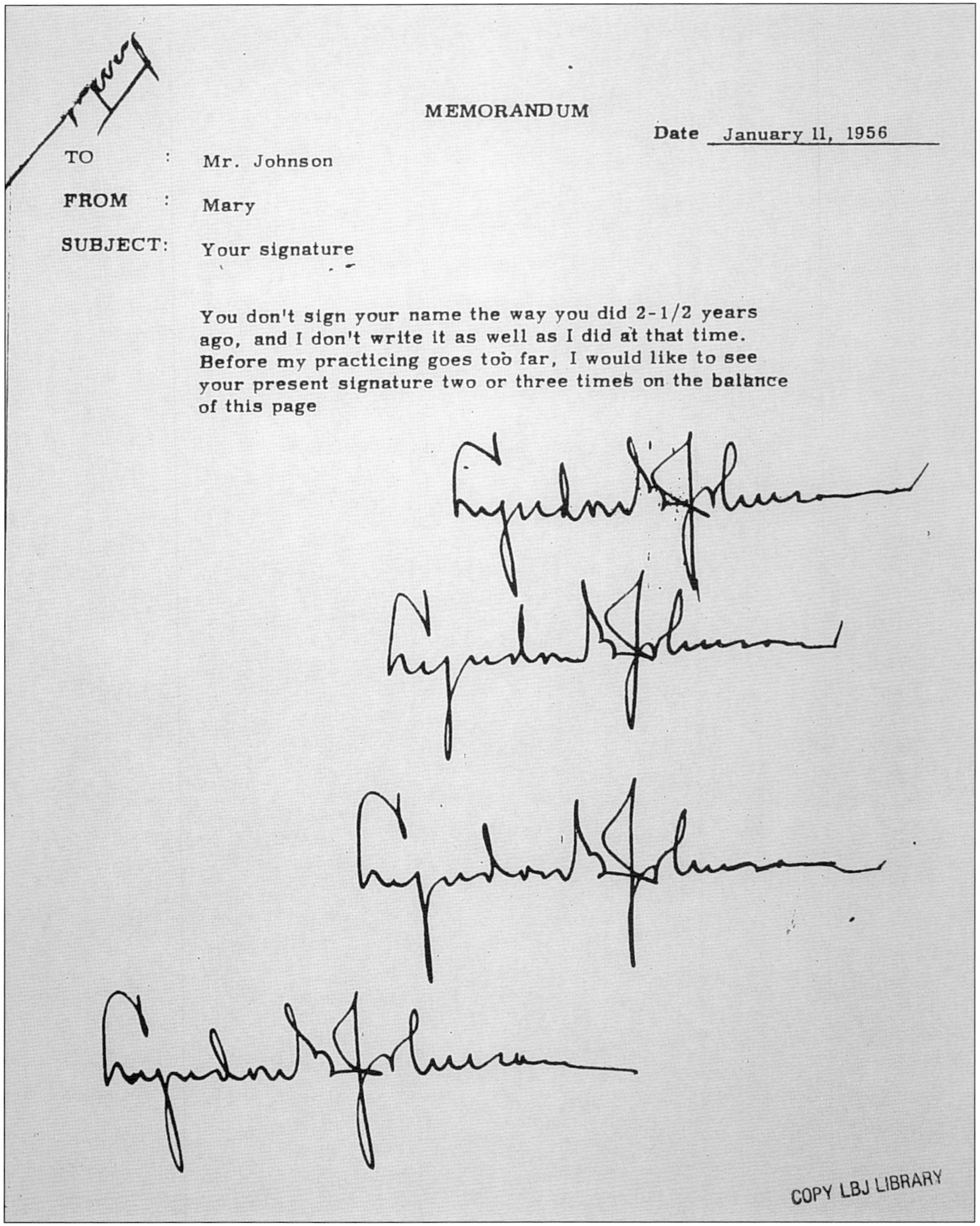

MEMORANDUM

Date   January 11, 1956

TO       :   Mr. Johnson

FROM     :   Mary

SUBJECT:     Your signature

You don't sign your name the way you did 2-1/2 years ago, and I don't write it as well as I did at that time. Before my practicing goes too far, I would like to see your present signature two or three times on the balance of this page

COPY LBJ LIBRARY

**Diagram #1**

Memorandum sent to Lyndon Johnson from his secretary

Mary Rather, January 11, 1956

Received by: TH

Assigned to: CA

Date completed: 12

## ORAL REFERENCE REQUEST

Name of researcher Claudia Anderson for

Address

Phone Number

REQUEST

has hypothesized that the autopen does not have the capability of inserting a "dot" after the "B" in LBJ's signature, and therefore an aide must have inserted the dot in a different pen after the autopen signature. Can we verify that?

RESPONSE

TH called CWC at home: the autopen was moved from the 4th floor cage to the Dorothy Territo Room adjoining Phase I. At that time there were templates with it in a large oversized (like a dress box). There were templates that had it both ways--with and without the dot. The autopen and templates were transferred to Char in the Museum.

CA checked w/Char and looked at the templates--wrote that we have them "both ways."

**Diagram #2**

Oral Reference Request from the LBJ Library concerning the Autopen Machine, December 12, 1999.

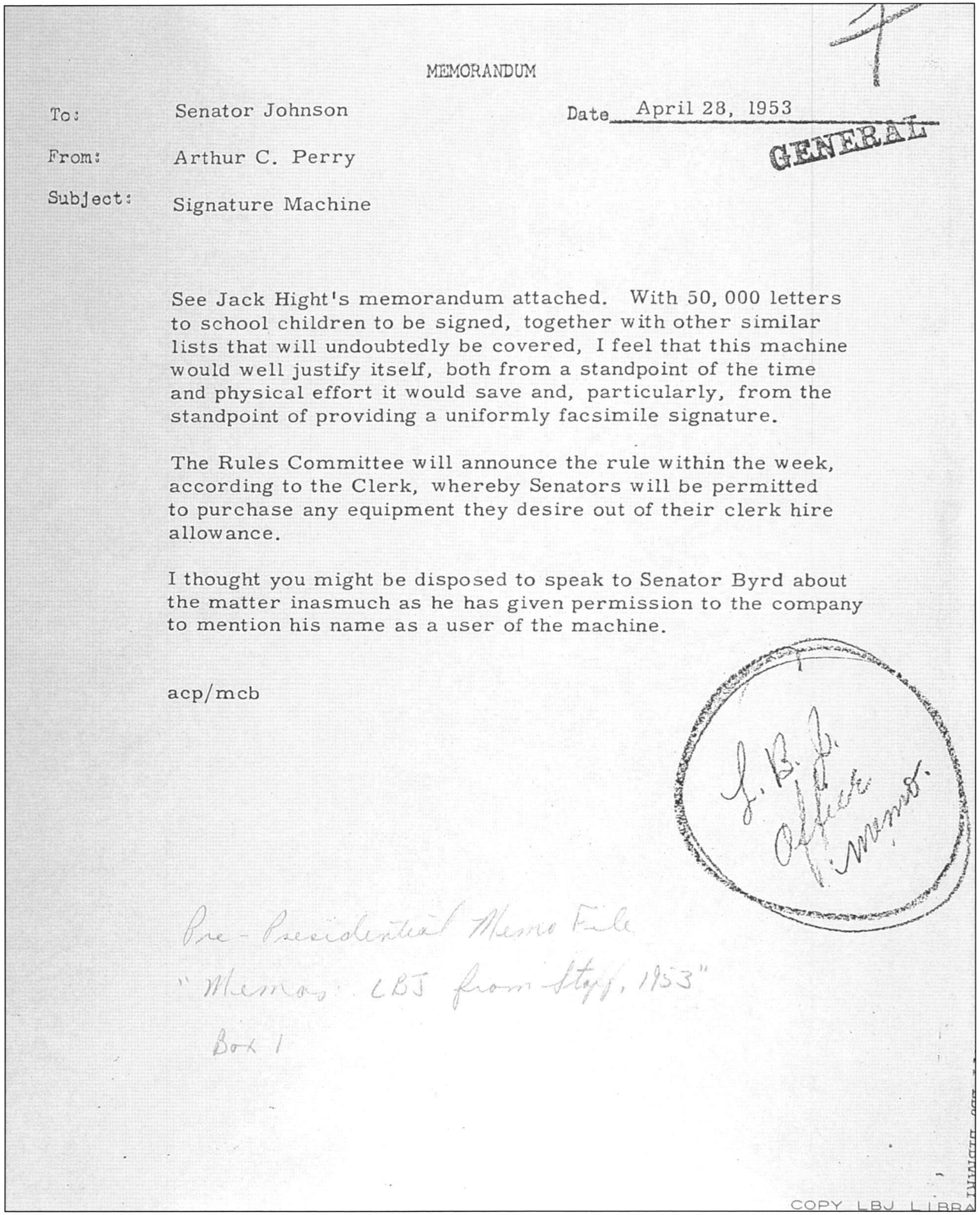

MEMORANDUM

To: Senator Johnson Date April 28, 1953

From: Arthur C. Perry

GENERAL

Subject: Signature Machine

See Jack Hight's memorandum attached. With 50,000 letters to school children to be signed, together with other similar lists that will undoubtedly be covered, I feel that this machine would well justify itself, both from a standpoint of the time and physical effort it would save and, particularly, from the standpoint of providing a uniformly facsimile signature.

The Rules Committee will announce the rule within the week, according to the Clerk, whereby Senators will be permitted to purchase any equipment they desire out of their clerk hire allowance.

I thought you might be disposed to speak to Senator Byrd about the matter inasmuch as he has given permission to the company to mention his name as a user of the machine.

acp/mcb

L.B.J. Office memo.

Pre-Presidential Memo File
"Memos LBJ from Staff, 1953"
Box 1



**Diagram #3**

Senate memo from Arthur Perry to LBJ recommending the purchase of the autopen machine April 28, 1953

**M E M O R A N D U M**

**TO:**      Harry Middleton/Charles Corkran

**FROM:**   Tina Houston

**SUBJECT:**  LBJ's signature

**DATE:**   11/22/88

Jack Taylor, Maxwell Taylor's son, is doing an article on LBJ's

signature.  Two questions have come up which I need a ruling on.

We have verbalized the following to researchers (since the Jennifer/

Fred Casoni research), but we have not put it in writing.  Is

is OK if we put it in writing to Jack Taylor?

1) Others signed LBJ's name during the Presidency, but the major

person who did so was Bruce Thomas.   Walter Jenkins may have done

so while he was on the White House staff.

2) The autopen was used during the Senate days, but was not used

during the White House period.


Also, can we write and/or tell people that we have an autopen

from the White House here at the Library?  In the future, if someone

wanted to look at it, could we show it to them?


Background information:

(and researchers have found in files)
We have written people, sending them documents which "reflect Bruce
Thomas' role as a 'signer' for President Johnson.  We have written
and told researchers that the dot under the "B" was reserved for
LBJ.  When other people signed his name, they were not supposed to
use the dot.  (This information about the dot has appeared in published
articles.)  We have told people that Walter Jenkins and Bruce Thomas
both signed for LBJ.

**Diagram #4**

Internal LBJ Library Memo from Archivist Tina Houston to Harry Middleton/

Charles Corkran, November 22, 1988

```
M E M O R A N D U M


     TO:      For the Record

     FROM:  Tina Lawson

     SUBJECT:   LBJ's signatures

     DATE:    10/28/85

Report of conversation with Dorothy Territo re LBJ's signatures:

LBJ autographed many copies of THE VANTAGE POINT, all of which
 have a dot under the "B" of his name.

Others who signed his signature were instructed not to use the
 dot.  However, it was not a foolproof system.

They were afraid to use the autopen much during the White House
 days, for fear that someone would say LBJ had not really signed
 a piece of legislation.
```

**Diagram #5**

Internal LBJ Library Memo from Archivist Tina Lawson (Houston)

*For the Record*, October 28, 1985

October 27, 1983

At last! I am so sorry for the long delay and thank you for your patience.

Here is the "Jack Dempsey" story. Mrs. Johnson remembers one time during World War II when the country was in the flush of citizen participation in the War -- about 1943. President Johnson was back at home after his naval service, a Lieutenant Commander, and rising young Congressman. He went on a tour to sell war bonds with some people from the screen world - Mrs. Johnson remembers Robert Taylor in particular - and with Jack Dempsey. Jack Dempsey was very popular with the people and a very colorful figure, and they were in Congressman Johnson's home District, the 10th. He was the host.

So, there were many citizens milling about in the little town they had stopped in. At one point, Mr. Dempsey said: "Congressman, you have to get me out of here and back to the airport by ___ o'clock, because it is my seven year old daughter's birthday, and I simply can't miss my flight, because she'd be so disappointed if I didn't get home."

Congressman Johnson was very mindful of the importance of all this to Mr. Dempsey and as it got later and later, and after repeated reminders that it was time to go, Congressman Johnson - a little exasperated - told Mr. Dempsey: "Now come on, you told me you had to catch the plane and if we don't leave now, I'm not going to be responsible."

To which Mr. Dempsey replied: "Congressman, after twenty-five years, if the people still care enough, than I have to sign these autographs."

Lyndon Johnson always remembered that every time he would weary of signing autographs and was very sensitive to the fact that it mattered to someone.

As for Mrs. Johnson's use of the autopen -- she really doesn't have much recollection about it, but believes it was not used until White House Days -- and only then when the volume of mail about a particular subject became so heavy that there simply wasn't time for her to sign every piece of correspondence -- something she always wants to do herself. Mrs. Johnson remembers, too, that the autopen was used to sign some of the signed calling or autograph cards that were sent to the general public (these would have been signature only items).

With the hope this is helpful to you and many good wishes,

Sincerely,

(Mrs.) Betty Tilson
Staff Assistant to
Mrs. Lyndon B. Johnson

4226 Vermont Avenue
Alexandria, Virginia 22304

**Diagram #6**

Letter from Betty Tilson to Jennifer Casoni,
October 27, 1983

# The M-60 Autopen Machine

The Lyndon Baines Johnson Library and Museum has in its archives an M-60 autopen machine that was used by Lyndon and Lady Bird Johnson. Along with the autopen machine, there remain eleven (11) original signature matrices. This particular M-60 autopen machine was built in 1969. We know this because of the number sequence on the serial plate. Thus, this machine would have been purchased and used by Lyndon and Lady Bird Johnson after they left office. However, this would have been the same type of autopen machine that LBJ and John Kennedy would have used when they were president because the M-60 model was built throughout the 1960s. Charles Hamilton, the most recognized and associated name in philography, had mentioned that Kennedy probably used the Model 50 machine as well.[10] Most likely, Johnson and Kennedy had employed the use of both machines during their years in public office.

The eleven original signature matrices stored at the LBJ Library with the autopen machine date back to 1967, with the latest matrix being manufactured in 1974. The signature matrices include signatures for Lyndon B. Johnson, Lady Bird Johnson, Harry Middleton, and Leonard H. Marks. Two of the eleven matrices have signatures that print the greeting "With best wishes."

The M-60 autopen machine was built by the International Autopen Company (IAC). The IAC was founded by the late Robert M. De Shazo, Jr., over fifty years ago. Today, the company is owned and operated by his family and is now called Automated Signature Technology or SigTech. A brief history of the company is presented on their Internet Web site.

*"Over 50 years ago, Robert M. De Shazo, Jr. had a vision that ultimately led to the creation of the signature machine industry. Until the business could support itself, Mr. De Shazo worked out of his Washington, D.C., home, traveling throughout the country selling signature machines, installing them, and training new customers. As his children grew, they would accompany him on his business trips, learning everything there was to know about this specialized equipment. Soon they were working in Mr. De Shazo's signature machine factory in the Washington suburb of Sterling, VA, traveling the country on their own, installing and servicing signature equipment and developing new ideas and products for the company.*

*Today Automated Signature Technology is owned and operated by Mr. De Shazo's four children."[11]*

The M-60 model autopen machine is large and quite heavy compared to the machines in operation today. Of course, technology has advanced in the thirty-four years since the M-60 machine was in service. The M-60 autopen machine measures 34" x 25" x 7" and weighs in excess of fifty pounds. Pictured on the following pages are several views of the M-60 autopen machine in its unrestored condition at the LBJ Library and Museum.

Originally, this machine had four removable wooden legs that fastened to the front and rear corners. Later, the rear legs were replaced with a solid wooden base called a "modesty panel." With the advent of the miniskirt and shorter dresses in the 1960s, the modesty panel was created to provide greater privacy and respect for the young ladies who sat and operated the machine.

A power cord and a foot pedal connect to the left side of the machine and provide electrical power and control to the autopen. Operating the machine is quite simple. There are only three toggle switches used for operation. First, the front and rear panels are opened, exposing the turntable. A signature matrix would be placed on the turntable. Closing the front and rear panels, the two guide pens located on the backside of the operating arm fall into the guide channels of the signature matrix. Once set, the operator flips the toggle switches on from right to left, turning the power on, then selecting to use either the foot pedal or the continuous signing mode. The operator would then place a document for signature under the operating arm. The light switch could be turned on allowing the table to be illuminated. This enabled the operator to see and place the document in the best position for signing. The remaining steps were to place a pen or pencil into the operating arm, hit the foot pedal, and begin signing.

The number of autographs this machine could produce was in the hundreds per hour. Newer machines today can produce as many as 400 signatures an hour, depending on the complexity of the signature.[12]

Front view of the M-60 autopen machine before restoration

## The M-60 Autopen Machine

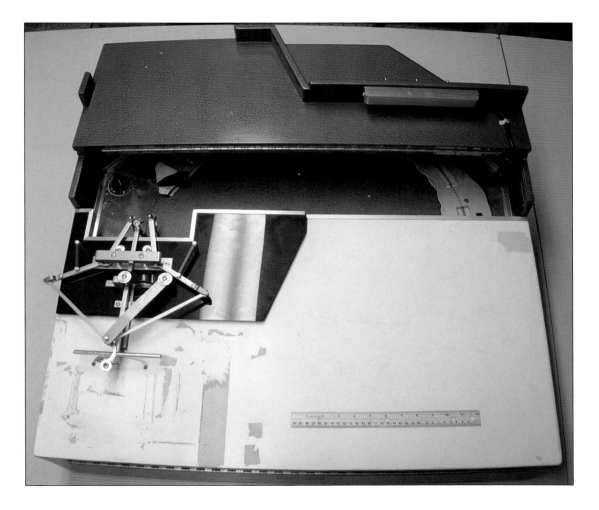

Top view of the M-60 autopen machine before restoration

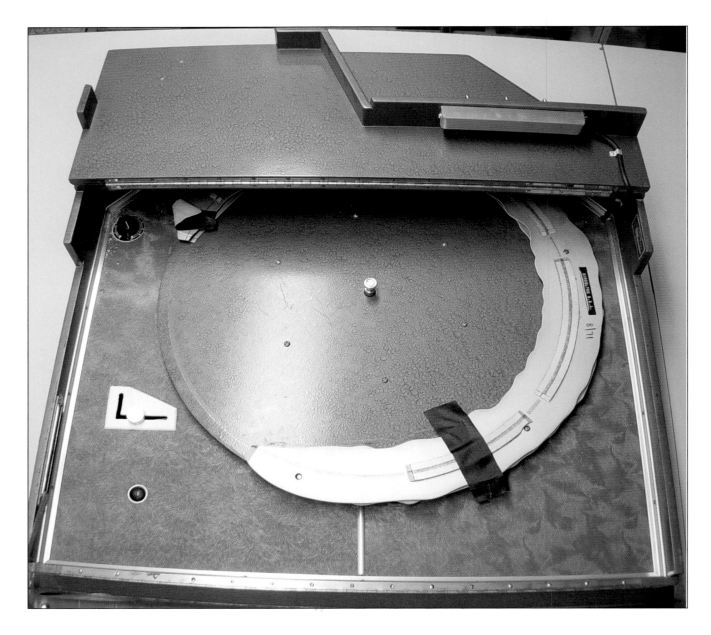

Top view of autopen machine with front and rear panels open showing the turntable and matrix

## The M-60 Autopen Machine

The control switches for the M-60 autopen machine

··*Dwayne Bridges*··

# The M-60 Autopen Machine

Top view of the M-60 autopen signature arm

# M-60 Autopen Signature Matrix

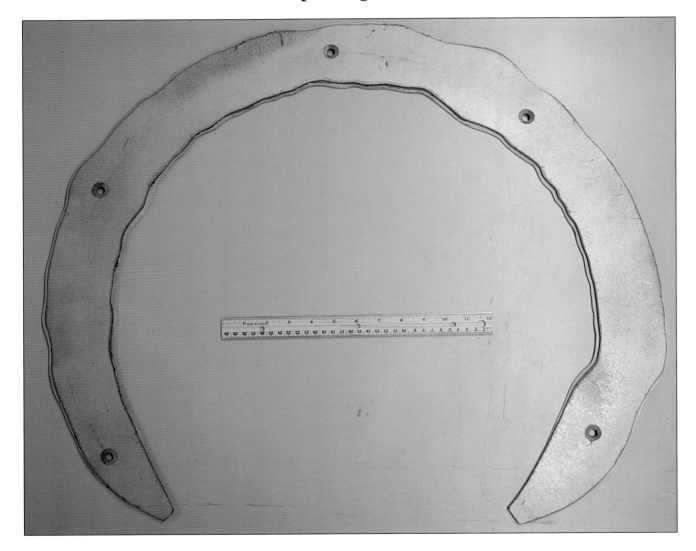

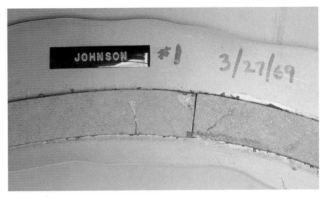

Close-up view of a signature matrix
—This matrix marked Johnson #1 3/27/69

Full view of an autopen signature matrix
—This matrix is marked Johnson White House 2/22/67

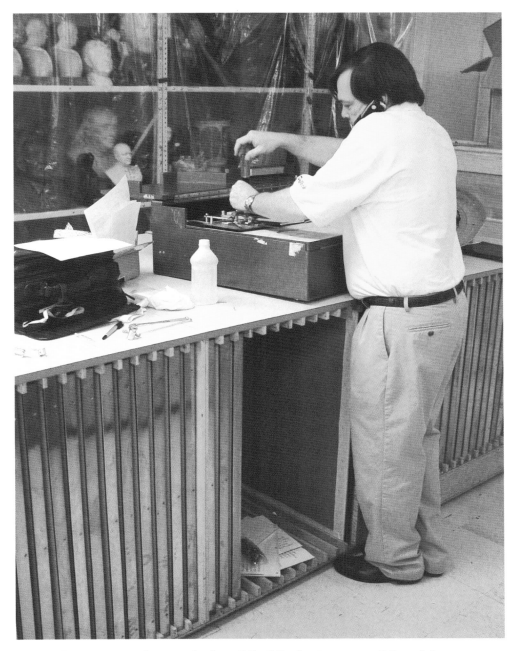

## Restoration of the M-60 Autopen Machine

Shown here is the son of the late autopen founder Robert De Shazo, Jr. His son, Lindsay De Shazo, is assisting the LBJ Library and Museum in restoring the M-60 autopen machine. The machine was found to be in its original condition. Only minor cleaning and adjustments were needed to bring the autopen machine back to full operation.

Taken December 5, 2003 ★ Photo by Dwayne A. Bridges

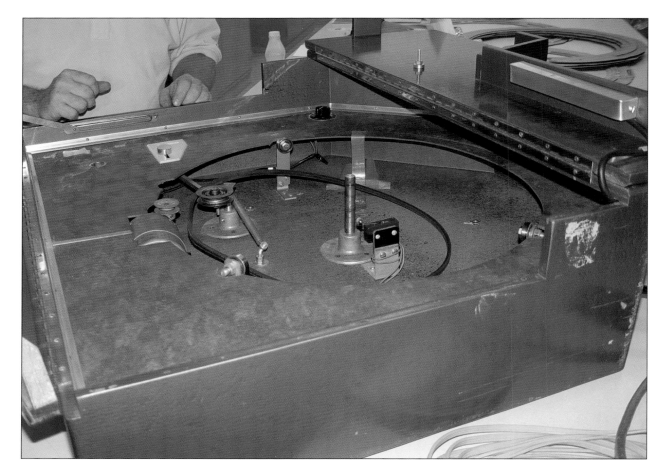

Unassembled view of the M-60 autopen machine with turntable removed for maintenance. The AC motor and turntable belt assembly can be seen along with the two turntable control levers located on the inside. The silver control lever located at the top left is the idler control. The black knob near the top center of the photo is the turntable speed control.

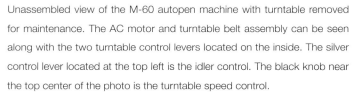

Front view of the fully restored M-60 autopen machine. Note the original foot pedal at the right.

⋆⋆Dwayne Bridges⋆⋆

## The Autopen Signature Matrices

As previously mentioned, the LBJ Library and Museum have eleven signature matrices stored in the archives with the M-60 autopen machine. These eleven signature matrices are all marked according to the date of manufacture and to signature type.

The eleven matrices are marked as follows:

1) Leonard H. Marks 1/74

2) Harry Middleton GSA 8/71

3) Harry J. Middleton GSA 5/73

4) Lady Bird Johnson (Special) GSA 4/73

5) Lyndon B. Johnson—White House 2/22/67

6) Lyndon B. Johnson #1 3/27/69

7) Lyndon B. Johnson #2 3/27/69

8) Lyndon B. Johnson #3 3/27/69

9) Lyndon B. Johnson #4 3/27/69

10) (LBJ) "With best wishes" #3 3/27/69

11) (LBJ) "With best wishes" #4 3/27/69

## M-60 Autopen Signatures

The following autopen signatures are from the original matrices housed in the LBJ Library and Museum. Each of these signatures was created with the original M-60 autopen machine on December 5, 2003, under the professional guidance and operation of Lindsay De Shazo from Automated Signature Technology. A blue medium-point felt tip pen was used for all signatures. Archivist Michael MacDonald from the LBJ Library and Museum, along with the author, recorded and witnessed each of the autopen signatures.

# M-60 Autopen Signatures

1. Leonard H. Marks    LBJ Library    1/74

Middleton    GSA    8/71

Harry Middleton    GSA    5/73

Johnson    White House    2/22/67

Lady Bird Johnson    (SP) [Special]    GSA    4/73

Johnson    #1    3/27/69

Johnson    #2    3/27/69

Johnson    #3    3/27/69

Johnson    #4    3/27/69

With Best Wishes    #3    3/27/69

With Best Wishes    #4    3/27/69

---

1. **Autopen signature of Leonard H. Marks dated January 1974**
   *Leonard Marks was the director of the U.S. Information Agency during the Johnson administration.*

2. **Autopen signature for Harry Middleton dated August 1971**
   *Harry Middleton was a staff assistant from 1967-69 and in 1970 became director of the LBJ Library.*

3. **Autopen signature for Harry Middleton dated May 1973**

4. **Autopen signature for Lady Bird Johnson dated April 1973**

5. **Autopen signature for Lyndon B. Johnson from matrix dated February 22, 1967**

6. **Autopen signature #1 for Lyndon B. Johnson from matrix dated March 27, 1969**

7. **Autopen signature #2 for Lyndon B. Johnson from matrix dated March 27, 1969**

8. **Autopen signature #3 for Lyndon B. Johnson from matrix dated March 27, 1969**

9. **Autopen signature #4 for Lyndon B. Johnson from matrix dated March 27, 1969**

10. **Autopen signature #3 "With best wishes" from matrix dated March 27, 1969**

11. **Autopen signature #4 "With best wishes" from matrix dated March 27, 1969**

# Signature Examples Lyndon B. Johnson

All signatures represented are to scale

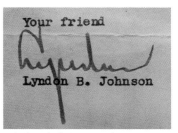

Authentic signature placed

on corner of a 5"x7" photograph

dated August 1946

## Signature as Congressman (1937–1948)

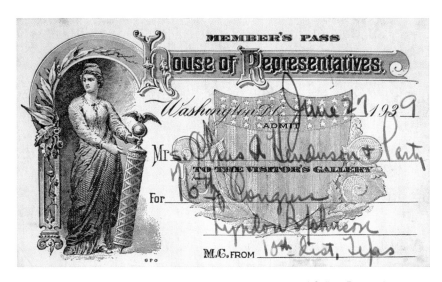

Very rare and authentic 1939 House of Representatives signed Gallery Pass written and

signed entirely in Lyndon Johnson's hand

Authentic first name signature on

letter dated August 1946

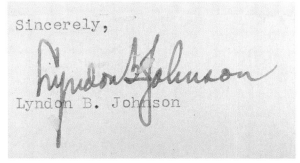

Authentic signature on letter dated July 1948

## Signatures as Senator (1949–1960)

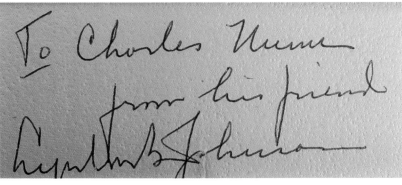

Authentic Senatorial signature on mat board dated early 1954 (signature is truncated at

bottom due to deterioration of the mat)

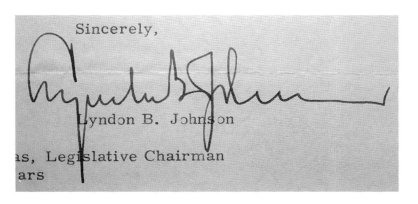

Secretarial signature from letter dated March 1958

# Signature as Senator (1949–1960)

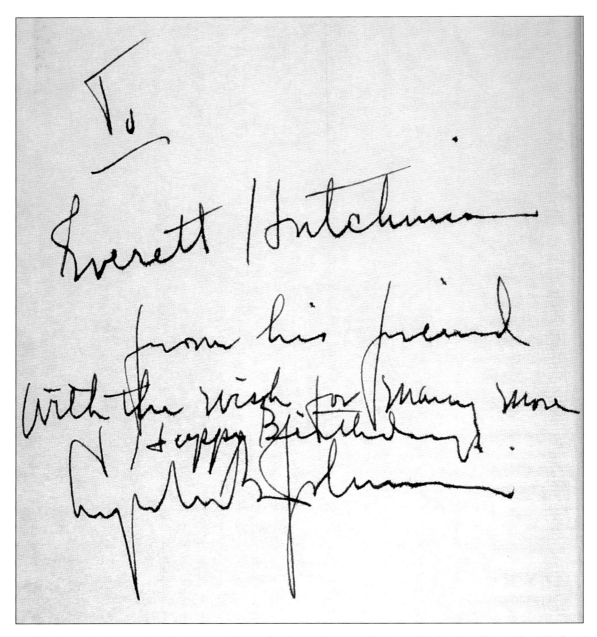

The above signature and sentiment was written on the first inside page of the book *Citadel – The Story of the U.S. Senate* by William S. White. The book was signed and given to Everett Hutchinson in honor of his birthday around 1956–1957. Everett Hutchinson had been a member of the Texas House of Representatives, chairman of the Interstate Commerce Commission, deputy secretary of the U.S. Department of Transportation and a former president of the Texas State Society of Washington, D.C.

This rare and authentic handwritten sentiment reads "To Everett Hutchinson, from his friend with the wish for many more Happy Birthdays," signed Lyndon B. Johnson.

## Autopen Signature as Senator (1949–1960)

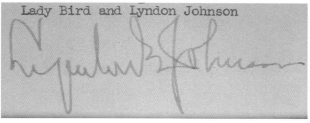

Autopen signature from a letter dated December 1960, as vice president elect. This same autopen can also be found during his later Senate years.

## Authentic Signature as Vice President (1961–1963)

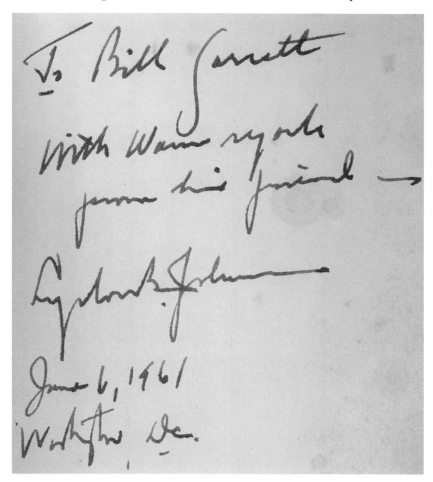

Authentic and very rare sentiment signed and dated June 6, 1961 by Vice President Johnson.

# Signatures as President (1963–1969)

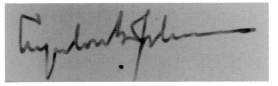

Authentic signature on signed photo dated early 1964.

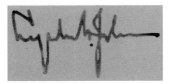

Authentic signature on signed photo dated December 1964.

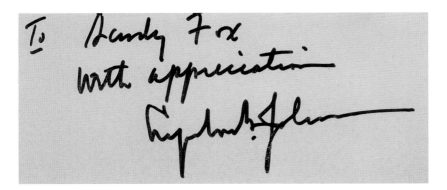

Authentic signature on photograph dated July 1966.

Authentic signature on photo mat board dated December 1966.

# Signatures as President (1963–1969)

Authentic signature from an *Air Force One* certificate dated

November 1967.

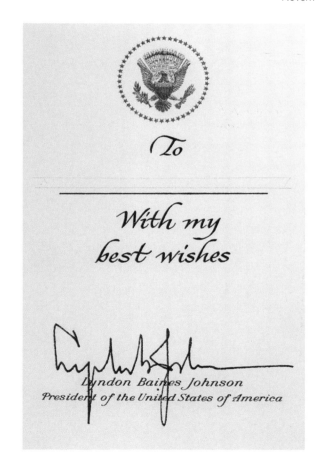

Pair of presidential bookplates with authentic signatures of President Johnson.

Note the bookplate on the left with handwritten calligraphy prepared by Sanford Fox.

These presidential bookplates are very scarce

The bookplates were prepared for the book *To Heal and to Build*
— *The Programs of President Lyndon B. Johnson*, published in 1968.

# Signatures as President

Believed to be an authentic signature in rare form on vellum paper, date unknown. Similar forms of this type of signature can be found on printed and franked material.

Autopen signature on White House card, date unknown.
Most likely a later presidential autopen.
Note the dot under the middle initial for this autopen.
Attributed to autopen Pattern III by Charles Hamilton.[13]

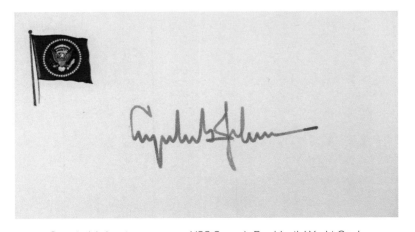

Secretarial signature on a rare *USS Sequoia* Presidential Yacht Card.
Date unknown, but most likely an early secretarial signature.
Most of these signature styles are attributed to Bruce Thomas.

# Signatures as President

Extremely rare autopen-signed 1968 presidential Christmas card.
Only 300 of these "unsigned" cards were produced by American
Greetings[14] (not to scale).

Full-scale photographs of the autopen signatures are shown
on the following page.

## Printed Signatures

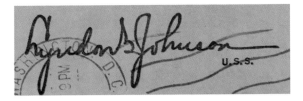

Printed franking signature on official government envelope as senator.

Printed franking signature on official government envelope as vice president.

Note—This same printed signature above can also be found on many of LBJ's Congress and Senate gallery passes. The use of this particular printed signature can be found in use as early as 1945.

Printed franking signature on official government envelope as president.

This was also used during his post-presidential years.

---

## Autopen Signatures

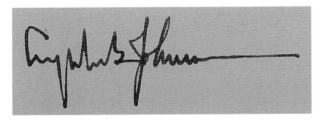

Autopen signature from 1968 presidential Christmas card.

Autopen signature from 1968 presidential Christmas card.

## Post Presidential Signatures (1969–1973)

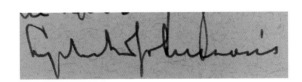

Authentic, post-presidential signature dated December 1970. Most LBJ post-presidential "full" signatures are found primarily on his bookplates.

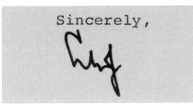

Authentic initials from a letter dated June 1971. This was his most typical way of signing during his retirement years.

Bookplate from *The Vantage Point* with authentic signature and date of signing

# Lady Bird Johnson

All signatures represented are to scale

## Signature from the Congressional years (1937–1948)

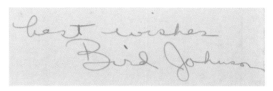

Early authentic signature from a personal note sent during
LBJ's candidacy for senator dated October 21,1948.

## Signature from the Senate years (1949–1961)

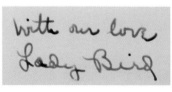

Sentiment and signature,
dated 1955.

## Autopen from the Senate years (1949–1961)

Autopen signature from a letter,
dated December 1960.

# Signatures as First Lady (1963–1969)

Early secretarial signature as first lady, dated December 10, 1963

This secretarial signature came from a letter that is considered to be one the first public correspondence by the first lady **(See page 132)**. A series of these letters were sent in response to the massive number of letters arriving at the White House concerning the death of John F. Kennedy. In her book, *Lady Bird Johnson – A White House Diary*, she mentions having several friends and associates over to The Elms to assist her in responding to the letters. Liz Carpenter also makes mention of this gathering in her book, *Ruffles and Flourishes*. Specifically, Mrs. Johnson mentions Wendy Marcus, Mrs. Oscar Chapman, Mrs. Eugene McCarthy, Mrs. Everett Hutchinson, Mrs. Hale Boggs, and Mrs. Frank Church as those that helped during this transition period.[15] Mr. George Meyer assisted with authenticating this particular signature.

Authentic signature on photograph,
dated December 1964.

Authentic signature on a letter sent to a congressman,
dated February 1965.

Authentic but unusual signature as first lady on a photograph,
date unknown.

# Signatures as First Lady

Authentic signature on White House letterhead sent to a personal
friend, dated August 23, 1967.

Autopen signature on letter dated February 14, 1968.
This is the same autopen signature that was used on the
1968 White House Christmas card.

Authentic sentiment and signature of Lady Bird Johnson, prepared for typesetting and printing.
From the Sanford L. Fox collection.

Note that the date of April 1968 was spliced into the sentiment and a 2" reduction request
was written on the left margin.

THE WHITE HOUSE
WASHINGTON

*With best wishes*
*Lady Bird Johnson*

Printed signature and sentiment on official White House card, date unknown.

*With best wishes*
*Lady Bird Johnson*

Authentic signature and sentiment on official White House card stock, date unknown. From the Sanford L. Fox collection.

This card may have been one of several that Mr. Fox had the first lady sign before choosing the most appropriate example for printing.

# Signatures as First Lady

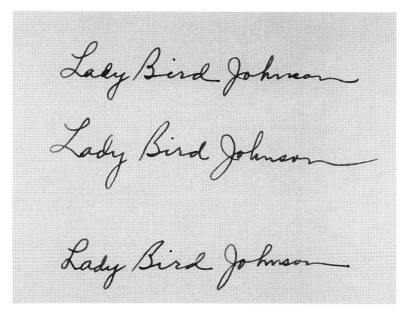

Three authentic signatures of Lady Bird Johnson on vellum paper, date unknown. From the Sanford L. Fox collection.

These signatures would have been sent to a printer and then used for White House cards, menus, invitations, state dinners, and other Programs.

Authentic signature on photo, signed during her final week as first lady, dated January 1969.

Merry Christmas ~ 1969!

We think of you often — and especially at Christmas! I remember with so much pleasure the beautiful and gracious things of those White House years — many

*Lady Bird and Lyndon Johnson*

from your talented hand. May 1970 bring you all the best —

*Lady Bird Johnson*

## Post-presidential Signatures (1969–Present)

Rare 1969 post-presidential LBJ ranch Christmas card, signed by Lady Bird Johnson.

This holiday card was sent to Sanford L. Fox.

# Post-presidential Signatures

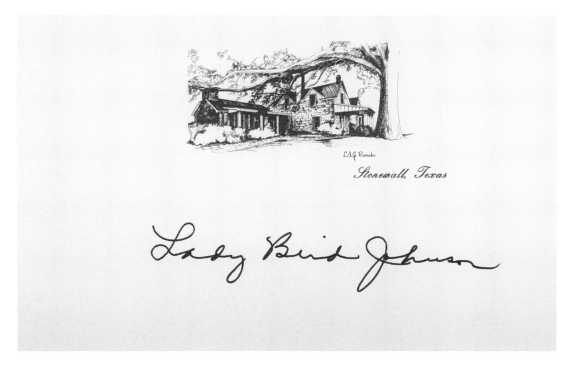

Authentic post-presidential signature on LBJ ranch card,

date unknown.

Authentic signature on photo mat board,

signed during the 1980s.

# Signatures of Lynda Bird Johnson

*Lynda Bird Johnson*

Authentic and early signature of Lynda Bird Johnson on vellum
paper, date unknown.

Sincerely,

*Lynda Johnson*

Lynda Bird Johnson

Authentic signature on a White House letter from Lynda Bird
Johnson. Dated October 4, 1967. Signed two months before she
became Mrs. Charles Robb.

*Lynda J Robb*

Authentic signature on White House photograph,
dated November 12, 1968.

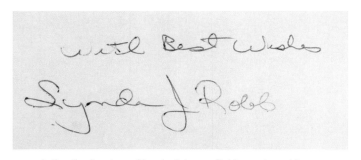

Authentic signature of Lynda Johnson Robb, post presidency.

# Signatures of Lynda Bird Johnson

THE WHITE HOUSE
WASHINGTON

May 15, 1968

Lynda:

Would you please do your signature -= in black
ink -- about 3 times on the bottom of this page.
We want to have a program for the children's
concert on Tuesday, the 21st -- and need to get
the signatures to the printers.    Thanks.
                                        Barbara
P.S. I think the news about the baby is wonderful!

Authentic internal White House letter to Lynda Johnson Robb requesting three

signatures for an upcoming children's program.

Dated May 15, 1968.

# Signatures of Luci Baines Johnson

Authentic signature of Luci Baines Johnson on
White House letter, dated June 20, 1966.

Authentic signatures on White House photo of both Luci Johnson
and Pat Nugent. Dated August 3, 1966, just three days before
their wedding.

Authentic signature and note to Sanford Fox from
Luci Johnson Nugent signed and dated in late 1966.

# Signatures of Luci Baines Johnson

Printed signature of Luci Johnson Nugent on White House card
stock, dated October 1967.

Authentic signature of Luci Baines Johnson, written on heavy card
stock, dated 1980s.

# White House Photographer
# Identification Stamps

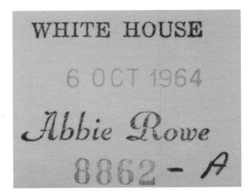

Scarce White House photographer's
stamp from a photograph by Abbie Rowe.

Reverse side photographer's stamp of Bob Knudsen,
taken during the Kennedy administration.

White House photographer's stamp of Cecil Stoughton, from the Johnson administration.

White House photographer's stamp of Michael Geissinger, from the Johnson administration.

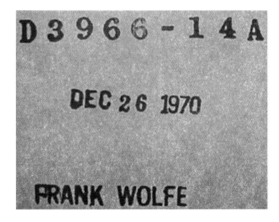

Photographer's stamp of Frank Wolfe, taken during the LBJ retirement years for the LBJ Library.

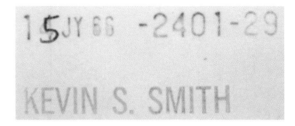

White House photographer's stamp of Kevin Smith, taken during the Johnson administration.

Scarce White House photographer's stamp of Don Stoderl, from the Johnson administration.

# Notes and Sources

## THE JOHNSON FAMILY

1   Robert A. Wilson, ed. *Character Above All.*
    Robert Dallek on Lyndon Johnson
    (New York: Simon and Schuster, 1995) p. 106.

2   Ibid, p. 106–107.

3   The White House
    <http://www.whitehouse.gov/history/presidents/lj36.html>
    July 16, 2002.

4   Lyndon Baines Johnson Library and Museum
    <http://www.lbjlib.utexas.edu/johnson/archives.hom/biographys.hom/
    ladybird_bio.asp>. July 6, 2003.

5   Doug Wead. "All the President's Children."
    <http://www.presidentschildren.com/list.htm#35>
    September 1, 2003.

6   Center for Politics at the University of Virginia.
    "Virginia Governor's Project - Charles S. Robb 1982–1986."
    <http://www.centerforpolitics.org/programs/govcon/robb_panelists-
    welcome.htm>. 2003.

7   Doug Wead. "All the President's Children."
    <http://www.presidentschildren.com/list.htm#35>.
    September 1, 2003.

8   Bill Wise. "Suddenly it's Teensville on Pennsylvania Avenue." *LIFE*
    15 May 1964, p. 94.

9   Doug Wead. "All the President's Children."
    <http://www.presidentschildren.com/list.htm#35>.
    September 1, 2003.

10  Carole Chandler. "Luci Baines Johnson – LBJ Holding Company"
    <http://www.utexas.edu/coc/journalism/SOURCE/adcouncil/johnson.
    html>.
    November 19, 1998.

## THE PHOTOGRAPHERS

1   "Frank Patrick Muto, 71, Photographer at Senate."
    *The Washington Post.*
    12 October, 1980, Metro Section, p. B6.

2   "Arnold Newman", PFA Newsletter
    *Photography in the Fine Arts Quarterly*, Vol 20, No. 1
    January 2003.

3   "Arnold Newman." A Gallery for Fine Photography.
    <http://www.agallery.com/Pages/photographers/newman.html>
    June 29, 2003.

4   "Robert Knudsen Dies; Photographer was 61." *New York Times*.
    January 31, 1989, p. D22.

5   "Terry Henion, Omahan Robert, L. Knudsen at the White House
    —Photographer of the Presidents."
    *Sunday World-Herald Magazine of the Midlands*.
    March 5, 1989, p. 16–17.

**6** Ibid. p. 17.

**7** "Robert Knudsen Dies; Photographer was 61."
*New York Times*. January 31, 1989, p. D22.

**8** Terry Henion, Omahan Robert L. Knudsen at the White House
—Photographer of the Presidents.
*Sunday World-Herald Magazine of the Midlands*.
March 5, 1989, p. 17.

**9** Ibid. p. 17.

**10** Ibid. p. 17.

**11** Personal interview with Cecil W. Stoughton. June 13, 2003.

**12** Cecil Stoughton and Major General Chester V. Clifton.
*The Memories – JFK, 1961–1963*.
(New York: W.W. Norton & Company, 1973) p. 199.

**13** Personal interview with Cecil W. Stoughton. June 13, 2003.

**14** "Picturing the Century: one hundred Years of Photography from the National
Archives."
<http://www.archives.gov/media_desk/press_kits/picturing_the_
century_kit.html>. June 22, 2003.

**15** Ibid.

**16** Personal interview with Frank L. Wolfe. August 15, 2003.

**17** Ibid.

**18** "Foggy Bottom Historic District"
*The National Parks Service – Washington, D.C.*
<http://www.cr.nps.gov/nr/travel/wash/dc20.htm>.
August 24, 2003.

**19** Personal interview with Kevin S. Smith. November 30, 2003.

**20** Personal interview with Michael A. Geissinger. July 31, 2003.

**21** Ibid.

## THE COLLECTION

**1** Guernsey's, A Division of Barlan Enterprises, Ltd.
*The Presidency, Rare Flags and Artifacts Relating to our Nation's History*.
(New York: Guerney's, 2002) p. 138.

**2** Ibid. p. 138.

**3** "Sanford L. Fox – White House Official." *The Washington Post*.
December 31, 1996, Metro Section, p. B4.

**4** Wanda Webb Evans.
*One Honest Man: George Mahon: A Story of Power, Politics and Poetry*.
(Texas: Staked Plains Press, 1978) p. 15.

**5** Ibid, p. 81.

**6** Oral History Interview between Joe Frantz and Congressman George Mahon
Lyndon Baines Johnson Library, Washington, D.C.
August 16, 1972.

**7**  Wanda Webb Evans.

*One Honest Man: George Mahon: A Story of Power, Politics and Poetry.*

(Texas: Staked Plains Press, 1978) p. 186.

**8**  Ibid, p. 16

## THE ART AND HISTORY OF PHOTOGRAPHY

**1**  Roger Hicks and Frances Schultz. *The Black and White Handbook*

*– The Ultimate Guide to Monochrome Techniques.*

(Great Britain: David & Charles, 1999) p. 130–145.

**2**  Michael Langford. *The Darkroom Handbook.*

(New York: Alfred A. Knopf, 1981) p. 112.

**3**  Ibid, p. 113.

**4**  Ibid, p. 56.

**5**  "Colour Printing Technique," *The Focal Encyclopedia of Photography.*

1971 ed.

**6**  Susan Kismaric.

*American Politicians – Photographs from 1843 to 1993.*

(New York: The Museum of Modern Art, 1994) p. 51.

## THE CONGRESS AND SENATE YEARS (1937–1960)

**1**  Kurt Singer and Jane Sherrod.

*Lyndon Baines Johnson – Man of Reason.*

(Minneapolis:T.S. Dennison & Company, 1964) p. 105.

**2**  Ibid. p.374–377.

**3**  Ronnie Dugger.

*The Politician – The Life and Times of Lyndon Johnson.*

(New York, W.W. Norton & Company, 1982) p. 299.

**4**  Merle Miller. *Lyndon – An Oral Biography.*

(New York: Ballantine Books, 1981) p. 135.

**5**  Ibid, p. 135.

**6**  Ibid, p. 136.

**7**  Ronnie Dugger.

*The Politician – The Life and Times of Lyndon Johnson.*

(New York, W.W. Norton & Company, 1982) p. 300.

**8**  Yoichi Okamoto. "Yoichi Okamoto and LBJ."

National Press Photographers Association, 1970.

**9**  Robert Dallek.

*Lone Star Rising – Lyndon Johnson and his Times 1908–1960.*

(New York, Oxford University Press, 1991) p. 285.

**10**  Ibid, p. 285.

**11**  Ronnie Dugger.

*The Politician – The Life and Times of Lyndon Johnson.*

(New York, W.W. Norton & Company, 1982) p. 141–142.

**12**  Merle Miller.

*Lyndon – An Oral Biography.*

(New York: Ballantine Books, 1981) p. 137.

13  Kurt Singer and Jane Sherrod.

*Lyndon Baines Johnson – Man of Reason*.

(Minneapolis: T.S. Dennison & Company, 1964) p. 182.

14  Merle Miller. *Lyndon – An Oral Biography*.

(New York: Ballantine Books, 1981) p. 143.

15  Paul K. Conkin.

*Big Daddy from the Pedernales*.

(Boston: Twayne Publishers, 1986) p.116.

16  Ibid. p. 116–117.

17  Doris Kearns.

*Lyndon Johnson and the American Dream*.

(New York: Harper & Row Publishers, 1976) p. 101.

18  Phillip Reed Rulon.

*The Compassionate Samaritan: The Life of Lyndon Baines Johnson*.

(Chicago: Nelson-Hall, 1981) p. 105.

19  Robert A. Caro.

*The Years of Lyndon Johnson – The Path to Power*.

(New York: Alfred A. Knopf, Inc., 1982) p. 170.

20  Jack Valenti. *A Very Human President*.

(New York: W.W. Norton & Company, Inc. 1975) p. 21.

21  Merle Miller. *Lyndon – An Oral Biography*.

(New York: Ballantine Books, 1981) p. 311.

22  G. L. Seligmann.

*The Vice Presidents – A Biographical Dictionary*.

ed. L. Edward Purcell.

(New York: Facts on File, 1998) p. 334.

23  Robert A. Caro.

*The Years of Lyndon Johnson – The Path to Power*.

(New York: Alfred A. Knopf, Inc., 1982) p. 92.

24  Theodore H. White.

*The Making of the President 1960*.

(New York: Athenem Publishers, 1961) p. 115.

25  Paul F. Boller, Jr.

*Presidential Campaigns*.

(New York: Oxford University Press, 1984) p. 298.

26  John Fitzgerald Kennedy Library, Address of Senator John F. Kennedy to the Greater Houston Ministerial Association Rice Hotel, Houston, Texas, September 12, 1960.
<http://www.cs.umb.edu/jfklibrary/j091260.htm>.
October 27, 2002.

27  The JFK Link, Remarks of Senator John F. Kennedy, Capitol Steps, Austin, Texas, September 13, 1960.
<http://www.jfklink.com/speeches/jfk/sept60/jfk130960_austin.html>.
March, 1999.

28  Press Release of Address by Senator Lyndon B. Johnson at Democratic Rally in Albuquerque, New Mexico.
Wednesday, September 14, 1960. Statements, Box 41, LBJ Library.

29  Transcript of 2nd Draft of Speech by Senator Lyndon B. Johnson for public address in Tucson, Arizona. Draft 9/10/60. Statements, Box 41, LBJ Library.

30  Ruth Montgomery. *Mrs. LBJ.*

    (New York: Holt, Rinehart and Winston, 1964) p. 147.

31  Transcript of Recorded Remarks by Senator Lyndon B. Johnson and

    former President Harry S. Truman in Kansas City, Missouri. July 29, 1960.

    Statements, Box 40, LBJ Library.

32  Transcript of Recorded Remarks by Senator Lyndon B. Johnson at

    Washington Park, Quincy, Illinois,

    September 27, 1960. Statements, Box 42, LBJ Library.

33  Ibid, Statements, Box 42, LBJ Library.

34  John Splaine.

    *The Road to the White House since Television.*

    (Washington, D.C.: C-SPAN, 1995) p. 54–55.

35  Transcript of Recorded Remarks by Senator Lyndon B. Johnson at City Hall,

    Columbus, Ohio,

    September 29, 1960. Statement, Box 43, LBJ Library.

36  Transcript of Recorded Remarks by Senator Lyndon B. Johnson at Democratic

    Rally in Jackson, Tennessee,

    September 30, 1960. Statements, Box 43, LBJ Library.

37  Bobby Baker. *Wheeling and Dealing.*

    (New York: W.W. Norton & Company, Inc. 1978) p. 134–135.

38  Transcript of Recorded Remarks by Senator Lyndon B. Johnson at Democratic

    Dinner in Knoxville, Tennessee,

    September 30, 1960. Statements, Box 43, LBJ Library.

39  John Splaine.

    *The Road to the White House since Television.*

    (Washington, D.C.: C-SPAN, 1995) p. 59–61.

40  Ibid., p. 61.

41  Theodore H. White. *The Making of the President 1960.*

    (New York: Athenem Publishers, 1961) p. 322.

42  Final Draft Dated 9/30/60 of Speech Delivered by Senator Lyndon B.

    Johnson to New Rochelle College in New Rochelle, New York,

    October 4, 1960. Statements, Box 44, LBJ Library.

43  Transcript of Recorded Remarks by Senator Lyndon B. Johnson at a Dinner

    Held at the Commonwealth Club in Richmond, Virginia,

    October 6, 1960. Statements, Box 44, LBJ Library.

44  Harry Provence. *Lyndon B. Johnson.*

    (New York: Fleet Publishing Corporation, 1964) p. 130.

45  Robert Dallek.

    *Lone Star Rising – Lyndon Johnson and his Times 1908–1960.*

    (New York, Oxford University Press, 1991) p. 586.

46  Harry Provence. *Lyndon B. Johnson.*

    (New York: Fleet Publishing Corporation, 1964) p. 130.

47  Final Draft dated 10/13/60 of Speech Delivered by Senator Lyndon B.

    Johnson in Allentown, Pennsylvania,

    October 18, 1960. Statements, Box 46, LBJ Library.

48  Final Draft dated 10/13/60 of Speech Delivered by Senator Lyndon B.

    Johnson in Sunbury, Pennsylvania,

    October 18, 1960. Statements, Box 46, LBJ Library.

**49** Transcript of Recorded Remarks by Senator Lyndon B. Johnson at the Democratic Rally Held at the Corpus Christi Airport in Corpus Christi, Texas, November 6, 1960. Statements, Box 50, LBJ Library.

**50** Transcript of Recorded Remarks by Senator Lyndon B. Johnson in Shamokin, Pennsylvania, October 18, 1960. Statements, pg. 9, Box 46, LBJ Library.

**51** Joseph Nathan kane. *Facts About the Presidents*. (New York, H.W. Wilson Co., 1989) p. 225.

**52** John Splaine. *The Road to the White House since Television*. (Washington, D.C.: C-SPAN, 1995) p. 62–64.

# THE VICE PRESIDENCY (1961–1963)

**1** Merle Miller. *Lyndon – An Oral Biography*. (New York: Ballantine Books, 1981) p. 338.

**2** William McGaffin. "The Quiet Man – Capitol Hill Wondering: What's Johnson Up To?" *Dallas Times Herrald*. 24 June 1962, p. 22-A.

**3** Kurt Singer and Jane Sherrod. "Lyndon Baines Johnson—Man of Reason" (Minneapolis, T.S. Denison, 1964) p. 288.

**4** Richard Harwood and Haynes Johnson. *Lyndon*. (New York: 1973) p. 57.

**5** Merle Miller. *Lyndon – An Oral Biography*. (New York: Ballantine Books, 1981) p. 342.

**6** Jack Bell. "LBJ becomes Strongest of U.S. Vice Presidents." *Dallas Times Herald*. 19 December 1962.

**7** Harry Provence. *Lyndon B. Johnson*. (New York: Fleet Publishing Corporation, 1964) p. 139–145.

**8** Ruth Montgomery. *Mrs. LBJ*. (New York: Holt, Rinehart and Winston, 1964) p. 160.

**9** Harry Provence. *Lyndon B. Johnson*. (New York: Fleet Publishing Corporation, 1964) p. 151.

**10** Doris Kearns. *Lyndon Johnson and the American Dream*. (New York: Harper & Row, 1976) p. 164.

**11** "Foreign Relations – Smoothed Feathers." *Time*. April 21, 1961, p. 19.

**12** William J. Jorden. "Texas Welcomes Adenauer with Cheers and Barbecue." *The New York Times*. April 17, 1961, p.1.

**13** J. A. Sierra. *The Timetable History of Cuba*. <http://www.historyofcuba.com/history/baypigs.htm>. March 18, 2003.

**14** Robert Dallek. *Flawed Giant – Lyndon Johnson and His Times 1961-1973*. (New York: Oxford University Press, 1998). p. 16–17.

**15** Jimmy Banks.
"Adenauer's Visit Spurs Austin Ticket Demands."
*The Dallas Morning News.*
April 16, 1961, Section 1, p. 7.

**16** *Journal of the Senate of the State of Texas.*
Regular Session, 57th Legislature.
(Austin, Texas: Von Boeckmann-Jones Co., 1961) p.752–756.

**17** Merle Miller. Lyndon – An Oral Biography.
(New York: Ballantine Books, 1981) p. 351.

**18** Tom Wicker. "Kennedy Renews Pledge to Taiwan."
*The New York Times.* August 3, 1961, p. 1–9.

**19** John Woolley and Gerhard Peters.
*The American Presidency Project.*
<http://www.presidency.ucsb.edu/site/docs/pppus.php?admin=035&year=1961&id=306>.
University of California, Santa Barbara, April 26, 2003.

**20** Lewis L. Gould.
*Lady Bird Johnson and the Environment.*
(Kansas, University Press of Kansas, 1988) p. 20.

**21** Lady Bird Johnson. *A White House Diary.*
(New York:Holt, Rinehart & Wilson, 1970) p. 20.

**22** Ibid. p. 115.

**23** Ibid. p. 127.

**24** Doris Kearns. *Lyndon Johnson and the American Dream.*
p. 145, Quoted from Lyndon Johnson, Speech before Senate Democratic Caucus, January 7, 1958.

**25** John Fitzgerald Kennedy Library, Special Message to the Congress on Urgent National Needs, Washington, D.C., May 25, 1961,
<http://www.jfklibrary.org/j052561.htm>.
May 24, 2003.

**26** "Space." *Time.* February 23, 1962, p. 26.

**27** Kennedy Space Center.
The Mercury Program – Friendship 7 MA-6.
<http://www-pao.ksc.nasa.gov/kscpao/history/mercury/ma-6/ma-6.htm>.
May 25, 2003.

**28** Ohio State University Archives. Celebration of the Flight of Friendship 7.
<http://www.lib.ohio-state.edu/arvweb/glenn/celebration/celebration.htm>.
May 25, 2003.

**29** John Glenn and Nick Taylor. *John Glenn – A Memoir.*
(New York: Bantam Books, 1999) p. 278.

**30** Ibid., p. 278–279.

**31** Ibid., p. 279.

**32** Ohio State University Archives. Celebration of the Flight of Friendship 7.
<http://www.lib.ohio-state.edu/arvweb/glenn/celebration/celebration.htm>.
May 25, 2003.

**33** Lt. Colonel USMC John H. Glenn, Jr. "A New Era."
Speech Delivered to a Joint Session of Congress, Washington, D.C., February 26, 1962. *Vital Speeches of the Day*, Vol. XXVIII, No. 11, March 15, 1962, p. 325–326.

**34** "The Space Challenge." John F. Kennedy, President of the United States.
Speech Delivered at Rice University, Houston, Texas, September 13, 1962. *Vital Speeches of the Day*, Vol. XXVIII, No. 24, October 1, 1962, p. 739–740.

**35** Alan Ladwig. "When Cape Crusaders Played Florida's Name Game."
*Space.com*.
<http://www. space.com/news/spacehistory/cape_kennedy_000511.html>.
May 13, 2000.

**36** Charles D. Benson and William Barnaby Faherty.
"Moonport: A History of Apollo Launch Facilities and Operations."
*NASA Special Publication-4204*, 1978.
<http://www.hq.nasa.gov/office/pao/History/SP-4204/ch7-7.html>.
May 28, 2003.

## THE TRIP TO TEXAS–NOVEMBER 1960

**1** Arthur M. Schlesinger, Jr.
*A Thousand Days – John F. Kennedy in the White House*.
(New York: Crown Publishers, 1965) p. 1019.

**2** Richard B. Trask. *Pictures of the Pain: Photography and the Assassination of President Kennedy*
(Massachusetts: Yeoman Press, 1994) p. 30–34.

**3** Ibid. p. 37.

**4** Ibid. p. 336.

**5** Oral History Interview between Joe Frantz and Congressman George Mahon, Lyndon Baines Johnson Library, Washington, D.C., August 16, 1972.

**6** Richard B. Trask.
*Pictures of the Pain: Photography and the Assassination of President Kennedy*
(Massachusetts: Yeoman Press, 1994) p. 45–49.

**7** Oral History Interview between Joe B. Frantz and Cecil Stoughton.
Lyndon Baines Johnson Library, Washington, D.C.
March 1, 1971.

**8** Wanda Webb Evans.
*One Honest Man: George Mahon: A Story of Power*.
Politics and Poetry.
(Texas: Staked Plains Press, 1978) p. 185–186.

**9** Lady Bird Johnson, *A White House Diary*. Photograph "Answering mail at The Elms."
(New York:Holt, Rinehart & Wilson, 1970).

**10** Public Papers of the Presidents of the United States: Lyndon B. Johnson, 1963.
(Washington, D.C.: Government Printing Office).

## THE PRESIDENCY (1963–1969)

**1** Paul F. Boller, Jr. *Presidential Campaigns*.
(New York: Oxford University Press, 1984) p. 308.

**2** Ibid. p. 308.

3   Evan Cornog.

    *Hats in the Ring: An Illustrated History of American Presidential Campaigns.*

    (New York: Random House, 2000) p. 259.

4   Paul F. Boller, Jr. *Presidential Campaigns.*

    (New York: Oxford University Press, 1984) p. 312.

5   John Splaine.

    *The Road to the White House since Television.*

    (Washington, D.C.: C-SPAN, 1995) p. 80, 209.

6   MacNeil/Lehrer Productions and KLRU.

    "Lady Bird Johnson – Portrait of a First Lady."

    <http://www.pbs.org/ladybird/epicenter/epicenter_report_train.html>.

    November 11, 2004.

7   Public Papers of the Presidents of the United States: Lyndon B. Johnson,

    1965, Volume II.

    (Washington, D. C.: Government Printing Office, 1965), entry 628,

    pp. 1215–1217.

8   Oral History Interview between Joe Frantz and Cecil Stoughton, Lyndon

    Baines Johnson Library, Washington, D.C.,

    Mach 2, 1971.

9   Public Papers of the Presidents of the United States: Lyndon B. Johnson,

    1963-1969.

    (Washington, D. C.: Government Printing Office).

10  Frances Spatz Leighton. *The Johnson Wit.*

    (New York: The Citadel Press, 1965) p. 15.

11  Liz Carpenter. *Ruffles and Flourishes.*

    (New York: Doubleday & Company, 1970) p. 102.

12  Robert Wallace. "A National Yelp Over an Earlift."

    *LIFE.*

    8 May 1964, p. 34A.

13  Traphes Bryant and Frances Spatz Leighton.

    *Dog Days at the White House: The Outrageous Memoirs of the Presidential Kennel Keeper.*

    (New York: MacMillan Publishing Company, 1975) p. 87.

14  Ibid, p. 166.

15  Ibid, p. 232.

16  Personal Correspondence with Virginia Travell Street,

    June 14, 2004.

17  Biographical Directory of the United States Congress,

    <http://bioguide.congess.gov/scripts/biodisplay.pl?index=R000295>.

    August 24, 2002.

18  Liz Carpenter. *Ruffles and Flourishes.*

    (New York:Doubleday & Company, 1970) p. 218.

19  Ellen Proxmire.

    *One Foot in Washington – The Perilous Life of a Senator's Wife.*

    (Washington, D.C., 1963) p. 40.

20  Lady Bird Johnson. *A White House Diary.*

    (New York:Holt, Rinehart & Wilson, 1970) p. 601.

21  Ibid, p. 599.

22  Liz Carpenter. *Ruffles and Flourishes.*

    (New York:Doubleday & Company, 1970) p. 291–293.

**23**  Wilbur Cross and Ann Novotny.

*White House Weddings.*

(New York: David McKay Company, 1967) p. 216–236.

**24**  Lyndon Baines Johnson.

*The Vantage Point:Perspectives of the President 1963–1969.*

(New York: Holt, Rinehart and Winston, 1971) p. 538.

**25**  Liz Carpenter.

*Ruffles and Flourishes.*

(New York: Doubleday & Company, 1970) p. 332–333.

**26**  Personal Interview with Kevin S. Smith.

November 30, 2003.

**27**  Charles Hamilton.

*The Robot that Helped Make a President: A Reconnaissance into the Mysteries of John F. Kennedy's Signature.*

(New York,1965) p. 22–23.

**28**  Mary Evans Seeley.

*Seasons Greetings from the White House.*

(Florida: A Presidential Christmas Corporation, 1998) p.93.

**29**  Personal Interview with Cecil W. Stoughton

June 13, 2003.

**30**  Mary Evans Seeley. *Seasons Greetings from the White House.*

(Florida: A Presidential Christmas Corporation, 1998) p. 102.

**31**  James MacGregor Burns, ed.

*To Heal and to Build: The Programs of President Lyndon B. Johnson*

(New York: McGraw-Hill Book Company, 1968) p. 293.

**32**  Mary Evans Seeley.

*Seasons Greetings from the White House.*

(Florida: A Presidential Christmas Corporation, 1998) p. 105.

**33**  Ibid, p. 109.

**34**  Ibid, p. 109-110.

**35**  Mary Evans Seeley. *Seasons Greetings from the White House.*

(Florida: A Presidential Christmas Corporation, 1998) p. 111.

**36**  Ibid, p. 114.

**37**  Lady Bird Johnson. *A White House Diary.*

(New York: Holt, Rinehart, Wilson, 1970) p. 759–760.

**38**  Ibid, p. 760.

## BACK AT THE RANCH—THE RETIREMENT YEARS (1969–1973)

**1**  Lyndon Baines Johnson.

*The Vantage Point:Perspectives of the President 1963–1969.*

(New York:Holt, Rinehart and Winston, 1971) p. X.

**2**  Paul K. Conkin. *Big Daddy from the Pedernales.*

(Boston: Twayne Publishers, 1986) p. 296.

**3**  Joint Committee on Printing.

*Memorial Services in the Congress of the United States and Tributes in Eulogy of Lyndon Baines Johnson—Late a President of the United States.*

93rd Congress, 1st session.

(Washington, D.C., Government Printing Office, 1973) pp. xvii–xxvi.

**4**   Ibid, pp. 33–34.

## SIGNATURE STUDY

**1**   Memo. Mary Rather to Senator Lyndon B. Johnson.
1/11/56, LBJ Library.

**2**   Letter. Gene Latimer.
9/4/83, LBJ Autograph Folder, LBJ Library.

**3**   Memo. Oral Reference Request from John Doe.
12/14/99, LBJ Autograph Folder, LBJ Library.

**4**   Charles Hamilton. *American Autographs*.
(Oklahoma: University of Oklahoma Press, 1983) p. 570.

**5**   Memo. Arthur C. Perry to Senator Johnson.
4/28/53, LBJ Autograph Folder, LBJ Library.

**6**   Memo. Tina Houston to Harry Middleton/Charles Corkran.
11/22/88, LBJ Autograph Folder, LBJ Library.

**7**   Memo. Tina Lawson to *For the Record*.
10/28/85, LBJ Autograph Folder, LBJ Library.

**8**   Letter. Betty Tilson.
10/27/83, LBJ Autograph Folder, LBJ Library.

**9**   John Reznikoff and Stuart Lutz. "Super Secretaries."
*Autograph Collector*. July 1977, p. 57.

**10**   Charles Hamilton. *The Robot That Helped to Make a President*.
(New York, 1965) p. 6–9.

**11**   Robert De Shazo.
"History." Automated Signature Technology.
<http://www.signaturemachine.com/company/about.htm>.
November 15, 2003.

**12**   David Laurell. "The Dreaded Autopen."
*Autograph Collector*.
December 2003, p. 47.

**13**   Charles Hamilton. *American Autographs*.
(Oklahoma: University of Oklahoma Press, 1983) p. 570.

**14**   Mary Evans Seeley.
*Seasons Greetings from the White House*.
(Florida: A Presidential Christmas Corporation, 1998) p. 114.

**15**   Lady Bird Johnson. *A White House Diary*.
First Photographic Section after Page 182.
(New York: Holt, Rinehart & Wilson, 1970)

# Bibliography

# BOOKS

Austin, Texas.
*Journal of the Senate of the State of Texas.*
Regular Session, 57th Legislature, Austin, Texas: Von Boeckmann-Jones Co., 1961.

Baker, Bobby.
*Wheeling and Dealing.*
New York: W.W. Norton & Company, Inc. 1978.

Boller, Paul F., Jr.
*Presidential Campaigns.*
New York: Oxford University Press, 1984.

Bryant, Traphes and Frances Spatz Leighton.
*Dog Days at the White House: The Outrageous Memoirs of the Presidential Kennel Keeper*
New York: MacMillan Publishing Company, 1975.

Burns, James MacGregor, ed.
*To Heal and to Build: The Programs of President Lyndon B. Johnson*
New York: McGraw-Hill Book Company, 1968.

Caro, Robert A.
*The Years of Lyndon Johnson – The Path to Power.*
New York: Alfred A. Knopf, Inc., 1982.

Carpenter, Liz.
*Ruffles and Flourishes.*
New York: Doubleday & Company, 1970.

Colour Printing Technique.
*The Focal Encyclopedia of Photography.*
1971 ed.

Conkin, Paul K.
*Big Daddy from the Pedernales.*
Boston: Twayne Publishers, 1986.

Cornog, Evan.
*Hats in the Ring: An Illustrated History of American Presidential Campaigns.*
New York: Random House, 2000.

Cross, Wilbur and Ann Novotny.
*White House Weddings.*
New York: David McKay Company, 1967.

Dallek, Robert.
*Flawed Giant: Lyndon Johnson and His Times 1961–1973.*
New York: Oxford University Press, 1998.

Dallek, Robert.
*Lone Star Rising—Lyndon Johnson and his Times 1908–1960.*
New York, Oxford University Press, 1991.

Dugger, Ronnie.
*The Politician—The Life and Times of Lyndon Johnson.*
New York, W.W. Norton & Company, 1982.

Evans, Wanda Webb
*One Honest Man: George Mahon: A Story of Power, Politics and Poetry.*
Texas: Staked Plains Press, 1978.

Glenn, John and Nick Taylor.
*John Glenn—A Memoir.*
New York: Bantam Books, 1999.

Gould, Lewis L.
*Lady Bird Johnson and the Environment.*
Kansas: University Press of Kansas, 1988.

Guernsey's, A Division of Barlan Enterprises, Ltd.
*The Presidency, Rare Flags and Artifacts Relating to our Nation's History.*
New York: Guerney's, 2002.

Hamilton, Charles.
*American Autographs.*
Oklahoma: University of Oklahoma Press, 1983.

Hamilton, Charles.
*The Robot That Helped Make a President: A Reconnaissance into the Mysteries of John F. Kennedy's Signature.*
New York,1965.

Harwood, Richard and Haynes Johnson. *Lyndon.*
New York: 1973.

Hicks, Roger and Frances Schultz.
*The Black and White Handbook: The Ultimate Guide to Monochrome Techniques.*
Great Britain: David & Charles, 1999.

Johnson, Lady Bird.
*A White House Diary.*
New York: Holt, Rinehart & Wilson, 1970.

Johnson, Lyndon Baines.
*The Vantage Point: Perspectives of the President 1963–1969.*
New York: Holt, Rinehart and Winston, 1971.

Kane, Joseph Nathan.
*Facts About the Presidents.*
New York: H.W. Wilson Co., 1989.

Kearns, Doris.
*Lyndon Johnson and the American Dream.*
New York: Harper & Row Publishers, 1976.

Kismaric, Susan.
*American Politicians: Photographs from 1843 to 1993.*
New York: The Museum of Modern Art, 1994.

Langford, Michael. *The Darkroom Handbook.*
New York: Alfred A. Knopf, 1981.

Leighton, Frances Spatz.
*The Johnson Wit.*
New York: The Citadel Press, 1965.

Miller, Merle.
*Lyndon: An Oral Biography.*
New York: Ballantine Books, 1981.

Montgomery, Ruth. *Mrs. LBJ.*
New York: Holt, Rinehart and Winston, 1964.

Provence, Harry. *Lyndon B. Johnson.*
New York: Fleet Publishing Corporation, 1964.

Proxmire, Ellen.
*One Foot in Washington—The Perilous Life of a Senator's Wife.*
Washington, D.C., 1963.

Public Papers of the Presidents of the United States: Lyndon B. Johnson, 1965.
Volume I, Washington, D. C.: Government Printing Office, 1965.

Rulon, Philip Reed.
*The Compassionate Samaritan: The Life of Lyndon Baines Johnson.*
Chicago: Nelson-Hall Publishers, 1981.

Schlesinger, Arthur M., Jr.
*A Thousand Days – John F. Kennedy in the White House.*
New York: Crown Publishers, 1965.

Seeley, Mary Evans.
*Seasons Greetings from the White House.*
Florida: A Presidential Christmas Corporation, 1998.

Seligmann, G. L.
*The Vice Presidents: A Biographical Dictionary.*
ed. L. Edward Purcell, New York: Facts on File, 1998.

Singer, Kurt and Jane Sherrod.
*Lyndon Baines Johnson: Man of Reason.*
Minneapolis: T.S. Dennison & Company, 1964.

Splaine, John, "The Road to the White House since Television," Washington, D.C.: C-SPAN, 1995.

Stoughton, Cecil and Major General Chester V. Clifton.
*The Memories: JFK, 1961–1963.*
New York: W.W. Norton & Company, 1973.

Trask, Richard B.
*Pictures of the Pain: Photography and the Assassination of President Kennedy.*
Massachusetts: Yeoman Press, 1994.

Valenti, Jack.
*A Very Human President.*
New York: W.W. Norton & Company, Inc. 1975.

White, Theodore H.
*The Making of the President 1960.*
New York: Athenem Publishers, 1961.

Wilson, Robert A., ed.
*Character Above All.*
New York: Simon and Schuster, 1995.

## Magazines, Newspapers and Periodicals

Anonymous. "Arnold Newman." PFA Newsletter.
*Photography in the Fine Arts Quarterly.*
Vol 20, No. 1, January 2003.

Anonymous. "Foreign Relations—Smoothed Feathers."
*Time.* April 21, 1961.

Anonymous. "Frank Patrick Muto, 71, Photographer at Senate."
*The Washington Post.* 12 October, 1980.

Anonymous. "Robert Knudsen Dies; Photographer was 61."
*New York Times.* January 31, 1989.

Anonymous. "Sanford L. Fox—White House Official."
*The Washington Post.* December 31, 1996.

Anonymous. "Space." *Time.*
February 23, 1962.

Banks, Jimmy. "Adenauer's Visit Spurs Austin Ticket Demands."
*The Dallas Morning News.* April 16, 1961.

Bell, Jack. "LBJ becomes Strongest of U.S. Vice Presidents."
*Dallas Times Herald.* 19 December 1962.

Henion, Terry. "Omahan Robert L. Knudsen at the White House—Photographer of the Presidents."
*Sunday World-Herald Magazine of the Midlands.*
March 5, 1989.

Joint Committee on Printing.
*Memorial Services in the Congress of the United States and Tributes in Eulogy of Lyndon Baines Johnson—Late a President of the United States.*
93rd Congress, 1st session, Washington, D.C., Government Printing Office, 1973.

Jorden, William J. "Texas Welcomes Adenauer with Cheers and Barbecue."
*The New York Times.* April 17, 1961.

McGaffin, William. "The Quiet Man—Capitol Hill Wondering: What's Johnson Up To?"
*Dallas Times Herald.* 24 June 1962.

Okamoto, Yoichi. "Yoichi Okamoto and LBJ."
*National Press Photographers Association.* 1970.

Reznikoff, John and Stuart Lutz. "Super Secretaries."
*Autograph Collector.*
July 1977.

Wallace, Robert. "A National Yelp Over an Earlift."
*LIFE.* 8 May 1964.

Wicker, Tom. "Kennedy Renews Pledge to Taiwan."
*The New York Times.*
August 3, 1961.

Wise, Bill. "Suddenly It's Teensville on Pennsylvania Avenue" *LIFE*. 15 May 1964.

## INTERVIEWS AND CORRESPONDENCE

Geissinger, Michael A. Personal Interview. July 31, 2003.

Mahon, George. Oral History Interview between Joe Frantz and Congressman George Mahon. Lyndon Baines Johnson Library, Washington, D.C., August 16, 1972.

Smith, Kevin S. Personal Interview. November 30, 2003.

Stoughton, Cecil. Personal Interview. June 13, 2003.

Stoughton, Cecil. Oral History Interview between Joe B. Frantz and Cecil Stoughton. Lyndon Baines Johnson Library, Washington, D.C. March 1, 1971.

Street, Virginia Travell. Personal correspondence. June 14, 2004.

Wolf, Francis L. Personal interview. August 15, 2003.

## PUBLIC TRANSCRIPTS

Anonymous.
Memo, Oral Reference Request from John Doe. 12/14/99. LBJ Autograph Folder, LBJ Library.

Glenn, John H. "A New Era." Lt. Colonel USMC John H. Glenn, Jr., Speech Delivered to a Joint Session of Congress, Washington, D.C., February 26, 1962. *Vital Speeches of the Day*, Vol. XXVIII, No. 11, March 15, 1962.

Houston, Tina. Memo, Tina Houston to Harry Middleton/Charles Corkran. 11/22/88. LBJ Autograph Folder, LBJ Library.

Johnson, Lyndon Baines.
Final Draft Dated 10/13/60 of Speech Delivered by Senator Lyndon B.

Johnson in Allentown, Pennsylvania. October 18, 1960. Statements, Box 46, LBJ Library.

Johnson, Lyndon Baines.
Final Draft Dated 10/13/60 of Speech Delivered by Senator Lyndon B. Johnson in Sunbury, Pennsylvania. October 18, 1960. Statements, Box 46, LBJ Library.

Johnson, Lyndon Baines.
Final Draft Dated 9/30/60 of Speech Delivered by Senator Lyndon B. Johnson to New Rochelle College in New Rochelle, New York. October 4, 1960. Statements, Box 44, LBJ Library.

Johnson, Lyndon Baines.
Press Release of Address by Senator Lyndon B. Johnson at Democratic Rally in Albuquerque, New Mexico. Wednesday, September 14, 1960. Statements, Box 41, LBJ Library.

Johnson, Lyndon Baines.
Transcript of 2nd Draft of Speech by Senator Lyndon B. Johnson for Public Address in Tucson, Arizona. Draft 9/10/60. Statements, Box 41, LBJ Library.

Johnson, Lyndon Baines.
Transcript of Recorded Remarks by Senator Lyndon B. Johnson at Washington Park, Quincy, Illinois. September 27, 1960. Statements, Box 42, LBJ Library.

Johnson, Lyndon Baines.
Transcript of Recorded Remarks by Senator Lyndon B. Johnson at City Hall, Columbus, Ohio. September 29, 1960. Statement, Box 43, LBJ Library.

Johnson, Lyndon Baines.
Transcript of Recorded Remarks by Senator Lyndon B. Johnson at Democratic Rally in Jackson, Tennessee. September 30, 1960. Statements, Box 43, LBJ Library.

Johnson, Lyndon Baines.
Transcript of Recorded Remarks by Senator Lyndon B. Johnson at Democratic Dinner in Knoxville, Tennessee. September 30, 1960. Statements, Box 43, LBJ Library.

Johnson, Lyndon Baines.
Transcript of Recorded Remarks by Senator Lyndon B. Johnson at a Dinner
Held at the Commonwealth Club in Richmond, Virginia. October 6, 1960.
Statements, Box 44, LBJ Library.

Johnson, Lyndon Baines.
Transcript of Recorded Remarks by Senator Lyndon B. Johnson at the
Democratic Rally Held at the Corpus Christi Airport in Corpus Christi, Texas.
November 6, 1960. Statements, Box 50, LBJ Library.

Johnson, Lyndon Baines.
Transcript of Recorded Remarks by Senator Lyndon B. Johnson in Shamokin,
Pennsylvania, October 18, 1960. Statements, pg. 9, Box 46, LBJ Library.

Kennedy, John F.
"The Space Challenge." by John F. Kennedy, President of the United States,
Speech Delivered at Rice University, Houston, Texas, September 13, 1962,
*Vital Speeches of the Day*, Vol. XXVIII, No. 24, October 1, 1962.

Latimer, Gene.
Letter, Gene Latimer, 9/4/83, LBJ Autograph Folder, LBJ Library.

Lawson, Tina.
Memo, Tina Lawson to *For the Record*, 10/28/85, LBJ Autograph Folder, LBJ
Library.

Perry, Arthur C.
Memo, Arthur C. Perry to Senator Johnson, 4/28/53, LBJ Autograph Folder,
LBJ Library.

Rather, Mary.
Memo, Mary Rather to Senator Lyndon B. Johnson, 1/11/56, LBJ Library.

Tilson, Betty.
Letter, Betty Tilson, 10/27/83, LBJ Autograph Folder, LBJ Library.

## INTERNET SOURCES

Benson, Charles D. and William Barnaby Faherty.
"Moonport: A History of Apollo Launch Facilities and Operations."
*NASA Special Publication-4204*, 1978.
<http://www.hq.nasa.gov/office/pao/History/SP-4204/ch7-7.html>.
May 28, 2003.

Center for Politics at the University of Virginia.
"Virginia Governor's Project—Charles S. Robb 1982–1986."
<http://www.centerforpolitics.org/programs/govcon/robb_panelists-
welcome.htm>.
2003.

Chandler, Carole.
"Luci Baines Johnson— LBJ Holding Company."
<http://www.utexas.edu/coc/journalism/SOURCE/adcouncil/johnson.html>.
November 19, 1998.

"Foggy Bottom Historic District."
*The National Parks Service – Washington, D.C.*
<http://www.cr.nps.gov/nr/travel/wash/dc20.htm>.
August 24, 2003.

JFK Link, Remarks of Senator John F. Kennedy.
Capitol Steps, Austin, Texas, September 13, 1960.
<http://www.jfklink.com/speeches/jfk/sept60/jfk130960_austin.html>.
March, 1999.

John Fitzgerald Kennedy Library.
Address of Senator John F. Kennedy to the Greater Houston Ministerial
Association, Rice Hotel, Houston, Texas September 12, 1960.
<http://www.cs.umb.edu/jfklibrary/j091260.htm>.
October 27, 2002.

John Fitzgerald Kennedy Library.
Special Message to the Congress on Urgent National Needs, Washington,
D.C., May 25, 1961. <http://www.jfklibrary.org/j052561.htm>.
May 24, 2003.

Kennedy Space Center.
The Mercury Program—*Friendship 7* MA-6.
<http://www-pao.ksc.nasa.gov/kscpao/history/mercury/ma-6/ma-6.htm>.
May 25, 2003.

Ladwig, Alan.
"When Cape Crusaders Played Florida's Name Game." *Space.com*
<http:/www.space.com/news/spacehistory/cape_kennedy_000511.html>.
May 13, 2000.

Lyndon Baines Johnson Library and Museum.
<http://www.lbjlib.utexas.edu/johnson/archives.hom/biographys.hom/ladybird_bio.asp>.
July 6, 2003.

Newman, Arnold.
A Gallery for Fine Photography
<http://www.agallery.com/Pages/ photographers/newman.html>.
June 29, 2003.

Office of the Clerk.
U.S. House of Representatives.
<http://www.clerk.house.gov/index.html>.
August 24, 2002.

Ohio State University Archives.
Celebration of the Flight of *Friendship 7*.
<http://www.lib.ohio-state.edu/arvweb/glenn/celebration/celebration.htm>.
May 25, 2003.

Picturing the Century:
one hundred Years of Photography from the National Archives
<http://www.archives.gov/media_desk/press_kits/picturing_the_century_kit.html>.
June 22, 2003.

Sierra, J. A.
*The Timetable History of Cuba*.
<http://www.historyofcuba.com/history/baypigs.htm>.
March 18, 2003.

The White House.
<http://www.whitehouse.gov/history/presidents/lj36.html>.
July 16, 2002.

Wead, Doug
"All the President's Children."
<http://www.presidentschildren.com/list.htm#35>.
September 1, 2003.

Woolley, John and Gerhard Peters.
*The American Presidency Project.*
<http://www.presidency.ucsb.edu/site/docs/pppus.php?admin=035&year=1961&id=306>.
University of California, Santa Barbara,
April 26, 2003.

# Yoichi Okamoto
## 1970 Slide Show Presentation

In 1970, Yoichi Okamoto presented a slide show before a live audience at a meeting of the National Press Photographers' Association. The presentation was an assemblage of his favorite photographs taken during his time at the White House. In the presentation, Oke offers, in his own words, a rare insight into the history and daily events that surrounded the administration of President Lyndon B. Johnson.

A DVD copy of this presentation can be found at the back of the limited edition series. A special thanks is extended to the National Press Photographers' Association in allowing the digital conversion and preservation of this important piece of history, so that it could be made available with this book.

Be sure to visit the National Press Photographers Association Web site at http://www.nppa.org to view their listing of many other fine presentations by distinguished photographers.

*(DVD available ONLY with the Limited Edition Hardback Series.)*